STEVE WAUGH'S
World Cup Diary

STEVE WAUGH'S
World Cup Diary

HarperSports
An imprint of HarperCollinsPublishers

Harper*Sports*
An imprint of HarperCollins*Publishers*

First published in Australia in 1996
by HarperCollins*Publishers* Pty Limited
ACN 009 913 517
A member of the HarperCollins*Publishers* (Australia) Pty Limited Group

HarperCollins*Publishers*
25 Ryde Road, Pymble, Sydney, NSW 2073, Australia
31 View Road, Glenfield, Auckland 10, New Zealand
77–85 Fulham Palace Road, London W6 8JB, United Kingdom
Hazelton Lanes, 55 Avenue Road, Suite 2900, Toronto, Ontario M5R 3L2
and 1995 Markham Road, Scarborough, Ontario M1B 5M8, Canada
10 East 53rd Street, New York NY 10032, USA

National Library of Australia Cataloguing-in-Publication data:

Waugh, Steve, 1965 —.

Steve Waugh's World Cup tour diary.

ISBN 0 7322 5720 4.

1. Waugh, Steve, 1965 — Diaries. 2. Cricket — Australia.
3. Cricket players — Australia — Diaries. 4. World Cup (Cricket).
I. Title. II. Title: World Cup tour diary.

796.358092

Printed in Australia by Griffin Press, Adelaide.

9 8 7 6 5 4 3 2 1
00 99 98 97 96

CONTENTS

Contents

THE PHOTOGRAPHS in this book come from three sources. Some are from my camera, but the majority are either the work of Sydney-based photographer Trent Parke or come from the superb resources of All Sport, courtesy of the Australian. *Trent, who covered the World Cup tour for the* Australian, *kindly provided some magnificent photographs that graphically capture aspects of life on the Indian sub-continent and also reflect his enormous skill with the camera. Most of the All Sport shots were taken by Shaun Botterill — my thanks go to him and all his colleagues who covered the tournament, and to John Mikulcic and his crew at APL, whose support and professionalism, as always, were fantastic.*

— Steve Waugh

Acknowledgements

Special thanks, plus my total respect and admiration, go to the members of the Australian World Cup squad. Their support, friendship and input during the tour are greatly appreciated.

Thanks also to:

- The people who contributed to the text — Mark Waugh, Mike Coward, Ray Farrell, the 'boys on tour' and James Knight.
- Rupert McCall, for kindly allowing me to include his poem, *The Last Bus Out of Lahore's Almost Gone*, which appears on page 24 and will be, he informs me, also included in his book, *Green and Gold Malaria*, to be released later in 1996.
- 'Crash' Craddock, for organising the Mother Teresa excursion.
- Scorer Mike Walsh, who never tired of me asking for information on match and tour statistics.
- HarperCollins *Publishers*, for giving me the chance to produce this book, and especially Harper*Sports*' Commissioning Editor Geoff Armstrong, for his dedicated support.
- Kylie Prats, of Brevier Design, for never complaining about the ridiculous deadlines Geoff Armstrong gave her.
- Ian Russell, for compiling the statistics that are featured at the conclusion of the diary.

PHOTO CREDITS

Front cover

Main shot: Steve Waugh in Jaipur, photographed by Shaun Botterill (APL/All Sport).
Others (left to right): Team celebrations after Australia's victory in the semi-final (APL/All Sport); Steve Waugh batting against New Zealand in the quarter-final (APL/All Sport); Steve Waugh congratulates Shane Warne during the final overs of the semi-final (APL/All Sport).

Back cover

Top: The jubilant Sri Lankans hold aloft the 1996 World Cup trophy (APL/All Sport).
Centre: The Australians at the Taj Mahal (Steve Waugh).
Bottom: A village cricket match in Nagpur (APL/All Sport).

Colour pages

Pages 49 to 56: Pages 49, 51–56 — APL/All Sport; page 50 — Steve Waugh
Pages 73 to 80: All pictures APL/All Sport
Pages 113 to 120: Pages 113–116 — APL/All Sport; pages 117–120 — Steve Waugh
Pages 153 to 160: All pictures APL/All Sport, except page 160 (bottom) — Steve Waugh
Pages 177 to 184: All pictures APL/All Sport, except page 184 — Steve Waugh
Pages 201 to 208: Page 201 (top), 203, 204 (top and bottom), 206, 207, 208 (bottom) — Steve Waugh; page 201 (bottom), 202, 204 (left), 205, 208 (top) — APL/All Sport

Note: the photographs on the black-and-white pages are acknowledged individually throughout the book.

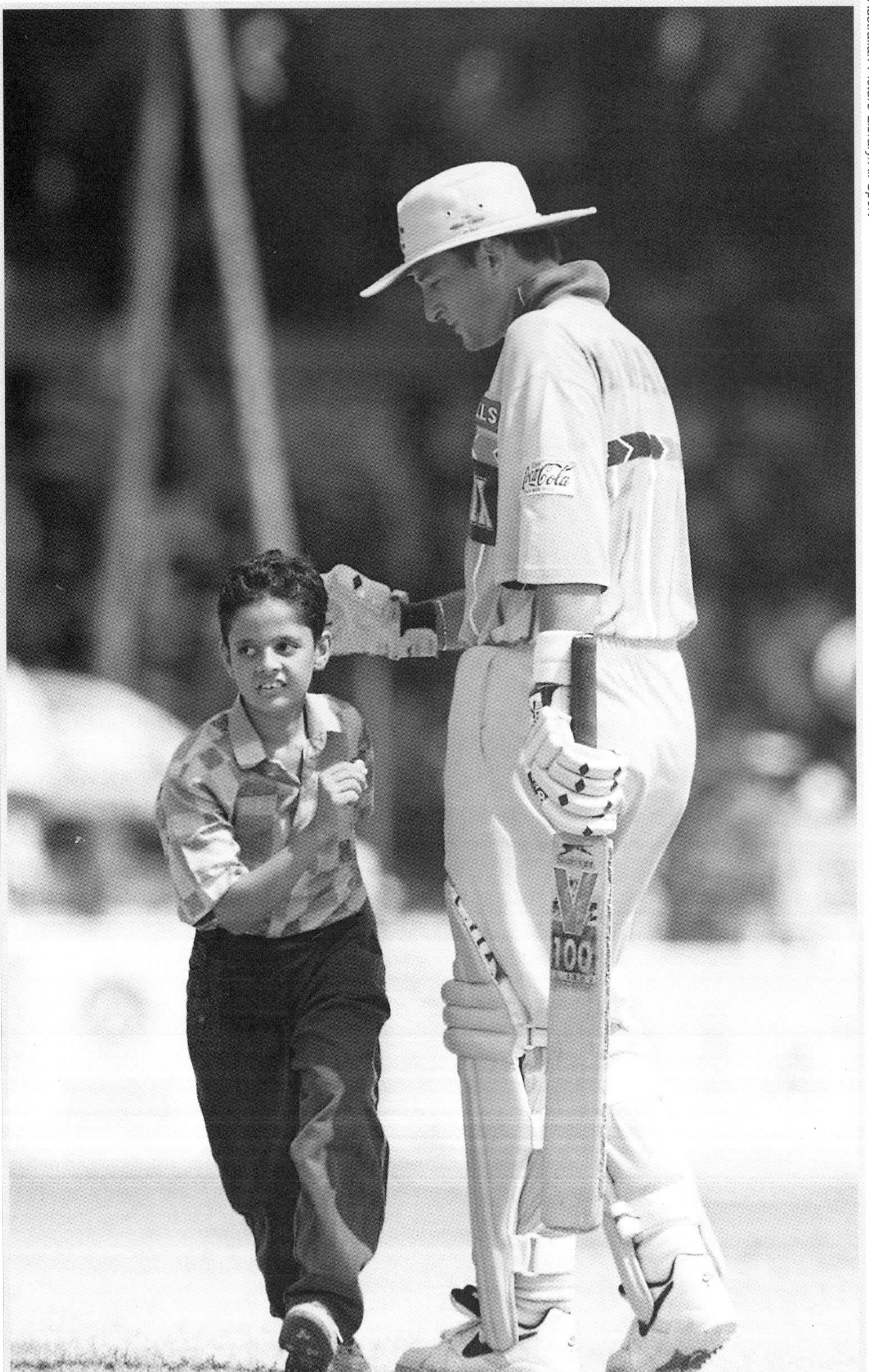

Australian Picture Library/All Sport

Foreword
by Mark Waugh

EVERYWHERE YOU GO there are autograph hunters. They're at the grounds, in the streets, in the hotel foyer, hiding on the team bus. Everyone wants your signature. Even the security guards, the room service guys and the hotel cleaners. I had one hotel worker charge into the bathroom at some unGodly hour of the morning — at a time that suited him a lot more than me — with pen and paper handy. But what could I do? After all, even at the worst of times cricket fans on the sub-continent are unbelievably passionate about their national sport.

One morning, my brother Stephen was running late for the team bus. This can happen from time to time, especially with Stephen. Inevitably, there were countless autograph hunters milling around reception, waiting for another of their heroes. Most of us were on the bus. Stephen, as yet, was not.

When he finally emerged downstairs he was met by a flurry of pens, papers, souvenir programs and the like. 'No,' he explained in the gentle voice he uses most early mornings, 'sorry guys, I haven't got time right now.'

'But Mr Wog,' one voice cried out (Indians just don't seem to be able to get their tongues around 'Waugh'), 'can we please have your autograph!!'

'Please, Mr Wog, just a second for your autograph??'

'Please, Mr Wog?!?!?'

'Please??!!??!!??'

By this time brother Stephen had nearly reached the exit. And this bloke was in tears. But Stephen couldn't stop. If he signed one autograph he would have had to sign a thousand.

'Mr Wog,' the fan sobbed. 'I know you are the greatest batsman in the world ... but you are not that great because you are making me cry!'

In India, cricketers really are bigger than movie stars. During the World Cup we saw countless billboards featuring Sachin Tendulkar and Mohammad Azharuddin. Superstars such as Brian Lara and Shane Warne are held in such high esteem. So, too, of course, is my brother.

And why not. The ratings have him as the world's number one batsman right now. Me? I'd put him at number three or four, just behind Lara and Tendulkar (which, of course, is nothing to be ashamed of). It's just that they bat with a touch more flair and style. That said, though, if I had to put my house on a batsman to score some runs in a crisis I'd be quite happy to put my hard-earned on Stephen. Perhaps even before the other two.

He gives the Australian middle order solidarity, in the way David Boon or Allan Border used to. In fact, he is very similar to AB — the way he occupies the crease, never gives in — and has been ever since the 1993 Ashes tour.

I don't think Stephen was ready for Test cricket when he was first selected, back in 1985. He really didn't know how to play at that level. But now he does. He's worked hard at his game, and appreciates his strengths and weaknesses. The flashy shots have gone, save for the occasional blaze in the one-dayers, and he has become very determined, very confident and a master of concentration. He now knows how to make runs, which, though it may sound simple, is the key to batting.

The 1996 World Cup was an amazing experience. The presence of so much security and the controversy over playing in Sri Lanka put a dampener on things for a while, but the tournament developed into an experience I will never forget.

My favourite memory is, inevitably, our epic come-from-nowhere win in the semi-final against the West Indies. I was fielding at backward point when the final wicket fell, and can remember clearly that bail tumbling off when Damien Fleming knocked over Courtney Walsh. It was a game we couldn't possibly win, yet we did, and is definitely the best victory I have been involved in in one-day cricket. The feeling immediately afterwards is difficult to describe — we were almost in shock after what had happened to us.

A lot of people have asked me if that sensational result left us flat for the final, but I don't think it did. To say so would be taking something away from the Sri Lankans. As I remember it, we were as keyed up as we could have been for the decider. The sad truth is they outplayed us on the night.

In many ways the World Cup was made for the Sri Lankans. Their batting plan was to look for big runs early, while the ball was hard and the field was in, which worked beautifully on the very good batting wickets and the small grounds. Whether such an approach would work in Australia I'm not so sure — sixes in the World Cup would have been caught in the outfield out here — but during the Cup their strategy worked just about perfectly.

Their bowling tactics were clever, too. The Sri Lankan attack lacks the class and variety to bowl out sides in Test cricket. But in the Cup they bowled at the stumps, and made you hit constantly towards one part of the field. Their captain, Arjuna Ranatunga, marshalled them well and (with the exception, ironically, of their portly skipper) they fielded athletically and with a passion. Quite clearly, they wanted to win.

I was more than happy with my form throughout the Cup, though I would have liked to score a few more runs in the semi and final. My hundred in the quarter-final against New Zealand was just about my best ever effort in limited-overs cricket, and one of the best innings I've played under pressure. But the funny thing is that early on, I wouldn't have backed myself to reach 20. Right at the start, I cramped up in my calves but fortunately some tablets eradicated that problem (it's hard to describe just how hot and humid it was). Then I scratched around for a while, until I moved into an

Mark Waugh acknowledges the Bombay crowd after his magnificent century in the Group A match against India.

unbelievable groove. I didn't think that much, just clicked into 'neutral' and followed my natural instincts. I really can't explain it. It was one of those special evenings when things work out just the way you would want them to.

I have one other special memory of the 1996 World Cup. On February 29, we were at our hotel in Nagpur, switching channels on the TV from one to the other of the two Cup games that were being played that day. Gradually our attention focussed more and more on the West Indies–Kenya match from Pune. No one, not even the Kenyans themselves could have given themselves a chance of beating the mighty Windies. But they were.

And they did.

We had been impressed by the Kenyans when we played them — they were clearly better cricketers than we had expected. This was especially true of their batting, though a couple of their bowlers went okay as well. But even so, it was both extraordinary and fantastic to see a tiny cricket country like Kenya overcome one of the great powers of the sport. At a time when cricket authorities are trying to lift the profile of the game across the world the repercussions of such a result can only be positive.

I have never been there but assume that the cricket infrastructure in Kenya is not flash. However, I know now, from first-hand experience, how naturally talented some of their cricketers are. Ten years ago, only Ranatunga's immediate family would have bet on Sri Lanka winning a World Cup final. Where the Kenyans will be a decade from now, who can tell? Perhaps they will be the new heroes of the cricket fans of India, fighting their way through hordes of autograph hunters as they struggle to get to the team bus on time?

I hope you enjoy Stephen's account of the '96 World Cup. The action photographs are brilliant, while some of the shots from off the field reveal a side of life on the sub-continent that few sports fans will ever see. And the words, like those from his previous three diaries, are revealing (but not too much!) and entertaining, and an outstanding record of a stressful but highly memorable time in the life of the Australian cricket team.

Introduction
by Mike Coward

AS SICKENING and frightening as it was, the bomb which ended or destroyed hundreds of lives in the Sri Lankan capital of Colombo on January 31, 1996, was not alone responsible for Australia's refusal to play their opening World Cup match in the beautiful but deeply troubled island republic.

Fatefully, the blast had come just two days after a tumultuous tour of Australia by Sri Lanka had concluded, and neither Mark Taylor and his men nor the directors of the Australian Cricket Board (ACB) could bring themselves to see such an act of terrorism in isolation.

This was not unexpected, given that the Australian Federal Police and other law enforcement agencies had been required to investigate a disturbing number of threats against Australian players, officials and cricket office staff during the white-hot international summer of 1995-96, which had also featured a visit by Pakistan. The threats, by mail and telephone and from within and outside Australia, came in the wake of a bribery scandal which had festered since Australia's tour of Pakistan in 1994; the seemingly baseless ball-tampering charges laid against the elite cricketers of both Pakistan and Sri Lanka; the highly contentious branding of Sri Lankan off-spinner Muttiah Muralitharan as a thrower; the ugliness of the second World Series final, when Sri Lankan players were jostled by spectators in Sydney and the consequent souring of cricket relations between Australia and Sri Lanka.

The decision of the Australians to boycott their match with Sri Lanka at the Premadasa Stadium in Colombo, which had been scheduled for February 17, polarised the international cricket community and seriously damaged Australia's relationship with the governors of the game throughout the Indian sub-continent.

Given historical enmities, it is rare for India, Pakistan and Sri Lanka to find common ground on any issue but in their disapproval of Australian cricket in 1995-96 they did so. Players and officials of Pakistan and Sri Lanka believed they were victims of a conspiracy in Australia and, in the name of solidarity, India quickly and loudly lent its voice to a claim of blatant harassment of sub-continent cricketers.

For example, in one of his widely-syndicated newspaper columns in India, peerless and influential Sunil Gavaskar wrote: "Funny how in most of the storms involving cricket the Australians are somewhere in the picture."

Then, for good measure, he listed every upheaval from bodyline in 1932-33 to the public humiliation of Muralitharan in 1995-96.

The traditional warm feeling towards Australia held by the cricket folk of India, Pakistan and Sri Lanka was replaced by a palpable iciness which cast a pall over the lead-up to the World Cup. Before a ball was bowled, Malcolm

Gray, a distinguished director of the ACB, was harangued by chiefs of the organising Pakistan India Lanka Committee (PILCOM) at a hostile meeting in Calcutta. Meanwhile, the Australian players and officials were being made to feel like outcasts. Suddenly, there was a potentially destructive division in the ranks of what is perhaps best described as the Greater Asian Cricket Basin (GACB) — the newest, richest, most innovative force in contemporary cricket.

As is so often the case, the antipathies were most evident among the game's politicians. The Indian people worried little about the machinations and petty politics of the game's rulers. Along with the Pakistanis and Sri Lankans, Indians have long had a fascination with Australian cricket and cricketers. Essentially, they wanted only to see the Australian players in action — particularly the brothers Waugh and Shane Warne.

However, while the imbroglio did not appear to deprive the Australians of popular support at the tournament, unquestionably it seriously undermined the impressive bridge-building that had been undertaken by Taylor in Pakistan in 1994 (his debut tour as Australian captain). In essence, Taylor's first duty as his country's leader had been a mission of atonement for the controversial tour of 1988, when manager Colin Egar and coach Bob Simpson accused Pakistan officials of incompetence and considered aborting the six-week tour after 15 days because of poor umpiring and pitch conditions.

Egar and Simpson were still in their jobs in 1994 and again at the World Cup in 1996, but it was Gray who represented the ACB at crisis meetings in Calcutta and endeavoured to placate PILCOM officials. One of Australian cricket's most worldly and visionary administrators, Gray is highly regarded throughout the cricket communities of the sub-continent. Indeed, as ACB chairman he played a vital diplomatic role when the 1987 World Cup was seriously threatened by the intransigence of both Rajiv Gandhi's Indian government of the day and the West Indies' more radical administrators on issues involving South Africa and its now defunct Cricket Union.

However, Gray's exceptional deeds at the negotiating table on that occasion counted for little in Calcutta in 1996 and he was assailed by luminaries of Indian cricket, Jagmohan Dalmiya and Inder Bindra, at a meeting at the plush Taj Bengal Hotel that was characterised by shouting and table-thumping. Gray listened with mounting dismay and anger as the ACB were blamed for the decision of the West Indies to boycott their match with Sri Lanka at Colombo on February 25.

At the height of the argument, officials from Zimbabwe and Kenya indicated they also wished to withdraw from their commitments in Sri Lanka. However, in the end, these matches were played without incident.

The Australian players, in particular, and the Australian cricket community in general were widely and often wildly criticised for their stand. It was noticeable, however, that the most strident critics either were oblivious to the extent of the underlying tension throughout Sri Lanka's Australian tour or living in societies apparently inured to violence and civil disobedience.

While they were affronted by the caustic comments which questioned their moral and physical courage, as well as their judgement, the Australian players were unrepentant. Instead the controversy strengthened their resolve to regain the title lost in Australia and New Zealand in 1992.

Certainly, in this instance, the vilification of Australian cricket was utterly unjust. Indeed, Australian cricket has been a strong supporter of the game on the Indian sub-continent since Billy Murdoch's Ashes tourists stopped off in Colombo in 1884. During the 1970s, 1980s and 1990s, Australian teams spread the cricket gospel despite delicate and sometimes potentially dangerous political situations throughout the region.

In 1979, an estimated 14,000 Indian troops were deployed to ensure the safe passage of Kim Hughes' Australian team when they played in the beautiful mountain city of Srinagar despite threats made against their lives by radicals said to belong to the Jammu-Kashmir Liberation Front and Pakistan Liberation Organisation. Similar security measures were in place seven years later, when Allan Border's Australians appeared in only the second limited-overs international ever played in Srinagar.

In 1988, Border led an Australian team into Pakistan in the wake of the apparent murder of President Mohammad Zia-ul-Haq at Bahawalpur and at a time when extremists were carrying out murderous acts in sections of Karachi and Hyderabad. Indeed, Karachi was not considered to be that much safer in 1994 and 1996.

Similarly, Australia has shown great faith in Sri Lankan cricket. In 1992, they were the first country to return to the troubled land after a five-year hiatus in international cricket that had continued while the civil war was at its height. During that tour, nine military chiefs were killed in one land-mine explosion in the war-torn north, but the Australian players stayed on and won many new admirers.

It was also on this tour that the Australians first played at what was then called the Khettarama Stadium, after the region in which it is located in Colombo. However, in May 1993, Sri Lankan president Ranasinghe Premadasa, who had a grand vision for the stadium, was assassinated by a member of the separatist Liberation Tigers of Tamil Eelam who had infiltrated his household. Now the cricket ground is known as the Premadasa Stadium.

That Taylor and his team were seen in some quarters as being directly responsible for the disharmony between the Australian and the Sri Lankan players irked the customarily imperturbable Australian skipper. Certainly, he was not alone in feeling that he and his men were expected to carry the can for some indecisive and inept administration both in Australia and England and, for that matter, the sub-continent.

While he was not publicly accusatory, Taylor's distress was obvious and he spoke out after Australia completed a whitewash of Sri Lanka in the 1995-96 Test series in Adelaide.

"I don't know what the answer is," he said forlornly. "They're (the ACB) probably upset with the ICC (International Cricket Council) as well. But I don't know where the buck stops, though. Do you blame the ACB, do you blame the ICC, do you blame Australian cricket, do you blame Sri Lankan cricket? I really don't know where the answer is. I just know it bounces back to the players and that is wrong."

Unlike the game's governors, Taylor had the courage to concede he had erred during the summer by not doing more to bring about a peace settlement between the two teams. At the time, Taylor said: "We took the time in the Adelaide Test match to go in and have a beer with the Sri Lankans. Probably the only mistake I made this summer I'd say, (is) that I didn't do it two weeks earlier. It's my fault. I made a mistake with that. If I could go back three weeks I'd have changed it in one night I reckon."

It had became obvious to outside observers that, almost to a man, the Australian players had grown weary of what they considered to be Sri Lankan captain Arjuna Ranatunga's niggling, niggardly and provocative demeanour and behaviour. Attempts were made to bring the teams closer together for the final Test in Adelaide, but Ranatunga and Graham Halbish, the dogmatic chief executive of the ACB, remained at odds.

Fearing an irreconcilable breakdown between the countries, Denis Rogers, barely five months into office as chairman of the ACB, found an ally in his then Sri Lankan counterpart, Ana Punchihewa, and they worked busily behind the scenes in an attempt to stabilise an old alliance. However, at the end of the Test match, the hierarchy of the Sri Lankan team pointedly released a statement rather than attend the customary post-Test and post-series media conference.

The portents were not encouraging. And two days later the bomb exploded at the Central Bank headquarters in Colombo.

The reaction to the Australian boycott would continue to reverberate around the cricket world long after Ranantunga held aloft the Wills Trophy after leading Sri Lanka to a famous victory over Australia at the Gaddafi Stadium in Lahore. Indeed, in all likelihood, the ramifications will be felt for many years to come. After all, as the Asianisation of Australia has intensified, Australian cricket has identified strongly with the region – elite teams have made 13 visits to India, Pakistan and Sri Lanka between September 1979 and March 1996, eight for Test matches. And four more visits — three involving Tests — are scheduled before Christmas 1998.

As was evidenced during the dark 1995-96 summer, the game's practitioners can teach officials and legislators a good deal about relationships across the cultural divide. One can only trust that Mark Taylor will get enough time away from bridge-building these next few years to ensure that his team can maintain their reputation as being the finest in the world.

Mike Coward is one of Australia's leading cricket writers, and the author of several outstanding cricket books including *Cricket Beyond the Bazaar* (1990), *Caribbean Odyssey* (1991) and *Australia Versus the New South Africa* (1994).

THE Daily Telegraph

SYDNEY, Thursday, February 1, 1996 — Weather: Dry, 28 degrees — Phone 288 3000 — *70 cents — M

BOMB BOYCOTT

World Cup doubts after 55 die in Sri Lanka blast

A police officer calls for aid for an injured man at the scene of the car bomb explosion in central Colombo yesterday. At least 42 were killed and hundreds injured

A SUICIDE bomb ripped apart the centre of Colombo yesterday, killing at least 55 people and threatening a boycott of the Sri Lanka leg of the World Cup by Australian cricketers.

A truck loaded with explosives was driven through the entrance of the nine-storey Central Bank building in the city centre, just one block from the Taj Samudra Hotel where the Australian

By RON REED in Colombo

cricket team is due to stay before its first match in about two weeks.

Police fear the death toll could climb into the hundreds, with a thousand more wounded, as they began searching the rubble.

The attack has exacerbated security concerns for the Australian World Cup side, which had already threatened to pull out of

the Colombo matches after death threats to team members.

Wicket keeper Ian Healy said last night: "It puts the Sri Lankan leg of the World Cup in jeopardy, that is for sure."

Test fast bowler Craig McDermott, who earlier in the season received a death threat that he would be "fed a diet of hand grenades", said: "A bomb one block from the hotel has to be looked into.

"We had heard everything had

settled down over there but obviously it has not."

Foreign Affairs officials were already locked in discussions with the Australian Cricket Board last night.

Witnesses to the bombing said a truck drove up to the bank building shortly before 11am, and gunmen jumped out and started firing. The truck then sped on, hitting the building and erupting in a fireball.

Charred and mutilated bodies

lay in the road while others were feared buried in rubble. Overturned cars and other vehicles burned in the street.

Plumes of black smoke billowed from at least a dozen buildings as hundreds of survivors, trapped on their roofs, waved for help.

Helicopters hovered overhead, trying to get low enough to pick up survivors.

Three hours after the blast **Continued Page 2**

METRO | Business: P59; Comics: P64; Crosswords: P63; Lottery (5876): P65; Television: P41; Weather: P66 | TeleClassifieds P67 (288 2000) | This newspaper participates in newspaper recycling

16

Prelude
by Steve Waugh

OF THE MANY, many games I have played in during my decade in international cricket, the one I enjoyed the least was the second final of the World Series Cup, against Sri Lanka, which was played in Sydney during the 1995–96 Australian season.

It was a game that will be remembered for all the wrong reasons. There was the ugly exchange between the Sri Lankan batsman, Sanath Jayasuriya, and our fast bowler, Glenn McGrath, which saw the pair pushing and shoving in mid-pitch. Then came a brief but angry conversation between Aussie keeper and vice-captain Ian Healy and the Sri Lankan skipper, Arjuna Ranatunga, which came about after Ranatunga called for a runner even though he didn't appear to be injured. Sure, he looked tired, even exhausted, and he was lathered in sweat. But he didn't seem injured.

'You can't call for a runner just because you're unfit,' Heals had bluntly informed him.

And, finally, after the match and the competition had been completed, the Sri Lankans refused to shake hands with Aussie captain Mark Taylor, or acknowledge the home team when we were presented with the Cup. In my opinion the whole episode was an absolute disgrace. Our win meant nothing to me. All I could think of was how little I had enjoyed being involved, and how sad it is when affairs reach the point where opponents can't shake hands after the contest has been won.

The summer had turned sour, with relations between the two countries strained and the Aussie team copping a great deal of criticism for this state of affairs. To us, this was inexplicable, unwarranted and grossly unfair. We felt we had been playing excellent cricket, in the right spirit.

The start of this predicament we found ourselves in occurred back in Perth, during the early days of Sri Lanka's Australian tour, when the umpires reported the visitors for ball tampering during the Test (a game I missed through injury). This claim was quickly dismissed, due to a technicality — the umpires hadn't reported the incident in the correct manner. Whether there was any truth in the initial accusation was never explored, so the bottom line was that the Sri Lankans were innocent and the matter should have been dead and buried. But some people couldn't forget what they saw as an attack on the Sri Lankans' integrity, and a wound began to fester among not only the touring team but also the Sri Lankan populations in Australia and abroad.

This persecution complex was compounded by the 'chucking' controversy that occurred on the opening day of the second Test, in Melbourne. The Sri Lankan off-spinner, Muralitharan, was called by Australian umpire Darrell Hair seven times in the match. This was a brave decision by the umpire, and one many believed to be correct. After all, the unfortunate bowler had been warned at various times over the years that his action was borderline, while over the previous two years more than one umpire had expressed doubts in their reports as to the legitimacy of his deliveries.

Forget whether that bowling action was legal or otherwise, it was dreadful to watch a sportsman being put through the torture and embarrassment that Muralitharan went through that day. Not only was he playing in front of a large Boxing Day crowd, but his humiliation was seen by millions of television viewers across the world. It should never have happened and in my opinion, the blame for his misfortune should have been shared by the authorities who must have known of the impending disaster and the coaches who refused to help Muralitharan modify his bowling action.

Whatever the rights and wrongs of this affair, it only helped to fuel the fire. Relations between Sri Lanka and Australia began to disintegrate, and the players began to feel the strain in the heat of the battle. There hadn't been much chat out in the middle during the series to that point, but now an undercurrent of frustration had built up, just waiting to come to the surface.

The tension finally reared its ugly head during the World Series Cup. Poor Muralitharan had been called again in Brisbane (in a match against the West Indies), and then their left-hand batsman, Asanka Gurusinha was reported in Perth for unsportsmanlike behaviour. By this point, Sri Lanka (both the team and many of their countrymen) thought everyone was against them and the result was the surly clash that was the second World Series Cup Final, in Sydney.

Just days after that turbulent fixture, we found ourselves in Adelaide, preparing for the third and final Test of the Sri Lankan series. Within two weeks we were to fly to the sub-continent to begin preparations for the sixth cricket World Cup, where our opening match was to be against ... Sri Lanka, in ... the Sri Lankan capital, Colombo. We were far from happy with what had gone on during the Australian summer and, to compound our unease, some of the Australian squad, among them Shane Warne, Craig McDermott and coach Bob Simpson, had received death threats.

It was under these trying circumstances that the team squad, plus the Chairman of the Australian Cricket Board, Denis Rogers, the ACB's Chief Executive Officer, Graham Halbish, and the ACB Treasurer and board member, Des Rundle, joined us three days before the Test to have an open discussion (call it a crisis meeting, if you like) about our concerns and queries on the World Cup tour. Naturally enough, the players who had been threatened were the most apprehensive. Overall, the feeling among the side was one of uncertainty; what we were after was the true (and hopefully reassuring) story. What was relevant, what wasn't? Were we going to be safe, or weren't we?

Mark Taylor began by asking the Board officials what were the players' alternatives. Could we have a part tour? A full tour? Or no tour? And what were the ramifications of those scenarios? The 'no tour' option was ruled out virtually straightaway — nobody wanted that, and nobody thought that might happen. The 'part tour' option appeared a more likely alternative, the idea being that the opening game in Colombo and our pre-tournament training week in Colombo would be shelved in favour of us going directly to Calcutta for the opening ceremony and then to Vizag for our scheduled game against Kenya.

Graham Halbish's reaction to this proposal was clear. After listening to some players' preferences for this course of action he said: 'I'm hearing what you're saying, but if you do decide to pull out of that first game, it will take 10 years at least to rectify the situation.' We all took 'situation' to mean the relationship between Australia and Sri Lanka. Graham also stressed that boycotting this leg of the tour would inevitably make the Sri Lankan people dislike us even more, and give further encouragement to the dangerous elements who had threatened some of us.

By the time discussion over this option was over, it didn't sound as if it was worth pursuing. So we moved on to the final alternative, that of completing a

Right: The controversial bowling action of Muttiah Muralitharan.

Below: The low-point of an angry summer — the Sri Lankan players refuse to shake Mark Taylor's hand after the second World Series final, in Sydney.

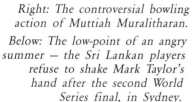

Both pics: Trent Parke

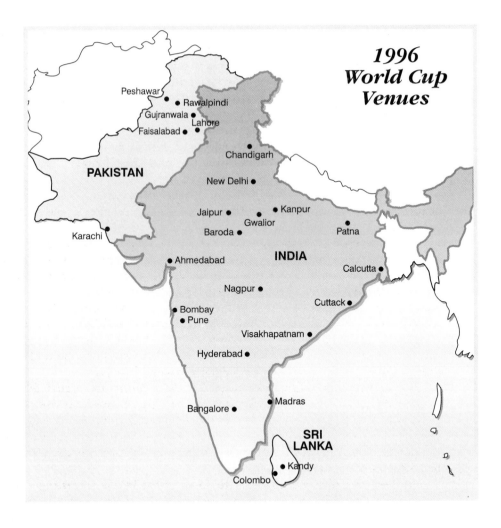

1996 World Cup Venues

full World Cup tour. If this was to happen, we wanted to know what measures would be taken to ensure us all a safe passage during our stay. And not just in Sri Lanka but also in Pakistan, where much ill-feeling had been caused by the bribery allegations that had followed the Australian tour of 1994.

On the issue of Pakistan, World Cup tour manager Col Egar (whom we knew had recently been to Pakistan to find out just what might be in store for us) alleviated most of the worry when he said simply, 'it was a dead issue now'. But what of Sri Lanka? Both Denis Rogers and Graham Halbish came up with a list of guarantees they had received from the relevant authorities.

If the tour went ahead, the status of the Australian cricket team while touring Sri Lanka would be upgraded to the equivalent of a visiting Head of State. We would depart the airport from a separate exit, after going through a separate passport control. Cars would be cleared from the sides of roads that we would be travelling on. Armed guards would join us on the team bus. There would be one bus for the players and another for their luggage. Security guards would stay with us 24 hours a day. The team would be given its own floor at the hotel, with that floor and the floors above and below secured by armed guards. Team lists would be checked off at the hotel, to make sure the right people knew where we were at all times. All incoming phone calls would be screened, and all practice sessions supervised by security guards. We were told the Sri Lankan Police Commissioner, Secret Service and a range of security firms had been involved in the development of this strategy. Their extensive and thorough nature were a reflection of just how real the threats to our safety had been, but even so, the ACB told us they were going to employ extra security from the worldwide security firm, Group 4, to ensure maximum safety.

All this was very reassuring, but while it meant that players would be reasonably safe, it didn't mean we would feel comfortable and able to concentrate on the job of playing good cricket. But, all things considered, it seemed the best solution to the whole problem.

And I must say that probably the most welcome comment came from ACB chairman Denis Rogers, who told us that the highest priority of the Board was the safety of the players.

One sobering moment came when we were told of a faxed message the Board had received during the week. The basis of the note was that on our arrival in Colombo, the Australian team would be greeted by a suicide bomber. Not even heads of state such as Gandhi could be completely protected, the fax read, and anybody could be had! You can't help but think about whether it's all worth it when you hear of threats such as this. We're only cricketers trying to play cricket! Then came the advice that if anyone received any threatening or suspicious articles or parcels, they should be handed to the Federal Police. ACB staff had been given the same instructions.

The meeting lasted some two hours. After it, most of the guys felt more comfortable about the situation but were still slightly apprehensive. We had ended with a decision to hold another team meeting towards the end of the Test, to monitor everyone's thoughts. This also would give both teams a chance to use the Test to try and patch up the relationship between the teams that had become so soured.

However, this plan was thwarted to some extent by the increasingly hostile Sri Lankan captain, who simply refused to come to the party. Instead, he managed to stir the situation up even more by saying how much Sri Lanka were looking forward to playing Australia in their country, in front of their crowds and with neutral umpires. Ranatunga's comments implied that the Sri Lankans had been hard done by in Australia, and that we would be getting some of our own back when we travelled there in a couple of weeks.

The Test match, fortunately, was played in tremendous spirit (Ranatunga was unable to play, with the captaincy being passed on to Aravinda de Silva). The teams even had a get together after the match for a beer and a chat, with all concerned getting on very well. We learned that they, like us, had been feeling the strain and that they, too, felt that the real problem had not been between the players but had been initiated and then exacerbated by the way the authorities had handled the controversies. It was a pity both sides didn't get together for this exchange earlier on, as it would probably have averted the ugliness of the Sydney one-day final.

The Australian players met before the resumption of the fifth day's play and unanimously decided to go ahead with the tour. The only change would be that our pre-tournament warm-up would be conducted in Brisbane and not Colombo.

Days later, this real-life game of snakes and ladders came to life again when, out of the blue, I received a call from a journalist who asked me: 'Steve, what is your reaction to the bomb blast that just occurred in Colombo?'

The Australian World Cup squad

Captain: Mark Taylor — Tubs or Tubby
Vice-captain: Ian Healy — Heals
Michael Bevan — Bev
Damien Fleming — Flemo
Stuart Law — Lawie
Shane Lee — Meadow
Craig McDermott — Billy
Glenn McGrath — Pigeon
Ricky Ponting — Ponts or Punter
Paul Reiffel — Pistol

Michael Slater — Slats
Shane Warne — Warney
Mark Waugh — Junior
Steve Waugh — Tugga

Coach: Bob Simpson — Simmo
Physio: Errol Alcott — Hooter
Manager: Col Egar
Media Manager: Ian McDonald
Scorer: Mike Walsh

My reply was simple: 'I don't know what you're talking about.'

However, I soon did, as the horrifying pictures from this despicable act were shown on Australian TV screens. That it had happened a mere five minutes walk away from our intended Colombo address left an inevitable thought in my head. It could quite possibly have been us, caught in the wrong place at the wrong time.

Ron Reed, a respected cricket writer with the News Limited group, was in Colombo at the time and sent a chilling report back to Australia, which was published in Sydney's *Daily Telegraph* on February 2. It read in part:

If the directors of the Australian Cricket Board had been in Colombo yesterday morning to accompany me on a grim walk through the horrific aftermath of Wednesday's suicide bomb atrocity, I have no doubt they would quickly arrive at a unanimous decision.

Australia must either forfeit the opening World Cup match against Sri Lanka or insist that it be moved to India or Pakistan ...

Long summers spent watching cricket from press boxes or official enclosures does little to prepare you for the sight of charred corpses, burnt beyond all hope of identification, piled one on top of the other on a city footpath.

While Colombo is one of the world's most cricket crazy cities, it is also a war zone. As such, sending the Australian team here represents an unacceptable risk ...

Media reports had the death toll as over 100, with further bombings highly likely. Given this fact, and our low popularity in Sri Lanka, we had to acknowledge that if we toured there we were a potential target; it seemed hardly worthwhile to put our lives at risk for a game of cricket.

I would have been willing to go if the Board insisted on us touring there, even though, frankly, I didn't want to. There were reports that six senior players were threatening to boycott the Sri Lankan leg, but these stories were 100 per cent fabricated. In fact, I took offence that my name was mentioned as one of the six — my attitude was that we were either all in or all out.

In the end, the sensible thing happened and the decision to abort the Sri Lankan leg was taken by the 13-man Executive of the ACB and not by the team. This decision was supported by the majority of the Australian population, who recognised that playing sport, even for your country, is not worth risking your life for. Unfortunately, this sentiment wasn't shared by PILCOM, the World Cup organising committee, by the people of Sri Lanka, or by quite a few influential people on the sub-continent.

I feel the criticism of the decision is ill-informed and unfair. Terrorism isn't tolerated or accepted in Australia, even though, sadly, it is a part of life in other parts of the world. But just because it is a part of life in other parts of the world surely does not mean that we, a sporting team, should ignore the dangers and hope we won't become involved.

For us, the abandonment of the Sri Lankan leg is both disappointing and unfortunate. We have learned that the decision is to be seen by the Cup organisers as a forfeit, with the two points on offer going to the Sri Lankans. However, I don't believe this setback will hinder our chances — in fact, it might do the opposite. No longer will we have to worry about death threats and bombings. We'll be able to concentrate on what we do best ...

Playing cricket and enjoying it!

1996 World Cup Draw

GROUP A	GROUP B
February	**February**
16 West Indies v Zimbabwe, Hyderabad	14 England v New Zealand, Ahmedabad
17 Sri Lanka v Australia, Colombo	15 South Africa v UAE, Rawalpindi
18 India v Kenya, Cuttack	17 Holland v New Zealand, Baroda
21 India v West Indies, Gwalior	18 England v UAE, Peshawar
21 Sri Lanka v Zimbabwe, Colombo	20 New Zealand v South Africa, Faisalabad
23 Australia v Kenya, Visakhapatnam	22 England v Holland, Peshawar
25 Sri Lanka v West Indies, Colombo	24 Pakistan v UAE, Gujranwala
26 Kenya v Zimbabwe, Patna	25 England v South Africa, Rawalpindi
27 India v Australia, Bombay	26 Pakistan v Holland, Lahore
29 Kenya v West Indies, Pune	27 New Zealand v UAE, Faisalabad
	29 Pakistan v South Africa, Karachi
March	
1 Australia v Zimbabwe, Nagpur	**March**
2 India v Sri Lanka, New Delhi	1 Holland v UAE, Lahore
4 Australia v West Indies, Jaipur	3 Pakistan v England, Karachi
6 India v Zimbabwe, Kanpur	5 Holland v South Africa, Rawalpindi
6 Sri Lanka v Kenya, Kandy	6 Pakistan v New Zealand, Lahore

Note: The games involving Australia v Sri Lanka (February 17) and West Indies v Sri Lanka (February 25) would not be played, because the visiting teams decided not to travel to Colombo. Sri Lanka would be awarded both matches on forfeit.

QUARTER-FINALS
March
9 First in Group A v Fourth in Group B, Faisalabad
9 Third in Group A v Second in Group B, Bangalore
11 Fourth in Group A v First in Group B, Karachi
11 Second in Group A v Third in Group B, Madras

SEMI-FINALS
March
13 Winners of March 9 Quarter-finals, Calcutta
14 Winners of March 11 Quarter-finals, Chandigarh

FINAL
March
17 Winners of Semi-finals, Lahore

The Last Bus out of Lahore's Almost Gone
(The Spirit of the Southern Cross)

There's something strange that separates the other tribes from us
    Just take this bunch of cricketers and put them on a bus ...
Warney's on the lookout for a feed of KFC
    While Junior's pretty keen to find the Bombay TAB
And Ponts is right behind him with a form guide full of tips
    Though the only dogs he'll get on here are prob'ly served with chips

Slats has packed his buttercup — he's heard the food here's fiery
    As Tugga makes an entry in another bloody diary
To tell the truth, I love those books — there's not a page I've missed
    And it's good to know that when they win, the boys can all get pissed

Now Stuey's telling Flemo that his goatee's much the sharper
    And Bevo's reminiscing how he stitched up Mr Harper
A four to win off Roger's spin — the perfect play of plays
    It's the sort of thing you dreamt of back in backyard cricket days

Billy checks the scenery — it's not quite Mermaid Beach
    In fact, the speedos and the surf ski seem a long way out of reach
Silence falls upon the bus as minds are thinking deep
    And Simmo thanks the Lord that he can finally get some sleep

Then Warney skulls his thickshake down and bowls the empty cup
    The youngster Lee is all at sea — he's beaten all ends up
The boys are sure he's got an edge — the bus goes up as one
    Simmo almost shits himself and reaches for his gun

'Bowling Shane — this bloke's a joke' says Heals to stir the Karma
    But the batsman just ignores him unlike Roshan Mahanama
Now Pistol's in a headlock and he's not all that impressed
    But sitting next to a Pigeon well he should have bloody guessed

The team has found the clown it needs — the kid's fair dinkum loony
    And though it isn't shouted out — the boys are missing Boonie ...
Tubby chews his juicy fruit in true Australian style
    They're a rowdy pack of bastards but they'll always make you smile

Cos the spirit of the Southern Cross is in the bus today
    It has been there from the start and it will be there all the way
The country that they fight for might be many miles afar
    And Pistol might be choking in the grip of 'Pidg' McGrath

But the mateship of this regiment is not in any doubt
    The confidence ignited by the fire in their shout
Their courage stands unchallenged in the hearts of those who count
    Only with the voice inside do expectations mount

For if they sell their talent short and bow out in despair
    They know they'll face an injury that Hooter can't repair
But no-one needs to tell them — it's a fact already learned
    The rest is on the outside and for now they're not concerned

For now there is a trophy in the shimmer of their eyes
    And every soldier understands — there ain't no second prize.

— 'Rupert' McCall

DAY 1 — *February 9*
(Sydney to Bangkok)

IT WAS THE SEA of emerald green blazers with blinding yellow vertical stripes, accompanied by the outrageously noticeable red ties, that stood the boys out from the rest of the passengers. Along with my wife, Lynette, I made my way towards them at Thai International Airways' counter number 53, in preparation for our World Cup adventure.

Only now did it all seem real. After the trials and tribulations of recent weeks, we were in fact going to be on our way. We knew that the West Indies had followed our lead and also declined their invitation to play in Sri Lanka, a double blow to the competition which had apparently thrown PILCOM into panic mode. But what the next few weeks held for us, cricket and otherwise, none of us knew. Our flight was Bangkok first stop, and then, after a brief respite, on to Calcutta for the opening ceremony two days later. After that, it was anyone's guess as to where we were to go. Nobody had any idea at all, not even, it seemed, the tournament organising committee!

Slats tests out his newly-acquired VCR, while Warney settles in for the long haul. In the row behind are Stuart Law (left) and Craig McDermott.

An airport farewell is never the ideal place to part company, particularly when the media is craving shots of loving couples saying goodbye to each other. This time was doubly tough for me, as Lynette and I are expecting our first child. Glenn McGrath, on the other hand, was busy posting numerous Valentine's Day cards, in anticipation of a bumper haul of replies awaiting him when he returns home on March 19. Mark Taylor, meanwhile, dealt with a last-minute press conference — his role was to subdue those keen for one more controversy before we departed.

Once customs was cleared, it was time for a spot of shopping, with adaptor plugs, blow-up cushion pillows, batteries, tapes and film the top priorities for the boys. Some unusual pieces of hand luggage adorned the arms of Michael Bevan and Shane Lee, who looked more like members of a rock group than a sporting team as their guitar cases swung with every stride. Meadow carried a guitar of an acoustic variety — an instrument which he is, apparently, quite adept at using — while Bev, being the apprentice of the two, possessed a

We'll get there eventually ...

On a flight of this length, each player has different ways of passing the time away. The alternatives include watching the in-flight movies to reading books (Simmo), playing game boys (Warney), listening to headphones (Flem), sleeping (Junior), video filming (Slats), being a nuisance (Pigeon), filling in diary entries (Heals), reading magazines (Billy), reading rules and regulations (Tubs), heaving an ale or two (team management), checking their guitars out (Lee and Bevan), to eating everything in sight!

The one section of the journey that bought everyone together was when Tubs asked the lads their thoughts on issues such as short-pitched bowling and umpiring standards, which were to be addressed in Calcutta by the members of the ICC (International Cricket Council).

I suggested that the umpires should become as professional in their attitude as the players and be available to be coached and take advantage of practice facilities. The obvious place for this is at an academy, and it wouldn't be too tough to attach a section onto the existing ones to improve the standards currently being displayed. On short-pitched bowling, we unanimously agreed that the question of whether it becomes intimidatory should be left to the umpires' discretion, rather than be governed by rules such as a limit of two bouncers per over. Such inflexible restrictions can take something away from the game, which is meant to be a test of all skills.

bass. However, while Bev might lack some skill on the guitar, we know he's exceptional on the vocals. In fact, anyone who has heard his mellow tones would agree he wouldn't be out of place in *The Phantom of the Opera*! My own hand-luggage included a few new toys — an IBM ThinkPad and a new Canon camera — to help me in the production of this diary. The only downsides are the instruction manuals that have to be read!

My travelling companion for the nine-hour flight to Bangkok was Ricky Ponting, and it wasn't long before I was wishing someone else had been allocated the number next door. Not long into the trip, he offered me his mouthwash from his travel bag which, when used, projected not a mint spray but a manly smelling scent accompanied by a foamy substance which I realised after tasting was in fact shaving cream! Needless to say the lads enjoyed the practical joke at my expense, but Punter will be well advised to check his food over the next six weeks before digesting it. Soon after, a face towel, flying at good pace and thrown by none other than McGrath, slapped into the back of my neck. What a start! We were still on the tarmac, waiting for take off! However, thankfully, the remainder of the journey was incident free, mainly because, to everyone's delight, that somewhat thinner version of Merv Hughes (Pigeon) fell asleep not long after we were in the air.

At the Amari Hotel, in Bangkok, the unthinkable happened — M. Waugh and S. Waugh rooming together. Not since the long-lost days of living in Picnic Point Road, in the Sydney suburb of Panania, had we been put in the same room. I guess the major change is now we own separate clothes and don't have to fight to see who gets the best shirt or the pair of socks without a hole in them. And there has been one other development — Mark has obviously spent many hours developing a healthy snore — and it did cross my mind to delve back into some of the underhanded tactics of our youth and re-introduce a Chinese burn or two. Or perhaps a crow peck to the scalp, or even a jab into the Adam's apple region. Anything to stop the racket from continuing.

DAY 2 — *February 10*
(Bangkok to Calcutta)

FEELING somewhat refreshed after a decent sleep, we assembled in the hotel foyer before making our way through customs again. On reaching the business-class lounge area, we were treated to the first mini jam session of the 'Travelling Blueberries' (Messrs Lee and Bevan). First impressions suggested the lads were 'short of a gallop' — they'll need at least a bit of fine tuning before their act can be considered destined for bigger things.

Once again, the plane trip turned into a scene from *Kindergarten Cop*. However, astonishingly, McGrath was the recipient rather than the purveyor of the abuse. The occupants of row 22 (S. Waugh, Lee and Ponting) decided to cash in on the 'Narromine Nightmare's' misfortune in being located in row 21 by sprinkling sugar, salt and pepper on his closely cropped dial. That was just for starters. The two sets of complimentary business-class socks were then expertly tied together and manoeuvred by Meadow and Punter to complete a classic strangulation. And our fun was capped off by a couple of jabs with some leftover toothpicks and a soothing cleansing from many a face-wash towel.

Looking to return these favours, Pigeon went to work on a slab of cheese, sticking toothpicks into it at all angles until it resembled a dangerous weapon

Both pics: Steve Waugh

Above: Well wishers, all suffering from Cup fever, line the streets of Calcutta as we make our way from the airport.

Below: A sign of things to come. Camera crews, security guards and huge crowds greet our arrival at the team's hotel.

Mark Taylor stated our position regarding the Sri Lankan matter very clearly at his first World Cup press conference today. Inevitably, this was the subject that dominated proceedings, and Tubby put up a very impressive display.

'The decision stands,' he explained to the media throng, when asked whether there was any chance of the game in Colombo going ahead after all. 'We are prepared to forego the tie and concentrate on the next match. We are just focusing on our practice.'

When asked if we were fearful of the type of reaction we would have received in Sri Lanka, Tubs replied: 'We love the Sri Lankan crowds. They are cricket loving. But it is the security situation which has compelled us to stay away.'

And of the reported guarantee from the Tamil Tigers, who have been blamed for the Colombo bomb blast, that they would not interrupt the cricket, Mark commented: 'We just take it as a statement. It is a statement issued from one office or another. There is no guarantee of security as far as we are concerned.'

used by soccer hooligans. It was, of course, thrown our way, and stabbed the unsuspecting Lee in the chest region much to McGrath's sadistic delight.

These pre-school activities continued until we began our descent into Calcutta. As we assessed all that was below us, what was instantly evident was the city's trademark smoggy, dusty haze. However, after we landed we were immediately surprised by the lack of humidity and heat in the air; it was, in fact, very mild compared to the scorching summer temperatures of Brisbane. My first contact with the locals came very quickly, as an obvious cricket fan stepped forward and exclaimed: 'Hello, Mr Wog. Very well played in 1987, all the best for '96.'

It's amazing how one comment can put everything into perspective, and this one did just that for me. Sometimes you forget how much this game can affect people. You take things for granted. But when you realise a guy like this remembers how you performed nine years ago and wants you to do well, even though you're part of a visiting team — that's a very effective reminder that you have an obligation to always give it your best shot. You're not only playing for yourself and your team, but also for the numerous people out there who care whether you succeed or fail.

Surprise number two verged on a miracle. We cleared customs without going through any formalities. Surprise number three — our hotel had been changed without anyone's knowledge or acceptance — was less remarkable, for such an occurrence is nothing new in these parts. Rather, it is part of the mystery of touring the sub-continent. Surprise number four, or should I say nightmare number one, came with the room announcements ...

Glenn McGrath and Steve Waugh together in number 269!

Our first get-together as a team happened at 6 pm, in Tubby Taylor's room, and quickly turned into a 'Claytons' meeting. Col Egar, the team manager, informed us that as things presently stood we were a team without a game, venue or schedule as well as being devoid of uniforms and friends. Good start! The one positive of the whole meeting came when our liaison manager, Sona, stormed into the room and announced that he had brought with him the official World Cup chewing gum sponsor's product, and that each player was to receive two boxes.

DAY 3 — *February 11*
(Calcutta)

WE LEARNED this morning that PILCOM had staged another meeting yesterday evening, to try and finally establish what to do with the increasingly ostracised Aussies and not-quite-so-ostracised West Indies. However, once again, nothing firm had been decided, although the latest twist in the plot revolved around World Cup minnows Zimbabwe and Kenya, who have both said they don't want to be the first team to play in Sri Lanka.

Our situation hasn't changed. We have become recluses in our own hotel, unable to do any sightseeing or shopping because of security concerns. And we are unable to find an adequate practice venue. The decision to bring with us over 70 videos from Australia has turned out to be a masterstroke, and room 269 has become something of a mini-cinema, showing anything and everything, even if it is too cramped a venue to hold a team of cricketers.

This afternoon the videos had to be put on hold, as today was opening ceremony day and a full schedule lay ahead of us. First up was the photo session, involving every team and, judging by the mayhem and madness on display once they had the green light to snap away, almost every photographer in India. Amazingly, this event took the allocated 45 minutes and not the expected two hours, which gave us the chance to go back to the hotel for a couple of hours.

As they had done since we arrived, huge crowds had gathered outside the team hotel, all desperate for a glimpse of the players and praying for a touch of one. But the latter was a virtual impossibility because of the tight security around every team. As each player stepped off the bus, a tumultuous roar filled the air, with waving, whistling and smiles in every direction. This was a show of affection that highlighted once again the Indian people's love of the game.

Before long we were back on the bus and making our way to Eden Gardens, Calcutta's huge and extraordinary cricket ground. Two top-class commandoes, each brandishing a submachine gun, came with us, along with the ACB-employed Group 4 security personnel. It was comforting to have them there, not so much

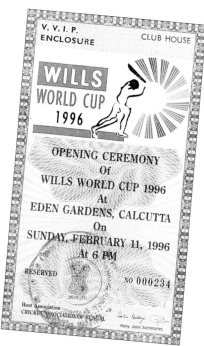

Although it might appear that Mark Taylor has just made a cash withdrawal from his bank account, he is, in fact, being escorted by Black Cat commandoes to the ICC's meeting in Calcutta.

because we felt under any threat because of any animosity towards us, rather there were so many people about we just weren't quite sure what could happen. It was evident by the huge numbers of people milling around outside the stadium that it was going to be a full house inside and, hopefully, a great show. Sure enough, the ground was jammed to capacity (and perhaps some more after that), which was a great sight to behold. This was an atmosphere that was intoxicating to all.

As we sat in the players' area waiting to be introduced to the masses, my mind was suddenly inundated with memories of our 1987 Cup triumph on this very ground. I could see the massive crowd all willing Australia to victory, the run out of Bill Athey I was involved in, Mike Gatting attempting his now infamous reverse sweep, our victory lap of honour and the buzz of excitement that emanated from the grandstands all day! These were great moments and I only hope, as a side, we will get a chance to experience it again.

Part of the evening's festivities involved all the teams walking onto the arena, one at a time. Australia received a fine ovation, but to liken our reception to the home team's would be like comparing a bumblebee to a Boeing 747. It was one of the great moments; one of those rare things you had to witness first-hand to appreciate. All I can say was that my body was covered in goosebumps and a surge of pins-and-needles tingled around my system.

Unfortunately, even at this stage of proceedings, the compere was beginning to botch things up. First he mixed up the UAE and South Africa, and then he almost forgot Sri Lanka. This from a bloke who had begun proceedings with the line: 'There's no need to introduce myself, you all know who I am.' He obviously rated himself pretty highly and kept telling us so, but in truth he was a complete shocker. The fireworks display was superb but the advertised highlight, a state-of-the-art 'Laser Show' went horribly amiss after strong winds tossed a crucial mesh screen around. This left the laser with nothing to project onto. It was hard to believe that no-one had thought it necessary to attach a few ropes to the screen to stop it flying aimlessly in the breeze, but it had obviously slipped past the organising committee's agenda.

The compere explained away the laser fiasco with the line: 'I'm sorry, but the wind seems to have broken the laser machine.' And his advice to the throng, when it seemed a riot might break out after they learned that they weren't going to see the laser show after all was simply: 'Why don't you all just sit and chat to the person next to you.'

Formalities over, it was back to the hotel, probably before any of the 120,000 people at Eden Gardens had departed, to have an hour's break before setting off for the official opening ceremony dinner. This turned out to be a relaxed, casual outdoor affair, ideal for everyone because it wasn't too formal. There were no speeches and the players had a rare opportunity to have a beer and a chat to men who would be their opponents in the coming days.

As I slipped between the sheets, after a long but enjoyable day, I made a vow to do everything possible to help Australia reach another World Cup Final and once again experience the unique joy of completing a victory lap.

Australians and Englishmen mingle before the 'all teams' group photograph to be taken at Eden Gardens. England's captain, Mike Atherton (front, right), is talking to Mark Taylor and Ian Healy. Lurking in the background (far left) is yet another Black Cat commando.

Steve Waugh

DAY 4 — *February 12*
(Calcutta)

BREAKFAST was once again very good, with canned orange juice, scrambled eggs, baked beans, tomato, grated potato, toast and a cup of tea among the choices. Also to the team's liking was the weather — mild temperatures under a hazy blue sky. But a downer was the air pollution, ever present in Calcutta, which is thick and greasy and seems to coat itself onto your skin.

Ever since we had arrived here, we had received the run-around from local authorities whenever we asked about a training venue. But finally such a facility was discovered, and though it wasn't of the calibre of an Adelaide Oval or SCG it was the best around, with a single wicket and a grassy area the size of a football field on which to practise fielding routines. The spectator facilities, however, were archaic. One side of the ground was lined with wooden planks that appeared ready to ignite at the slightest hint of a spark, while the remainder of the ground looked like something out of a Flintstones episode. The paths, steps and risers seemed to be made of concrete, but were decaying quicker than a dodgy wisdom tooth.

Aesthetics aside, the wicket proved to be more than adequate. Under the watchful eye of physio Errol Alcott, the boys settled down to an enthusiastic session which was interspersed with a punching-bag routine. The highlight was a high-quality fielding session which had all the trademarks of a 1987 workout — there was lots of chat, support and spirit, ingredients that will be extremely valuable in the heat of the battle. We were all aware that any small edge could be the difference between winning and losing.

With a couple of hours spare, Slats and I gained permission from our security staff to have a look around the Ganges River. Our two commando guards joined us, along with Manoj from Group 4 (who'll be travelling with us for the entire competition).

The river was not only alive with vessels but was full of people going about their everyday chores. This was in spite of the fact that the murky brown water was covered in a thin film of what seemed to be extremely unhygienic material, and the river bank was littered with rubbish ... broken pottery, plastic bottles, bricks, decaying food and waste products. We saw a group of three who were washing themselves and their clothes. As they beat their garments violently on the nearby rocks, soap splattered everywhere ... it seemed they were striving to breathe life into these well-used items.

As we made our way along the river bank, a crowd gathered around us, in ever-increasing numbers. We presumed this was because they recognised us, though we had noticed that it took little — a minor disturbance or a buzz of excitement — for these well-natured people to attract each other like magnets. But we quickly realised that the first scenario was the correct one, which was not surprising, considering most of the population is cricket mad and players

The only available practice facility in Calcutta was not quite the equivalent of the SCG. However, after the days of controversy and conjecture, it was brilliant.

are idolised in much the same manner as pop stars in our part of the world. Further on, there were families washing their dinner plates, kids eating plates of rice, adults enjoying a cigarette together and, most commonly, people using the mud banks as a portable toilet. This might sound pretty gruesome, but in reality it is no more than a reflection of the impoverished circumstances in which these desperately poor people live. There aren't any other options; survival is the name of this game.

Food is the number one priority, and there is no opportunity to conform to the ways of the western world. Rather than denigrating their way of life, I admired their spirit and toughness, and over an hour had flown by before either Slats or I checked our watches.

We both wanted to see more of this raw human element that is on display every day in this part of the world, but we were required back at the team hotel, where Hooter had scheduled a team aqua-aerobics workout. The boys were literally jumping out of their skin in eager anticipation of this joyous experience. Sounds professional? The truth was that we were cowering at poolside, unable to convince ourselves that the water was going to be anything other than icy cold. Our worst fears were soon confirmed, and we 'frolicked' about in the water in a state of semi-shock.

Worse was to follow when we began our first 'Nerds v Julios' contest of the tour — a swimming relay race. These contests are normally tough tussles, but due to Ricky Ponting's inability to do anything but sidestroke, we Nerds succumbed to a superior outfit on the day. After this debacle was completed, our illustrious physio suggested we finish with a variety of stretching routines and a fitness workout, and this proved to be an inspirational move. Afterwards, the entire exercise was deemed a major success, if a rather unpleasant one.

Our management accepted a dinner invitation tonight, to visit the Calcutta Swimming Club. Unfortunately, it turned out to be a signathon and snapathon, with autograph books and cameras coming from all directions. On a more positive note, the food was good and the Travelling Blueberries made their long-awaited debut.

You don't want to become paranoid about the food you eat on the sub-continent, but at the same time a commonsense approach is required. Food such as chicken, beef and pork must be served piping hot, while salads are a definite no-no, as they are washed under tap water. And most importantly, only ever drink water from a bottle. You should never, ever drink water out of a tap or else your cricket activities will be curtailed very abruptly.

A surprise announcement was made before the Blueberries began. The duo, it seems, have become a trio. After a mere two hour's tuition on the bass guitar, Slats has joined the fame-bound Lee and Bevan, apparently on the insistence of Bev who wanted to concentrate on his singing. The bass, he felt, was a burden rather than an asset to his performance. Tonight, Lee's guitar playing was a revelation, Bevan's singing deserved a standing ovation and Slater's bass playing was an abomination. Those who were there won't forget it and all are looking forward to gig number two ...

Wherever that might be!

This is supposed to be serious!
Hooter (centre, at back) struggles to keep our focus
on the team's pool fitness workout. The McGrath/S. Waugh combination
(second from left) is in complete control, while the Slater/McDermott (far right) and
M. Waugh/Healy (centre) appear to be in all sorts of trouble.

DAY 5 — *February 13*
(Calcutta)

THE TRAINING SESSION we survived today was one of the toughest I have ever been involved in. The emphasis, pure and simple, was on physical fitness.

The activities revolved around a five-station fitness circuit which had been created by Hooter and his cohorts, Bevan and McDermott, who had somehow found themselves on the team fitness advisory panel. Great news, that, especially when you consider Billy works out with iron men and Bevo is something of a gym junkie, capable of lifting weights Arnie Schwarzenegger would baulk at.

True to their credentials, the boys had us all but hallucinating as we struggled around the circuit, which went as follows:

Station 1 — 50 crunch sit-ups; run 25 metres to get to ...
Station 2 — 30 push-ups; run 25 metres to get to ...
Station 3 — 30 grade-four sit-ups (arms crossed); run 25 metres to get to ...
Station 4 — 30 burpees; run 25 metres to get to ...
Station 5 — 30 squats and jumps; run back to station 1 and repeat twice more!

I know I should, for the uninitiated, try and explain what things like 'crunch sit-ups' and 'grade-four sit-ups' and 'burpees' are, but to do so would only bring back painful memories. Let's just say they are things normal people don't do. While five or six of the boys were performing this routine, another five or six would be working out in the nets, with the remaining few involved in fielding exercises. Though difficult, today's session was once again intense and highly motivated, and clearly sent out a message to anyone watching. This team is intent on having an excellent tournament.

At 5 pm, the team was summoned to Col Egar's room for yet another meeting. This time, thankfully, some light was shed on our situation. We are heading to Bombay, to spend the next six days, before leaving for Visakhapatnam, the location of our first game in the World Cup, against Kenya. One still gets the impression that we aren't too popular and today's show of solidarity game between a combined Pakistan/India team and Sri Lanka, in Colombo, will further enhance this unwanted reputation.

I guess our best answer to the whole fiasco is to go out and play good cricket. After all, we are cricketers. We shouldn't be used as political puppets by people wanting to reassure their public that everything is okay — when it isn't. Sri Lanka is currently a dangerous place, and no cricketer should have to risk his life by playing there.

Late this afternoon, our squad was nearly trimmed to 13, when my roomie tried to charge himself up with 110 volts of electricity during an unsuccessful attempt at changing a light bulb. If only he'd asked me whether or not the switch was on, he wouldn't have had to recoil back in shock. This may sound sadistic, but I laughed as the sparks illuminated the room ... this, I thought, was some form of pay back for the years of nuisance tax he has imposed on us all!

Kangaroo justice

BY SABYASACHI BANDOPADHYAY WITH JOY CHAKRAVARTY IN BOMBAY
AND RITA SEBASTIAN IN COLOMBO

The jubilant Aussies after the dismissal of Sri Lankan Hashan Tillakratne at a recent Test: The accused

MOHAMMED Azharuddin, Wasim Akram, Sachin Tendulkar, Aamir Sohail, Waqar Younis, Anil Kumble. It was the dream team of the subcontinent which aimed to play a goodwill match with Sri Lanka on February 11 to express solidarity with the island nation. Results were unimportant, so when the Indo-Pak team clinched a four wicket victory over the best nation. Sri Lankans shed tears, not over the defeat, but over the camaraderie and the bond that South Asia had expressed in the face of the blatant act of perfidy that two other cricketing nations had done.

"Stone them, lash them," said Sunil Fernando in pithy Sinhala who has no second thoughts about the punishment that he feels should be meted out to the Australian and West Indian cricket teams for opting out of the World Cup fixtures in Colombo for security reasons.

Sunil, a staunch Sri Lankan supporter who has his small pocket radio almost pasted on to his ear whenever the Sri Lankan team plays a match at home or abroad, is an angry young man. "How dare they do this to us when everything was prepared for them and we were looking forward to watching them play."

His sentiments are echoed by people like Lalitha Susanda, a domestic aide who has grown up with cricket since she watched her young brothers play on the village green using a hard slice of coconut bark as bat.

"I would like to stone them myself. That is what they deserve. If the Australians had come they would have been booed and jeered till they left for what they did to our boys in Australia. Cheats. That is what they are."

It's not the Sri Lankans alone. In India too strong sentiments were expressed against the Aussies and the West Indies team for their forfeiting matches in Colombo. Said C. K. Khanna, Hony. Secretary, Delhi and District Cricket Association. "It's foolish of the two countries not to play in Sri Lanka. As a punishment they should not be allotted the World Cup for next two editions."

Another person who also was angry with the two countries was Ram Babu Gupta, former international umpire. "I conducted matches in Pakistan during the Indian tour in 1987. At some places the situation was so tense, but we never thought of boycotting any match citing security reasons. The Australians and the West Indies should have been awarded minus 2 points—instead of 0—for forfeiting their matches."

Suggestions for punishments vary. Former Sri Lankan Test Captain Michael Tissera feels that there should be a major fine or a ban. "One of the two. A fine would be more appropriate in this instance because of the financial losses incurred like TV rights, gate money etc. The ICC should have some stringent rules when this kind of thing happens."

P. A. Selvarajah who played cricket at school and later for his university, participated in the Indian Robinson-Baria tournament for three successive years in the 1940's and played for the Tamil Union in Colombo, emphatically says that the Australians should be banned for at least one year.

He is harsh in his condemation of the West Indians for taking the cue from Australia. "They have demonstrated the servile mentality of slaves bowing to their white masters," says Selvarajah.

But the punishment that 12-year old Susil Ekanayake would like to inflict on the two teams is frightening. He rolls his big eyes, looks pretty ferocious and delivers his verdict, "Skin them alive."

But not everybody is likely to declare war on the Australians and West Indies. Some people are quite sympathetic with them. Like former Test cricketer Dilip Sardesai. According to him, the Australians and West Indians were not totally at fault. "They must have recieved some report about insecurity in the island country and thus have pulled out. It doesn't look nice and the Sri Lankan government and fans may feel bad about the decision, but why should one play under constant threat. I feel no fine or penalty should be imposed on them this time. But there should be a penalty clause added in the rule books from next time onwards," says the former cricketer.

Sardesai finds support in celebrated coach Ramakanth Achrekar who says that the sentiments of the countries who are playing should be respected. "The Australians and the Caribbeans must have arrived at the decision after giving it some thought. I really won't like to put the fault on them," says Achrekar.

V. S. Hariharan, an equity research analyst with Prime Equities endorses his views. "While the Australian pullout can be considered as genuine, one really can't explain why the Windies pulled out. But even the Aussies were more threatened because of the death threats against players on Muralitharan and Malik issues. The bomb blast was just a convenient excuse.

"I feel a monetary fine should be imposed and not suspension. If you suspend West Indies and Australia what is left in world cricket?"

Like public opinion, there were great contrasts in the various newspaper editorials and reports on our decision to bypass Colombo. Some comments we felt were fair and balanced, others seemed illogical, wildly emotional, even bizarre. One Sri Lankan official allegedly responded to a remark by Shane Warne that shopping in the streets of Colombo would be dangerous by questioning Shane's manhood. 'Shopping,' this bloke is supposed to have said, 'is for sissies!' In London, the award-winning columnist Simon Barnes, in The Times, *wrote what I thought was a ridiculous piece in which he suggested that our decision to forfeit the Sri Lankan game amounted to no more than a 'comic subplot'. We were, he reckoned, 'unaware of the priorities of a greater world,' and should have 'blithely' accepted what he quite calmly describes as 'life's turbulence'. He went on to compare the Australian reaction to the Colombo bomb blast to David Campese complaining about the way the English rugby team play their football, and to describe the Australian complaints about bodyline back in 1933 as being no more than a whinge about the 'accurate, professional execution' of a shrewd plan. Over the years Simon Barnes has written some outstanding columns and articles. This wasn't one of them.*

The article reproduced above illustrates the extent of some negative opinion our decision generated. 'Stone them, lash them,' was one view. 'Skin them alive!' cried another. But this is a story that does put both sides. The former Indian Test batsman, Dilip Sardesai, is quoted as saying: 'It doesn't look nice and the Sri Lankan government and fans may feel bad about the decision, but why should one play under constant threat?'

Checking out of a hotel and paying your account is a relatively easy process in Australia but in India it's tougher than completing a faultless gymnastic routine on the balance beam! Many a mysterious charge appeared on the McGrath/S. Waugh printout. A 'miscellaneous' charge being just that. Miscellaneous!! There was a bill for video machine use, which we had thought was complimentary, and then there was the crowning jewel ... the hire of a car for an afternoon. Pretty fanciful, that one, considering we hadn't been allowed out of the hotel without tight security. Closer inspection revealed that the car had been hired at exactly the same time we were in a team meeting. With such a watertight alibi, the hotel management had no choice but to relent — a major achievement in itself — and some joy was thankfully had in our quest for a realistic bottom line.

DAY 6 — *February 14*
(Calcutta to Bombay)

AN OBSCENE WAKE-UP call arrived at 5 am and only just had the desired effect. And it was Pigeon, and not I, who was finally coaxed out of the sheets. To compound our ugly moods, the designated departure time of 5.45 am drifted out to 6.15 am, not because of any late arrivals, but because the usual half a dozen chiefs couldn't agree on what actually was the correct time for our farewell, or even who was supposed to load the bags onto the bus.

Mishap number two was never going to be far away but came even quicker than we could have thought. We ended up at the wrong airport. Thankfully, however, this wasn't too costly as the correct one wasn't too far away.

Once there, we were escorted to a private lounge, which had been carefully disguised as a private autograph session for the local police. That mission accomplished, we thought the coast was clear to board the plane. Incorrect! Next stop was the airport security system, which required us to take our hand luggage through metal detectors and an X-ray machine and then turn around and come out the same way we entered in order to collect our bags and again board the bus, which would take us out to our plane. Then, when we boarded the plane, a few players' seats were already occupied.

Our original schedule had us in Colombo for the first 10 days of the World Cup, so it was almost impossible to find any accommodation in Bombay at short notice. Our choice of the Centaur Juhu Beach Hotel was determined on the grounds of availability and not preference.

Simmo soon had us into action with a practice session at Bombay's Gymkhana Club, which happens to be one of the most exclusive clubs in all

What we're all fighting for

The World Cup trophy is an antique, sterling silver trophy that was actually made 118 years ago by the London crown jewellers, Garrards, an establishment that is still going strong today. After Garrards' design concept was accepted by PILCOM (who had a bevy of alternatives to choose from), the jewellers crafted and modified that original Cup to suit the demands of the organisers, and then presented it to be fought for by the 12 competing nations.

The Cup weighs in at four kilograms, and stands 12 cm high. Its most elaborate feature is an etching of a 1785 painting, which depicts a game of cricket played on an English village green and is based on a painting that is part of the magnificent cricket museum at Lord's.

Although the victorious captain will be handed the original trophy at the presentation ceremony after the final in Lahore, the Cup they get to take home will be a replica. The original trophy will remain the prized possession of the people who paid for it ... the sponsors.

Australian Picture Library/A

The sixth World Cup finally began today, in Ahmedabad,
where New Zealand defeated England by 11 runs. Nathan Astle, who scored 101,
and opening bowler Dion Nash (3-27) were the heroes for the Kiwis, while Graeme
Hick managed 85 for the Englishmen. Here Nash auditions for a part in the next
Toyota commercial after taking the wicket of Dominic Cork.

of India. The only negative to this move was the distance of the Club from our
hotel — a good one hour and 45 minutes away. The practice wickets, though,
were very good, and a tough uncompromising session was turned in — proof
again that all the lads are jumping out of their skins after our days of inactivity.

Not surprisingly, the trip back to the hotel saw the lads starting to flag due
to exhaustion, and our mood wasn't helped by the news we were to change
hotels as soon as we got back. Then our departure from the Centaur Juhu
Beach was delayed by around 45 minutes because the porters couldn't decide
how to load our bags onto the bus. Or, more likely, they didn't like the idea of
lifting these metal monstrosities that carry all our equipment.

The hour-long drive to the centre of Bombay was made more enjoyable by
the musical talents of Shane Lee, who produced his guitar and gave us the
opportunity to join in for a sing-a-long. Songs that were butchered included
Jesse by Joshua Kadison and *American Pie* by Don McLean. By the time Bon
Jovi's *Wanted Dead or Alive* had been attempted and discarded, we had made
our final destination for the day, the five-star Oberoi Hotel.

The Telegraph

28 PAGES CALCUTTA WEDNESDAY 14 FEBRUARY 1996 RS 2.30

IN BRIEF

Sensex crosses 3,500 with 56-point gain

Mumbai, Feb. 13: The Bombay stock exchange sensitive index opened 15.68 points below its overnight level at 3,456 but finished at the day's highest point of 3,527.84 today. This was 56.16 points above its previous close, reports our special correspondent.

The composite national index, in a similar pattern, opened 11.08 points below its previous level at 1,584.41 but closed above the 1,600-mark at 1,607.70, 12.21 points above its previous close. The BSE-200 and the dollex gained 4.97 and 2.33 to 357.04 and 160.75, respectively. The NSE index gained 0.74 to 77.91 and the 51-scrip CSE index lost 4.36 to 459.05.

Details in Business Telegraph

The Telegraph

Included free with The Telegraph today is World Cup Plus, the first of several four-page cricket specials we will publish in the course of the tournament. Also, joining Ian Chappell on The Telegraph's exclusive team of experts are Sir Richard Hadlee, Greg Chappell and Ashok Mitra (from tomorrow).

J&K attack

Jammu (PTI): Militants attacked a village in Mughal Maidan in Doda district on Monday night, looted over a dozen houses and kidnapped a youth, official reports received here said. Over 10 militants raided the village and stormed into selected houses at gunpoint.

Indo-Nepal ties

New Delhi: The Nepalese Prime Minister, Mr Sher Bahadur Deuba, said on Tuesday his country will continue to demand scrapping of the security clause in the Indo-Nepal treaty of 1950, says our special correspondent.

Full report on Page 4

Haj quota raised

Jaipur (PTI): Haj pilgrims quota has been increased to 56,000 this year. The minister of state for external affairs, Mr R.L. Bhatia, said all applicants from Rajasthan would be accommodated.

Thackeray suit off

New Delhi (PTI): The Supreme Court on Tuesday dropped contempt proceedings against the Shiv Sena chief, Mr Bal Thackeray, for derogatory remarks against some of its judges, reports our legal correspondent. The court accepted his unconditional apology

Jaya files plea

New Delhi (PTI): The Supreme Court on Tuesday referred to a constitution bench two appeals filed by the Tamil Nadu chief minister, Ms Jayalalitha, and Tamil Nadu state, challenging an order of the Governor, Mr M. Channa Reddy. Mr Reddy had sanctioned prosecution of Ms Jayalalitha on corruption charges.

QUOTE OF THE DAY

Neighbours in need are neighbours indeed

A banner at Premadasa Stadium, venue of the Indo-Pak solidarity match

3 flags unfurl as Lankans celebrate cricket; World Cup starts today

India, Pak forget bitterness to call Australia's bluff

FROM SUMIT MUKHERJEE

Colombo, Feb. 13: Arch foes India and Pakistan fielded an unprecedented joint team against Sri Lanka here today to prove that only sportsmanship could conquer fear of terrorism.

The display of solidarity between the co-organisers of the Wills World Cup, India, Pakistan and Sri Lanka, came as a fitting rebuttal to Australian and West Indian fears of lack of security and touched the hearts of millions of cricket fans here.

Australia and West Indies boycotted their matches here after a bomb blast on January 31 killed 86 people and wounded more than 1,300.

In the hastily-arranged goodwill match, the Wills XI, boasting the best Indian and Pakistani cricketing talent, defeated Sri Lanka by four wickets. After restricting the Lankans to 168 for nine off the allotted 40 overs, they scored 171 runs in 34.3 overs. For the visitors, Anil Kumble took four wickets for 12.

It was a bit like the Eden Gardens. The crowd stayed back after Waqar Younis hit the winning runs to cheer the victorious team. Azhar got a standing ovation when he received the Wills Solidarity Cup.

The Indian skipper and captain of the goodwill team, Mohammad Azharuddin, summed up the mood after the game when he said: "We came here for a cause and showed the world that cricket was the winner today. I think a point has been made and it was worth coming all the way."

Tendulkar, who had problems meeting Akram's high five after catching Romesh Kaluwitharna, agreed. He said: "It was a tremendous experience, all of us playing together. I am glad I was a part of it."

The dream team's manager, Intikhab Alam, gushed: "It's history being made here."

It was all about cricket but, for once, the game itself took a back seat. The mood here was festive and emotional. As one of the banners said, "Neighbours in need are neighbours indeed."

Thousands of fans lined up patiently to catch a glimpse of the cricketers. Shouts of "India, Pakistan zindabad" rent the air as the bullet-proof air-conditioned bus whizzed past en route to the Premadasa Stadium.

CALLING A SPADE A SPADE: This poster may not be great poetry but sums up the mood at the Premadasa Stadium in Colombo, venue of Tuesday's Wills XI-Sri Lanka solidarity match (AFP)

The entire route was dotted with banners proclaiming, "We salute your magnificent gesture of solidarity" and "Sri Lanka welcomes the golden sons of India and Pakistan."

A five-year-old elephant, Kandula, draped in a gold-brocaded sheet, greeted the players as they got off the bus. Children wearing traditional dresses of the three ethnic-religious communities of Sri Lanka, the Sinhalese Buddhists, Tamil Hindus and Muslims, danced to the beat of drums.

Inside the stadium, cricket-crazy Lankans ensured a carnival atmosphere. Nearly 14,000 spectators sang Hindi film songs and danced to their tune to set aside resentment and disappointment at the Australian and West Indian boycott.

Another poster said: "The Wills World Cup belongs to Asia", indicating that regionalism, rather than nationalism, was the order of the day.

Some could not help taking a dig at the Australians. "Aussie Prime Minister is Keating, Australians are cheating", said a poster. Four men jogged around the stadium carrying the flags of India, Pakistan and Sri Lanka and shouted: "India, Pakistan zindabad, Australia very, very, bad."

The fiercely-patriotic Sri Lankans cheered Azharuddin and Tendulkar as they dazzled with the bat. Even the self-appointed flag-bearer of the home team, Percy Abesekhara, was seen waving all three flags; and nobody did it better than him.

The Indian High Commissioner to Sri Lanka said: "It was a wonderful and spontaneous gesture of solidarity by the cricketers."

And members of the Wills XI disregarded personal inconveniences to make the political point. After attending the opening ceremony in Calcutta on Sunday, the players arrived here early today, went to bed a little before dawn and were on the field about six hours later.

Before the game Azharuddin stressed the immense discomfort the players willingly underwent. He said: "It is great to be here. I only hope we don't fall asleep on the ground."

All members of the Wills XI boast a hysterical following in the sub-continent, but their participation in today's match cemented an emotional attachment with fans here.

On their part, Sri Lankans threw an elaborate security blanket around the Premadasa Stadium. A truck laden with 180 kg of explosives was yesterday found inside a pagoda, only 2 km from the stadium, leading to the unprecedented security arrangement.

The stadium was guarded by commandos with M-16 automatic rifles, mounted policemen and sniffer dogs. Fans entering the stadium had to go through six checkposts and only labelled vehicles were allowed into the stadium. The bomb squad and 10 sniffer dogs searched the terraces, the Army patrolled the outer perimeter and the police controlled the crowd inside.

The players were accorded security usually reserved for visiting heads of states. But the best thing about the massive bandobast was that it did not restrict players' movement inside the pavilion.

Pakistani skipper Wasim Akram said he was not bothered about yesterday's discovery of the explosive-laden truck. He said: "We came here to play cricket and that is what we did."

Sri Lankan board officials looked relieved after the match went off smoothly. The treasurer of the board, Mr Hillary Marcelline, said: "If the Australians and West Indians don't come even now we have nothing to say."

In Calcutta, the Australian coach, Bobby Simpson, reiterated his country's decision not to go to Colombo. He said: "Our decision has already been made official. There is no change in our stand."

The West Indians also stuck to their position. The president of the West Indies Cricket Board of Control, Mr Peter Short, yesterday said in Bridgetown: "I cannot conceive of any measure that would absolutely guarantee the safety of our players."

WORLD CUP

REPORTS

PAGE 8
- Parents resent bitter Cup
- Cricket, books no sops for CPM voters
- CAB stands to strict test

PAGE 14
- Greg Chappell's column
- Cricket proves to be great leveller
- Battered Lankans enjoy a place in the Sun
- Raj hangover at Ahmedabad
- It's boom time for bookies
- Former Bengal cricketers not optimistic about Eden wicket
- Dream team mesmerises Lanka

PAGE 16
- England, NZ set to kick off cricketing extravaganza
- Security for English team beefed up
- Windies most disciplined team, says Wes Hall

TODAY'S MATCH

England vs New Zealand, Ahmedabad

TELECAST TIMINGS

PRIME SPORTS
- 8 am: Wills World Cup preview
- 9 am: Live telecast
- 10 pm: Highlights
- 2 am(Thursday): Highlights' repeat

DOORDARSHAN I & 7
- 8.50 am Live telecast

DOORDARSHAN METRO
- 2pm-2.25 pm: Live telecast

EXPERT EYE

Boycott puts Australia, WI on razor's edge

BY RICHARD HADLEE

Finally, following many months of media speculation about the 1996 World Cup, the time of reckoning has arrived. After the opening ceremony in Calcutta on Sunday evening, all teams are going through their final warm-up sessions and anxiously awaiting their first round matches. Today is the showdown between New Zealand and England, who meet at the Gujarat Stadium in Ahmedabad.

Having won six of their last 12 one-day International encounters against India, Pakistan and Zimbabwe, New Zealand will be feeling more confident than England who lost five of the six one-day matches on their recent tour of South Africa. This is an important game for both teams.

New Zealand's tour of India in 1995 gave them the opportunity to experience the conditions which will have assisted their preparation and build-up to the World Cup. However, New Zealand has made some changes to the team which toured before Christmas and they appear positive in their approach. Players like Spearman, Astle, Fleming and Cairns are potential match winners.

England may be buoyed by their impressive World Cup record, even though they have been the losing finalist in 1983, 1987 and again in 1992. Maybe this year they feel they can go all the way.

The host nations, India, Pakistan and Sri Lanka, will enjoy considerable advantage. Pitch conditions, climate, health, changes in diet and the large fanatical partisan crowds, which the visiting nations must adapt to, could be very influential.

Without a ball being bowled, Sri Lanka have already qualified for the quarterfinals. This is a big advantage. However, they will miss out on match play from two hard games which may in fact handicap them for future advancement in the tournament.

On current form, Australia appear to be the best allround team in both Test and one-day cricket but they have put their chance of becoming world champions at risk through forfeiting their match against Sri Lanka. They now cannot afford to lose a match to lesser-rated Kenya or Zimbabwe.

Like Australia, the West Indies have put their chances at risk by not playing Sri Lanka. Their recent form has been erratic and they do not appear to be the powerful and dominating force in the cricketing world they were in the 1970s and 80s. They should, however, still be respected, especially with the world's premier batsman, Brian Lara, back in the team who could be a very positive influence on both the senior and junior players in their side. The West Indies, winners in 1975 and 1979, have a competitive nature and a proud record to uphold which could prove to be just the motivation they need.

South Africa have a hard and uncompromising approach to the game and their recent form over the last two years shows that they will be difficult to beat. Zimbabwe, Holland, UAE and Kenya may have difficulty going beyond the preliminary rounds but any of these teams could cause a major upset.

While India have heroes in Sachin Tendulkar and Azharuddin, players like Manoj Prabhakar and Kumble could be just as influential. Wasim Akram and Waqar Younis are potent strike bowlers for Pakistan but it will be the batting of players like Inzamam and the experience of Miandad that will add stability to Pakistan's effort to retain the World Cup.

Sri Lanka have experience in their captain, Arjun Ranatunga, and vice-captain, Aravinda de Silva, but I have also been impressed with the fast improvement of Chaminda Vaas as a left arm pace bowler.England's trump card could be Graeme Hick while South Africa's could be Daryll Cullinan and Fanie De Villiers.

I was very impressed with Zimbabwe's Heath Streak during their recent tour of New Zealand. Australia's three Ws, Shane Warne, Mark and Steve Waugh, are all wonderful players who complement a well balanced team. In Curtly Ambrose and Courtney Walsh, they have experienced bowlers who can pick early wickets. This will help inspire the West Indies.

All teams have match winning players and this 1996 World Cup will be an important time for them to cement their authority on the game.

Meet backs Rao on hawala

FROM OUR SPECIAL CORRESPONDENT

New Delhi, Feb. 13: The Prime Minister, Mr P.V. Narasimha Rao, today succeeded in getting all state party leaders to endorse his "cleansing drive" against hawala tainted politicians.

In a cleverly worded resolution passed at the end of the PCC(I) and Congress Legislature Party leaders' meeting, the Congress(I) appealed to all political parties not to draw mileage from the hawala scam.

"The reality, as it has emerged, has revealed that when a social or economic malaise strikes, it makes no distinction between one party or group and another, whatever the claims. Instead of trying to paint each other black, leaders of society would do well to realise the facts and make all possible efforts to find remedies in the common interest of the people," it said.

The meeting was a well planned move by Rao loyalists to rally state leadership behind the drive against corruption and shows little sympathy for hawala-tainted ministers.

Though no direct reference was made to the hawala issue, most leaders expressed solidarity with Mr Rao's current initiative. "This meeting welcomes the decision of the Prime Minister to give a free hand to the investigating agencies in discharging their duty of bringing out the truth," the resolution said.

It also noted: "The Prime Minister has always stated that the law will take its course and indeed the legal process is being allowed to take its own course, no matter who is involved therein. This attitude alone will help cleanse the society in general and the political process in particular."

The resolution made it clear that the move initiated by Mr Rao needs to be given support by everyone.

Mr Rao set the tone of the meeting when he said that for the past few weeks the mood of the Congressmen had been on the "upswing" and party workers appeared to be much more "ethusiastic" than what they were in the previous years. He also spoke about the various schemes undertaken by his government to give relief to the poor and weaker sections of society.

Though nobody directly made any demand for denying party tickets to tainted leaders, many wanted candidates with a clean image. This indicated Mr Rao will continue to keep partymen and Cabinet colleagues on tenterhooks about their political future.

Delhi court dismisses case against Rithambara

New Delhi, Feb. 13 (UNI, PTI): A Delhi court today acquitted the Vishwa Hindu Parishad activist, Sadhvi Rithambara, of charges of whipping up communal sentiment saying they were "politically motivated."

The sadhvi has been charged with making inflammatory speeches against Muslims at Vishwas Nagar Chowk in November 1990. The then deputy secretary (home), Mr M.S. Siddiqui, had requested the special branch of Delhi police to initiate criminal proceedings against her.

The metropolitan magistrate, Mr Sanjay Agarwal, said in his 12-page order today: "The court is of the opinion that registration of the case against the accused is influenced by political forces." He added the case was registered haphazardly and the chargesheet filed without proper scrutiny.

Mr Agarwal ruled that after hearing the prosecution and the defence no prima facie case under Section 153 A of the Indian Penal Code could be established.

Earlier, the defence counsel, Mr Alok Kumar, contended the prosecution did not have proof the speech had hurt Muslim sentiments.

He also argued the prosecution could not prove the case against his client in the absence of witnesses and proof like audio or video recordings of the speech.

Mr Agarwal then ruled: "I have no option but to discharge the accused Sadhvi Rithambara of the offence as prima facie no case is made out."

The order further said: "The accused stated nothing against any particular community so as to insult it. There is no evidence on record to suggest that feelings of any particular community or persons were hurt by the alleged speech."

Swami sits pretty as cases drag on

FROM R. VENKATARAMAN

CENTRE YET TO GET VITAL RECORDS

New Delhi, Feb. 13: The Centre has not been able to proceed against Chandraswami despite several prima facie cases against him.

The government's documented submissions to the Supreme Court detail his involvement in the St Kitts case, Fera violations and cases of cheating NRIs.

The document obtained by The Telegraph says the letter rogatory sent to St Kitts "has not yet been executed". Chandraswami is accused of forging bank documents to implicate Mr Ajay Singh, son of the former Prime Minister, Mr V.P. Singh. He is charged with committing "illegal acts of forgery and fabrication of false evidence, framing false records, with a view to show that Mr Ajay Singh maintained a foreign account no. 29479 worth $ 21 million with First Trust Corporation Limited (FTCL)".

However, six years after registration of the case, the government has told the Supreme Court that the original document "available in the almirah of Mr T.V. Byron, a solicitor and one of the founder directors of the FTCL, have not been made available so far despite repeated requests and personal visits".

The status report, an annexure, says, "It has not been possible to secure the original records either by the CBI officer who had visited St Kitts during 1990-91 or through letters rogatory sent". Thirtytwo letters rogatory were sent to various countries, including the US, Canada, St Kitts and Spain since 1988 and 10 show-cause notices issued to the accused for Fera violations.

The document is a comprehensive list of cases against Chandraswami as the Supreme Court has decided to club all cases against him to take a decision on whether he should be arrested and whether the government and its investigating agencies are proceeding in accordance with the law.

The public interest litigation seeking Chandraswami's arrest was filed by advocate Anukul Chandra Pradhan. The apex court appointed senior counsel Anil Dhiwan as amicus curiae assisted by lawyer A.K. Sahu. The duo have been amicus curaie in the hawala case.

The document says, "There is no further information available from St Kitts and the investigation can only be finalised on receipt of the results of execution of letters rogatory sent to St Kitts".

On a Fera case accusing Chandraswami of acquiring foreign exchange worth 6000 pounds (which he deposited in the High Court of Justice Queen's Bench Division in defamation suit no. 6353 of 1984), the status report says, "On completion of investigation, the allegation was proved and SP's report was sent to the Director of Enforcement, New Delhi on 29-12-1989 for initiating necessary action".

Action is yet to be taken as the joint secretary of the home ministry, vide his letter dated December 20, 1995, forwarded a letter indicating "no evidence" to the effect that the amount in pounds was deposited by Chandraswami and his former PA, Kailash Nath Aggarwal.

The Fruit of Love

About 12 months back, cricket writer, Robert 'Crash' Craddock invited me to fill in a 'player profile'. It was one of those question-and-answer type things that feature questions such as 'favourite drink', 'favourite movie', 'most memorable moment in cricket', 'which person in the world would you most like to meet?' ...

My first choice for that final question was born Agnes Gonxha Bojaxhiu, in Skopje, Yugoslavia, on August 27, 1910. But she is known throughout the world as Mother Teresa. I guess this was an unusual selection, but that was it, and afterwards Crash and I decided that if we were ever together on tour in India, then we would make all attempts to meet this revered and admired, almost saint-like figure.

After we arrived here for the '96 World Cup, numerous calls were put through to the relevant authorities, and finally an early morning meeting was arranged to coincide with yesterday's 6 am service at Calcutta's Sisters of the Missionaries of Charity Mission.

I don't mind confessing that I hardly slept at all, owing to a mixture of excitement, nerves and anticipation at seeing first-hand a person loved across the planet. Mother Teresa has devoted her whole life to helping those less fortunate than herself. This, of course, is a difficult concept for the average person to comprehend, for it is always easier to look after yourself than worry about others. But not this remarkable lady, who resists the temptation of material objects. Instead, she gives away everything she receives to the needy of the world.

Our driver for the morning took a group of us through the streets of Calcutta, at a time when the city was beginning to come to life.

I saw workers carrying their tools of trade atop their heads. Animals were lugging huge loads, while school kids travelled to school in rickshaws. The homeless were warming themselves up with open fires that had been lit by the side of the road, as their young children playfully ran about despite the fact they had barely a strand of clothing on their backs.

When our driver exclaimed, 'We're here!' I was somewhat surprised. Looking around, I couldn't see anything out of the ordinary — just low-storey buildings in poor condition, the same as everywhere else. There were no security guards, all, it seems, are welcome. We were led down an alley way and then told to take a right into an open doorway. Discretely placed on the concrete walls were signs: 'No photography or video cameras allowed.' However, fortunately, we had gained permission to bring a photographer (Trent Parke) in with us, to take one or two shots for a newspaper story.

By the time we'd been escorted up the two flights of well-worn concrete stairs by a sister, mass had begun. The room used for the service reminded me of an old schoolyard classroom, with wooden shutters all along one side and open doors on the other. The floor was more than half full with the sisters, every other vantage point was crammed to the limit by a mix of locals and overseas visitors. It was an eerie experience seeing the sisters sitting on the floor as the early morning sun streamed through the open shutters — these filters of light glistened across the top of the sisters' heads, giving them an 'angelic' appearance.

Moments later they were all on their feet, shuffling forward to receive their communion. What I will never forget is how varied were the ages and races of the sisters; no two looked alike. This was, it occurred to me, in itself a show of solidarity for their faith and beliefs.

From where I was, just outside the open doors in the walkway, I had a slightly obscured view of proceedings and still hadn't spotted the woman I had wanted to see. Then it seemed the service had ended, and what had seconds earlier been eagerness now changed to severe anxiety. Where to go? I spun around, and was about to point the group to what I thought might be a better position when suddenly our team liaison officer propped, his jaw hit the deck and then he dropped to his knees and assumed the prayer position.

In my haste to turn around and see what

ail the fuss was about, I nearly bumped into a hunched-over sister, not more than one-and-a-half metres tall. Only now did I realise what was happening. Mother Teresa was in our midst.

Our team liaison officer jumped quickly to his feet, hustled himself into a position where he could gain Mother Teresa's attention, and quickly introduced me as a member of the touring Australian cricket team. She replied with a polite 'hello', while I managed to blurt out 'pleased to meet you'. Then she shuffled off to the masses who were eagerly awaiting her presence.

The extent of her status and respect was evident everywhere. People were genuinely awestruck, none more so than a lady near me who broke down and cried.

I thought our meeting had ended, but was delighted to see Mother Teresa head back towards us. As she walked, she handed out what seemed to be tiny pieces of paper. It was extraordinary — you could feel her calming influence, and an aura only special people exude. I noticed she moved with some difficulty. Her mangled and deformed toes and fingers betraying the ravages of arthritis, while her arched back reflected both her

age and the sicknesses (and three heart attacks) that have plagued her in recent years. But she did not look ill. It was as if her great inner strength was coming through.

She shuffled to within a metre of me, and stretched out here hand. 'Here,' she said, 'have one of my business cards.' Then she moved on, and out of sight, back to her living quarters.

The card read: 'The fruit of silence is prayer, the fruit of prayer is faith, the fruit of faith is love, the fruit of love is service.'

Through all of this, Trent Parke had been a total nervous mess. Photo opportunities had been rare, and he was unsure whether he had the photo he was after. Not many people get the chance he had, to photograph Mother Teresa in her own backyard.

We all went back to the hotel, totally uplifted by this morning's events. I now hold her in even higher esteem than before. All the way home, and for most of the day, I reflected on the unique vow that makes these remarkable women so special ...

'To give whole-hearted free service to the poorest of the poor ...'

DAY 7 — *February 15*
(Bombay)

OUR PRE-TOUR strategy of training as hard as, if not harder than, any of our opponents, much in the same way as we did in 1987, was once again put in place this morning. The easy and probably preferred option for most of the lads would have been to have a rest and relaxation day today after the shambles of yesterday, but another toughening-up session was the call from team management. This clearly suited the sadistic mind of Errol Alcott, who had plotted a series of torturous upper-body exercises — this time there were six stations of sickness, the first being a two-minute boxing routine. Then came ...

2. Two minutes of push-ups
3. Two minutes of cycling — elbows to knees
4. Two minutes of shoulder work (arms to stay horizontal)
5. Two minutes of stomach work (one of crunches, one of leg lifts)
6. Two more minutes of boxing combinations

Hooter, being an intelligent man, decided that if we were each allocated a partner, it would be of some physiological benefit. His thinking was that we would encourage each other in the quest for better results. However, I can vouch for the fact that the pairing of S. Waugh and S. Warne failed to reach the expected heights; in fact, we walked away with a couple of injuries. The push-up leg saw yours truly damage a wrist in the search for excellence, while Warney stumbled on the boxing routine when a poorly-timed right uppercut sent a shooting pain down his already cortisone-injected right-hand ring finger.

Spurred on by our sterling efforts, the following pair, Healy and McDermott, carved up the course and it was whispered afterwards that they may look to the Atlanta Olympics as their next challenge. But the rest of the squad didn't give the impression that they were the cream of Australian cricket. Many a move was poorly executed, with perhaps the worst being that of Ricky Ponting, who managed to squeeze a straight right past the intended target of Paul Reiffel's gloves and smack poor Pistol on his not insignificant 'bugle'.

Who is this 'Step Wog'?

Our squad has three players sporting goatees — Ricky Ponting, Stuart Law and Damien Fleming — and the trio are continually throwing the locals, who pride themselves on recognising each and every member of the squad. And the Indians are once again unable to wrap their tongues around the name 'Waugh'. No matter how hard they try, 'Wog' is always the outcome. After touring here four times now, I am beginning to feel at home being called 'Step Wog'!

Ricky Ponting (left) and Paul Reiffel in happier times, during the 'six stations of sickness' fitness routine. Soon after the photo was taken, Ponts put Pistol down for the count, after a solid straight right missed its intended target.

Needless to say, it was hard work having to fire up for a net session after these strenuous activities. But we all somehow found the inner strength, with all the batsmen in the squad beginning to adjust to the slower Indian wickets.

Lunch at the Gymkhana Club was as good as anywhere in Australia and almost all the lads tucked in. The two exceptions were Warney and Punter, who had by this point succumbed to stomach problems and headaches.

Such setbacks are all part of touring places like India and Pakistan. They are all but unavoidable, and must be seen as such, and not as mini disasters. In most cases, the body comes to grips with the unaccustomed stomach bugs and the symptoms fade away after a couple of days of the appropriate treatment. Medication, though, is vital, especially anti-malaria tablets. Two international cricketers, Saeed Anwar of Pakistan and the West Indies' Carl Hooper, have contracted malaria in the past 12 months.

By mid afternoon, my roomie was showing signs of becoming victim number three, as he made frequent visits to the bathroom to drive the large white porcelain bus. Pigeon's facial complexion began to take on a distinctive ashen look, and it was soon apparent that he would miss tonight's official function — a cocktail party put on by the hotel management.

And to give you an idea of the lack of social activities on offer over here, the team stayed at the cocktail function for a full hour after the required time. This kind of devotion to duty is unheard of in countries such as Australia, England and South Africa.

The main discussion at the function was, of course, the Sri Lanka boycott. No matter how hard we try, we just can't get away from it. Reports today suggested that Australia and the West Indies may be fined up to $US3 million each for refusing to play in Colombo. One senior Indian official was quoted as saying that the agreement between PILCOM and the 12 teams competing stipulated that a financial penalty could be imposed in the event of a team forfeiting a match. Our management doesn't agree, so there may be some more arguments between administrators before the matter is finally sorted out.

Ironically, although the decision to award the two points from the game to Sri Lanka was made four days ago and there is no chance of us changing our minds, technically we still haven't 'lost' the match. That, under the rules of the World Cup, cannot happen until the scheduled day of the game.

The Cow who lived on eighth floor

I read this newspaper report a couple of days back, and have decided to reproduce it here, without comment.

This is the story of a cow that once lived on the eighth floor of a building in south Calcutta. The gentle looking creature belongs to Mr Hari Prasad (not his real name), a businessman from Uttar Pradesh. Three years ago, when Mr Prasad's son got married, he joked with the bride's parents: 'People get cats and dogs for dowry, the least I can get is a cow!'

Not in his wildest dreams did Mr Prasad imagine that his off-the-cuff remark would be taken seriously. Lo and behold, within a few days he got a call that a cow, with a calf in tow, were on their way to his house. 'My first reaction was one of fright,' he says. Where on earth was he going to keep them? Mr Prasad lived in an eighth-floor apartment.

He lived in dread, regretting his joke. Till he saw the cow and the calf. And then, he says, it was love at first sight. He adored them and wanted them, even if it meant giving up part of his eighth-floor flat for them. He named the cow Sherni (a lioness).

Now the next hurdle: how to cart the pair all the way up to the eighth floor. The building did not even have a lift. The calf was literally carried up, cradled in a man's arms. The cow followed meekly, slowly and steadily, up the eight floors.

Mr Prasad doted on his new companions. Unfortunately, the calf did not really take to living in an apartment and died within a few months. The cow, however, didn't mind the high-rise living. It was Mr Prasad who got a bit tired of handling a cow in an apartment. He got in touch with a friend who owned a farmhouse in a Calcutta suburb, and decided to shift her there.

Now the next problem: how to get Sherni down the eight floors. At the end of each flight of stairs he spread gunny bags to act as cushions in case the cow tripped. It took hours to get her down — the climb down was far riskier than the walk up.

Sherni was moved to her new home at the end of last year, where she is thriving in the company of other bovines. Mr Prasad has now decided to shift her to a new property he has bought near his friend's farmhouse. But he still misses her. Each time he talks about her there is a twinkle in his eyes. 'She is really good-looking and has an exceptional figure.

'Don't you think so?'

DAY 8 — *February 16*
(Bombay)

OUR RELENTLESS pursuit of excellence continued again this morning, as we left for the Gymkhana Club at nine o'clock. We were without Shane Warne and Ricky Ponting, who were both bedridden with stomach viruses.

The journey to the ground (now only five minutes — thank goodness for the hotel swap) was an eye-opening experience, as the massive population scurried to work in all directions, like ants coming out of the mounds in search of food. The smog is everywhere — an accepted part of life here — but it doesn't make it any easier on your eyes, which smart from the fumes, or on the asthmatics, who struggle as they inhale the toxic air. Animals such as goats, buffaloes and cows roam the streets, oblivious to all happenings around them. But even they would have noticed the wall of a building that had collapsed overnight and landed on a couple of parked cars not far from the Gymkhana Club.

Training today revolved around fielding routines, which have so far been relatively sparse. We certainly made up for lost time, though.

To begin with, the squad was broken up into two groups. The first exercise was a repetitive one, as it concentrated on speed to the ball, a clean pick-up and a clinical execution, which ended with a throw to the stumps. There was a fair degree of running involved in this exercise, as it required the boys to continually rotate and repeat — I like that, skills and fitness all in one. After this 15-minute warm-up period was over, we split up into three even groups, one headed by Simmo, another by Heals, and the third by Tubs.

Being interviewed at the Gymkhana club. It turned out that the female reporter knew more about me than I did!

Australian Picture Library/All Sport

Simmo handled the long and high ball catching, again tormenting all with his deft touch and innate sense of when a player is beginning to falter under his assault. Perhaps Simmo's finest hour occurred in India during our 1986 tour when he had wicketkeeper Tim Zoehrer back-pedalling with catch after catch until he strained every muscle in his body trying to apprehend another steepling high ball. This Tim accomplished, but unbeknown to him, he had strung himself up on a barbed wire fence, and he needed assistance from fellow players to free himself from the mess.

Going global

Australian Picture Library/All Sport

The second match of the tournament, between South Africa and the United Arab Emirates made the afternoon pass reasonably quickly, with South Africa's opening bat Gary Kirsten's 188 not out a superb effort (right), even considering the poor quality of the opposition's bowling. This was the highest score in World Cup history, and only one run short of the all-time one-day internationals record, held by Viv Richards.

The UAE are an unusual team, with only one home-grown player, their captain Sultan Zarawani. He's a Sharjah-based property magnate worth more than $A10 million, who usually takes his own personal doctor and physiotherapist on tour with him. Mr Zarawani was obviously trying to show some defiance and bravado when he came out to bat minus a helmet. His side might have been in dire straits, but this move appeared to be bordering on suicidal, considering South Africa's fastest bowler, Allan Donald, was operating at very good pace at the time. Sure enough, the first ball to the man wealthy enough to own a garage full of Ferraris clocked him on the forehead before the UAE skipper had even attempted anything resembling a stroke, or even an attempt at protection. To Zarawani's credit, he remained at the crease, although he was by now a mere shell of a man and fell victim to a timid shot soon after.

Even though teams like UAE, Holland and Kenya are highly unlikely to beat any of the Test-playing nations, it's great to see them involved. It not only encourages other countries to try and qualify for the next World Cup, but if cricket is to prosper in the future against other sports it will need to become more 'global' than it currently is.

From this energy-sapping routine, the group of Reiffel, Fleming, McDermott and S. Waugh fell into the clutches of the ex-physical education teacher, Mr Healy, who drilled us extensively. Then we were catapulted into the captain's domain of executing run outs from short distances. The work was tough but rewarding, and I felt that it was sharpening my game up just that little bit that could make all the difference in a match situation.

A small-scale net session followed, with all the bowlers having a hit in the middle. Pigeon's reverse drive that splayed the stumps everywhere was a standout stroke. Perhaps I'm being a little harsh on him, as his batting is definitely on the improve, and this little mishap was the result of frustration at the deteriorating state of the wickets, and one or two average strokes.

I visited the physiotherapist's room this afternoon for treatment to my right shoulder, which has flared up a little in recent times. However, there is nothing to be concerned about, so long as I keep up my strengthening program.

While the West Indies were beating Zimbabwe tonight in Hyderabad, we headed to a function hosted by Star TV, Asia's leading pay-TV network. Star-TV is currently run by an Australian, John Swinstead, which is a huge personal success story as he started from the very bottom in the media some years back. The highlight for many of the lads was the quality of the rum on offer, which brought back many fond memories of our recent Caribbean tour. The evening was capped off by a team get-together at the Taj Hotel Bombay, where we enjoyed a couple of very expensive nightcaps. Just one example: a nip of Baileys set me back 400 rupees (around $US12).

DAY 9 — *February 17*
(Bombay)

ORIGINALLY today was going to feature our opening match of the Cup, but the game in Colombo has, of course, been long abandoned. Instead, a much needed and deserved day off was on the agenda, but it got off to a poor start when a reporter from an Australian radio station rang at 6.30 am to request an interview. When I explained that this was an unsatisfactory time, the guilty party claimed ignorance, saying: 'I didn't realise it was so early.' This was a lame excuse, but you'd be surprised just how many times it's been used. One would have thought it was part of their job to know such things.

I'm sure people sense when you have a day off, because the phone rings more often than Commissioner Gordon's and a sleep-in is out of the question. However, one phone call which is always welcome is from my wife, and this morning's call was of extra significance as she rang to give me details of her 18-week ultrasound. This was an event I would have loved to have been involved in, especially as this is our first pregnancy. Missing moments like these is tough, but we all realise these sacrifices are part and parcel of the job.

My days off on tour are usually spent having a look around the town I'm in, but today was a non-adventure day, as I've succumbed to a stomach bug.

Steve Waugh

A young Bombay coconut seller waits patiently for his next customer.

Bombay is a cruel mix of some opulence and much grime and poverty.

The thought of an unexpected attack while shopping or seeing the sights was too much of a risk. So the first half of the day in room 1405 saw both Waugh and McGrath venturing no further than the doors of the mini-bar and expending energy only via the index finger which operated the remote control for our only entertainment — the TV.

My only other worthwhile activity of the day was to book a half-hour massage at the Health Club. Luckily for me, a local legend, Dessi, was given the job, and his 16 years of experience at working in these small plain locker rooms was put to good use in 30 minutes of whirlwind action.

Dessi is very proud of the fact that he has massaged many champion cricketers in his time. He has names such as Viv Richards, Allan Border, David Boon, Malcolm Marshall and Bob Simpson to his credit, and it seems that these occasions have all been great moments of his life, judging by the excitement and tone of his voice when he mentions them. Dessi uses many a unique method to revive tired and aching muscles, and his work was of a high quality, but it must be said that if you visit his massage table and your pain threshold is less than Mike Tyson's, then you are in for an experience you will be unlikely to forget. His fists moved like pistons and had the hardness of steel as they pulverised my calf and hamstring muscles in much the same way a chef would prepare veal for a schnitzel. And he used his elbows and thumbs to carry off some other tricky manoeuvres.

The choice of dinner for a partially recovered Warne, a struggling S. Waugh, a now healthy McGrath and an always healthy Reiffel was of the Mexican variety, and turned out to be the feed of the tour so far. But somehow I don't think this was a very wise move on my part. Putting this somewhat spicy meal into a stomach that felt like a hessian bag full of kittens virtually guaranteed that a large part of tomorrow would be spent in the bathroom.

Speaking of diets, Warney has none — well, not quite, but he's finding it tough to track down a quality toasted cheese sandwich and fries in this neck of the woods.

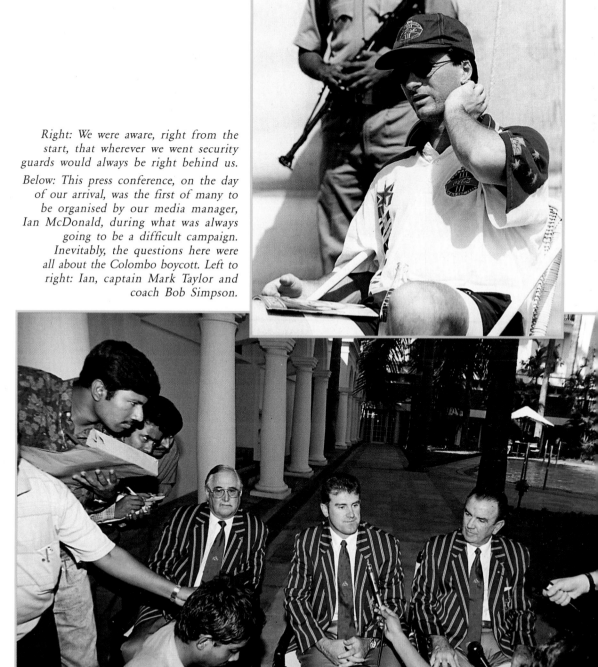

Right: We were aware, right from the start, that wherever we went security guards would always be right behind us.

Below: This press conference, on the day of our arrival, was the first of many to be organised by our media manager, Ian McDonald, during what was always going to be a difficult campaign. Inevitably, the questions here were all about the Colombo boycott. Left to right: Ian, captain Mark Taylor and coach Bob Simpson.

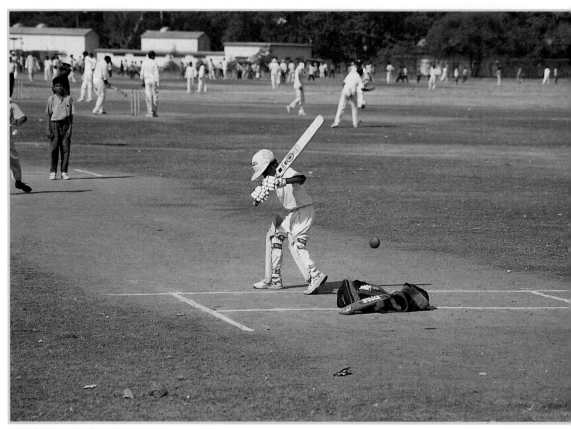

Above: A young Gavaskar or Tendulkar protects his makeshift wicket on the playing fields of the Gymkhana club in Bombay.

Below: A street kid in Bombay, outside the Gymkhana club. This young bloke would chase our team bus everyday, looking for any spare rupees.

Whatever might be happening in the world, cricket is always the lead story.

The opening ceremony in Calcutta, February 11, 1996. The state-of-the-art laser show is in full swing.

Above: Armed guards (foreground) watch the action in Visakhapatnam during our opening match of the World Cup, against Kenya.

Below: The end of my innings in Vizag, caught by the Kenyans' impressive opening bowler, Martin Suji, for 82.

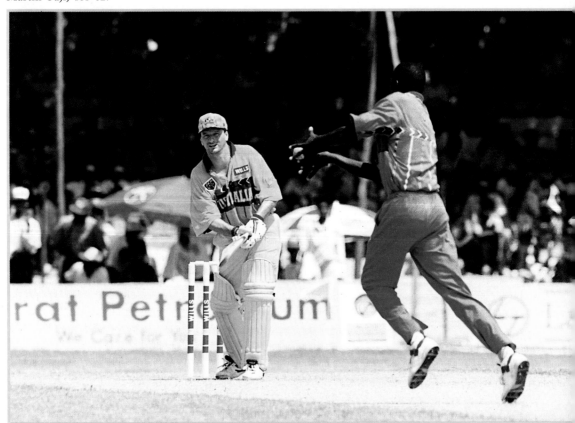

Above: Shane Lee (left), Ricky Ponting (in white cap) and Glenn McGrath (behind) enjoy a rickshaw ride through the streets of Bombay, 24 hours before our match against India.

Below: India's captain Mohammad Azharuddin (left) and Ian Healy enjoy a 'private' chat before our evening practice in Bombay.

Above: Mark Waugh puts India's Venkatapathy Raju into the crowd in Bombay, one of three sixes he hit during his glorious 126.

Below: Glenn McGrath, dismayed, frustrated and angry, after missing a difficult caught-and-bowled chance against Sachin Tendulkar.

DAY 10 — *February 18*
(Bombay)

IT'S AMAZING what a short break away from the game can do for one's enthusiasm and clearness of thinking. It was something I touched on in Australia recently when I said that the injury problems that have caused me to miss a couple of weeks of cricket in recent seasons have ultimately done me a favour, as I had come back into the team feeling revitalised and ready for action. I believe that this week of relative inactivity for the side will have a similar effect on each player. Today's practice match was our chance to get back into the swing of things.

The game took place at the scene of the first ever cricket Test match played in India, the Bombay Gymkhana club. These playing fields are famous throughout India for it was here, on this oasis in the middle of an area dominated by row after row of neglected-looking high-rise apartments, that such champions as Sunil Gavaskar and Sachin Tendulkar began their cricketing careers. With playing fields at a premium, I have seen as many as 10 matches in progress at once, on an area suitable for three or four at the most. It is not uncommon for players from different contests to collide when in pursuit of balls, or for games to be halted momentarily when a fielder chases a ball across the wicket of a neighbouring match. It is watching these games that drives home to me the love of the game of cricket over here — things such as adequate facilities and equipment aren't the number-one priority. Just getting a game started is!

The many fans of Tendulkar would have been more than pleased with his performance today in Cuttack — a man-of-the-match winning 127 not out in India's seven-wicket thrashing of Kenya. In today's other game, England had their first win of the competition, an eight-wicket defeat of the UAE in Peshawar.

Our practice match involved all the members of our squad (minus Warney and Billy, who are both nursing injuries) being split up among the local Gymkhana team to produce two evenly matched sides. The Gymkhana side was captained by a man known as 'Singh', and took to the field armed with six Aussie players — M. and S. Waugh, Healy, Lee, Slater and Reiffel. From the outset we knew we had a leader full of knowledge and great confidence in his own ability. This was evident when he asked of Paul Reiffel: 'From which end would you like to bowl?'

'I'm easy,' Pistol replied, 'it doesn't really bother me. But I'll take the top end!'

The top end was the one facing the Pavilion, and came complete with a gentle downward slope to the wicket and a nice breeze behind it.

However, very swiftly and unexpectedly came this retort from Captain Singh. 'No, you bowl from the other end. This one is mine!'

By the time the first ball was bowled a large crowd had congregated, keen for a first-hand look at the 'Kangaroos', as we were called. The wicket,

The field may have been open, but the background was spectacular and the match practice invaluable.

thankfully, played pretty well, except for a couple of rearing lifters that appeared later on (unfortunately, one of these caused the end of my brief innings, just as I was feeling comfortable). Highlights of the day included an encouraging partnership between Law and Ponting, two players of different techniques but similar ability. Punter is more of a dasher and smacker of the ball, whereas Stuart tends to guide and caress his strokes with effortless power. It's always good to have players in your line-up with different approaches to batting, as it doesn't allow the opposing bowlers a chance to settle into a rhythm or to employ a game plan that they can re-use without having to improvise.

The other encouraging performance was turned in by the highly promising Shane Lee, who hits the ball as cleanly as anyone I've ever seen. His 96 not out was an indication that he may be about to fulfil his undoubted potential, and fill the role in our one-day side that Simon O'Donnell occupied with distinction for many years — the bowling all-rounder who can change the tone of a match with his aggressive batting. Other players to do well included M. Waugh, Healy and Bevan, who all looked good with the bat, and Damien Fleming, who showed glimpses of his repertoire with some subtle changes of pace. It wouldn't surprise me to see Flem play an important role in this competition.

Although this game wasn't the ideal preparation for the big games ahead, a practice hit in the middle is always more beneficial than any net session, as it is as close to duplicating a real match situation as you can get.

The evening was spent at the Gymkhana club. So prestigious is the club that, although there are currently over 5,000 members, the only new members being admitted from now on are the children of the current members. Their hospitality was first class, with only the seafood items given the thumbs down, because of our pre-tour instructions on what to eat and what not to eat. Significantly, our suspicions about the prawns were confirmed when we realised that even the locals were giving them a miss.

Left: 'Heals,' I said, 'don't you have any idea how to spell your name correctly?' In fact, most of our shirts had to be sent back and altered, owing to the ordinary spelling ability of the manufacturer.

Below: Getting down to the serious stuff ... Ricky Ponting cover drives, with Heals keeping wicket.

Both pics: Australian Picture Library/All Sport

DAY 11 — *February 19*
(Bombay to Madras)

IN KEEPING with our aim of being physically strong for the upcoming five weeks, Hooter summoned the boys to the gym at 9 am sharp. Today's agenda saw the team split into two groups. One concentrated on an aerobic workout — 15 minutes on a variety of machines such as the stair master, a rowing machine, an exercise bike and a treadmill. None of these devices bring any joy to my world. Meanwhile, the other group had their work cut out negotiating a searching examination on the gym circuit, while the eagle eye of Alcott surveyed their every move. Remarkably, my early desire to fake stomach cramps or claim a migraine headache was soon forgotten, as I, along with all the boys, got into the swing of things. At the conclusion of the session I even had to concede that it might have been a beneficial one.

We boarded the team bus at lunchtime for a one-hour trip to the airport. We were heading for Madras, en route to Visakhapatnam, but by the time we had settled into the airport lounge, Warney had realised he'd left or lost the bag that carried all his cash and credit cards. Needless to say, he was in a state of panic until the missing item was located back at the Oberoi.

As usual, we experienced another plane delay, a fact that begins to niggle away at you when it becomes a regular thing. Two hours later we landed in Madras, feeling a little tired and very hungry, especially as the meal offerings on the flight had resembled play dough and smelt uneatable.

At our overnight hotel, we received the usual friendly welcome, with a garland of flowers placed around each player's neck and a facial makeover with red dye splashed between the eyes. Then, after a quick Chinese meal, it was straight to bed.

Both pics: Steve Waugh

Left: The secret behind the world's greatest slow bowler ...
endless chocolate bars. Right: Pigeon (left) and Lawie, complete with flowers and make-up,
trying to impress the locals in Madras.

DAY 12 — *February 20*
(Madras to Visakhapatnam)

PLANE TRAVEL on the sub-continent never fills anyone with great enthusiasm, especially when it comes after a 6 am departure from the hotel (which had necessitated a dreaded 5.30 am wake-up call). My new roomie, Slats, stirred first, while I remained motionless until it was deemed necessary to get my act together.

All was going fine as we prepared to board our flight to Visakhapatnam until we heard the announcement that our flight had been put back by 105 minutes due to bad weather. This was a somewhat surprising excuse, considering the whole of India was devoid of rain or cloud, but there wasn't much we could do except head off to the airport breakfast lounge. By this point it was evident that this wasn't going to be a good day, a fact that was underlined when our initial order of tea and toast proved too much for the staff to handle. Some 45 minutes later, our hunger pains were satisfied when some scrambled eggs made a surprise but pleasant appearance on the buffet table.

If one thing can put you off your food here it is the poor state your cutlery and crockery is often in. This morning, the waiter noticed that my cup looked distinctly dirty and tried to rectify the situation by inserting a couple of fingers and running them around the inside of the rim in the hope of removing the foreign debris. That he did achieve, but I'm not sure whether I was any better off for the whole exercise.

Our flight eventually left at 9.30, though we were travelling in a distinctly rust-riddled Boeing 747, whose appearance didn't instil any confidence in the dodgy flyers in the team, most notably Tubby Taylor. Once on board, it quickly became apparent that if you were 180 cm in height or over, you were in for one very uncomfortable trip as the seats were packed almost on top of one another. One almost had to laugh at the sight of McDermott and McGrath, their knees almost around their ears, struggling to come to terms with the lack of leg room.

The hour-long journey couldn't pass quickly enough, and when we arrived at this city by the sea we were met once again by the traditional flowers and red dot between the eyes welcome. It was on to our hotel, where, not long after my room-service tomato soup and southern fried chicken had been digested, it was time for another fitness session, this time by the pool.

Treading water with stomach cramps isn't easy, and I don't recommend it to anyone who has a dislike of pain, but 45 minutes on and a series of exercises later, I felt just about ready to make an assault on any number of the swimming events in Atlanta in late July.

To fill in the afternoon I opted for a haircut, shave and head massage. The haircut was performed with a reasonable display of skill. The shave was okay, at least until the second attempt, minus any shaving cream, relieved me of a

The 'Travelling Blueberries' – Slater, Lee and Bevan. Or is it the 'Land of the Giants'?

few layers of skin. But this minor irritation was merely a warm-up for the severe pain that lay ahead. I was expecting a nice soothing massage, and was quite taken aback by the early pulverising blows to the back and side of the skull, which set the tone for more of the same to follow. For a while I felt as if I was in a *Three Stooges* skit, with eye gouges, clips around the ears, knuckles on the crown of my head and slaps to the temple being the norm. The massager then moved on to a series of agonisingly brutish attempts at lifting my hair and skin from my skull. When this agony was finally over, I sat crumpled in my chair in a lather of sweat, not feeling at all well.

'How was that, Mr Wog,' my torturer enquired, 'very good?'

'Good' wasn't quite the adjective I was thinking of, but I happily handed the rupees over and made a dash for the exit before he could offer me a body massage.

In Faisalabad, South Africa were beating New Zealand by five wickets, with Hansie Cronje scoring 78 and Allan Donald taking three wickets. Meanwhile, my roomie was busy in room 602 (the abode of Bevan and Lee) trying out the guitar he had acquired in Bombay. The Travelling Blueberries have certainly had their share of ups and downs recently, with a major split nearly occurring last week. Meadow had volunteered his deft musical ear to tune Bevo's bass guitar, but tragedy soon struck when, in searching for excellence, Shane pushed the tautness of a string that little bit too far and snapped it. This might not sound too bad, but when it was revealed that the boys had no spare strings things grew a little tense. And they stayed that way until Meadow agreed to try and track another one down for his despondent partner.

Another setback to the band's mega stardom aspirations occurred when Bev lost his 'Learn How To Play Bass' instruction book. But from there the boys have bonded together in the face of adversity and are now regularly having what they call 'jam sessions' (we call them 'bedlam' sessions). Slats also keeps telling me he's improving with every strum.

He is also a believer in the tooth fairy!

DAY 13 — *February 21*
(Visakhapatnam)

TODAY'S EDITION of the *Hindu* newspaper contained two very interesting articles concerning safety. The first concerned safety measures that have been put in place for our stay here:

'In all, five Assistant Commissioners of Police, 20 Circle Inspectors, 48 Sub-Inspectors, 130 Head Constables, 431 Constables, and eight Armed Platoons, equivalent to three companies of Andhra Pradesh Special Police (APSP) besides an anti-sabotage squad and a pack of sniffer dogs specially requisitioned, will guard the Australians from the time their plane lands till they fly out to the venue of their next match. The players would be advised to lodge themselves on a common floor in their five-star hotel on the beach road and move about only in groups. Every bush and garbage bin around the hotel and the stadium will be inspected with metal detectors and by sniffer dogs for any explosive substance.

'Routes have been ear-marked for the players to motor down to the hotel from the airport and to the stadium for net practice and the match. They would be transported in buses, each having armed police on board and escorted and piloted on the road by trained personnel.'

A couple of pages further on, under the headline 'SCHOOLS TO OPEN' ran a story about the current state of unrest in Sri Lanka. It read:

'All schools in the country, other than those in Colombo district, will re-open on Monday.

Mark Taylor is being well looked after, as he talks to the press in Vizag.

Trent Parke

Schools had been shut down island-wide on February 14 amid fears of a possible attack by the Liberation Tigers of Tamil Ealam (LTTE) on educational institutions, though no official reason had been given for the closure.

'In a related development, a hand grenade was found close to Ananda College in Colombo city today. It was of a make used by the Tigers, but police appear mystified as to why it was left outside the college.'

This decision to close down schools came as something of a surprise to us, since the government had been telling the world that Colombo was a safe venue for international cricketers to play their World Cup matches.

These articles highlight that safety and security are both still a major concern over here and it does make you a little bit paranoid to read about it. It seems to me that Sri Lanka is too dangerous a place to visit for everyone except cricket teams, a fact I can't come to terms with!

When I woke this morning, I discovered a bunch of faxes beneath our door, all addressed to my roomie, who turned 26 today. Slats celebrated this occasion with a practice session this morning, on a ground that appears to have a very good wicket and reasonable outfield, and that does have adequate practice facilities. One peculiar sight for all of us was that of a group of ladies, dressed in traditional sari dresses, rolling the wicket in preparation for the Kenya match, which is still two days away.

The team completed an intensive workout, without any health or injury concerns. To finish the session off, we were put through a series of fielding drills reminiscent of a workout from a decade before, when Simmo first took over the coaching reins. It went for around 45 minutes, and was very physically draining, with match situations simulated to ensure maximum benefit.

I'm sure all the lads are keen for some match time after waiting so long for a game. After Sri Lanka and Zimbabwe made their tournament debuts today (the Sri Lankans won easily, by six wickets, with Aravinda de Silva making 91 and Asanka Gurusinha 87), only Pakistan and ourselves have yet to take the field. The reason for the Pakistanis' inactivity is a result of Ramadan, a religious festival that lasts for a month and forbids any food or drink intake between daybreak and sunset.

In today's other match, India comfortably defeated the West Indies, in a match billed as the clash between the world's two greatest batsmen. Brian Lara made only 2 for the Windies (out of 173), though he was apparently the victim of a dodgy umpiring decision, while Sachin Tendulkar took advantage

The Vizag groundstaff, female and male, share the pitch-rolling duties.

Heals, Warney and Tubs pray to Errol Alcott for 'no more!' during our team workout, while a group of hotel employees appear to take great pleasure in the trio's agony.

of a couple of early let-offs to hit a match-winning 70 as the home team won by five wickets.

Tonight saw the mobile casino swing into action in the manager's room, with Warney, Heals and myself looking after the bank. This involves providing drinks, music and gambling equipment. On one table a roulette wheel attracted some of the seasoned gamblers, most notably Junior, while the other game on offer, blackjack, was nearby and also drew a large crowd. The situation looked grim early on for the bankers, as roar after roar went up from the gambling fraternity, but when the dust had settled 90 minutes later, and the sums had been done, the loss to each of the bankers was a mere 300 rupees, or about $11 Australian — good value considering the entertainment and bonding it provided. Nights like these are invaluable on tour. They break the boredom and get the lads together, which is a much better alternative than everyone staying in their rooms watching television and/or getting homesick.

Security continues to be unbelievably tight, with armed guards manning the floor 24 hours a day. Sometimes it gets on your nerves, especially when a guard follows you down in the lift, then escorts you to the breakfast room. He might leave you to eat, but you're always aware that he's waiting for you outside the door. I guess it is necessary, but it does give you the feeling that something may happen. And the worst part is that I'm unable to leave the hotel and have a look around at the local environment.

Col Egar has claimed something of a coup by securing a couple of slabs of Foster's beer. This part of India is a dry area (no alcohol in public), so the manager's efforts are particularly noteworthy. It is not surprising how good the Aussie beer tastes. The local Kingfisher variety tends to be unfriendly to the palate and even harsher on the head the following morning.

DAY 14 — *February 22*
(Visakhapatnam)

I WOKE early with severe stomach cramps, after tossing and turning for most of the night. Hopefully this will be no more than a 24-hour problem, and one that doesn't affect my performance in our World Cup opener tomorrow.

Practice was once again the order of proceedings for us this morning, with a 9.30 session at the ground. The virtually all-female ground staff were hard at work by the time we arrived, with half a dozen girls on their hands and knees scouring the match-day wicket, and brushing the grass upwards with their palms in preparation for the mower to trim the excess off later on. Others were marking out lines by hands, another group fixed the boundary rope to the ground with metal clips. Later on, the pitch would be rolled, while all the time heavy loads were carried atop some of the women's heads. This was to be Vizag's first limited-overs international, so nothing was being left to chance.

Another good session was turned in by the team with the only concern centring on Billy, whose calf strain is still niggling away at him. Despite my

Groundstaff in Vizag make their final preparations for tomorrow's game.

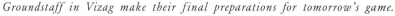

Trent Parke

ailing health, my form with the bat today was encouraging and I'm really looking forward to having a great World Cup. And I'm also looking forward to being able to put the feet up for a while, once the Cup is over. We'll be starting again in August, when we begin a period where the Australian team will be playing or touring for 21 months out of 22.

Due to popular demand, the casino was on again tonight. Unfortunately, the bankers were immediately in trouble, losing seven blackjack hands in a row to the delight of the group of Lee, McDermott, McGrath, Ponting and Taylor, who were all as humble as ever in their time of victory. However, much to the distress of these lads, we clawed our way back and would have recorded a healthy surplus except for the remarkable efforts of Punter, who walked away with enough cash to buy a weekender at Burnie, on the northern coast of Tasmania.

It will be a relief to finally get among the action against Kenya tomorrow. It's hard to believe that this will be our first game, while England, who defeated Holland by 49 runs in Peshawar today (England 4–279, Graeme Hick 104 not out, Graham Thorpe 89; Holland 6–230, Noortwijk 64, de Freitas 3–31), have already played three times. We expect to execute a handsome first-up victory, but at the same time we are aware our opponents have a lot of natural talent, and will be coming at us as hard as they can, in the hope of a fairytale victory.

Playing to others' expectations

The size of the media contingent seems to have doubled in the last 24 hours, as the game draws nearer. This, of course, means endless interviews, photos and demands on your time. Ironically, it seems the only media not here are the Channel Nine commentators, whose flight was cancelled this morning and isn't due here until one hour into tomorrow's game. Apparently, this means that one or two of our reserves might make their debuts in the commentary box.

Unfortunately for my roomie, he's one of the unlucky ones whom Channel Nine might be approaching. Flemo has also been left out, which, when you consider the calibre of these two players, shows just how strong our squad is.

It's an interesting period in Michael Slater's career, as it is really the first time he's experienced a bit of a form slump and is not an automatic selection since he made his international debut on the 1993 Ashes tour. In my opinion, he's had too much advice from people willing to offer instant remedies. In fact, the answer must come from within, as is always the case. An honest self-assessment will provide him with the necessary solutions.

From my vantage point, it appears that Slats began to believe he had to play to everyone else's expectations. I had a similar problem at a similar stage in my career. People told me I was a dashing, debonair strokemaker, who must always thrill the crowds with exciting and dangerous play. Only trouble was, I was getting out too often, too early. While there is no doubt Slats has the ability to electrify the masses, it is a tactic fraught with danger — no-one, except perhaps a Viv Richards or a Gary Sobers, can stay at the top playing this way.

I believe Slats has an excellent technique, and doesn't need to hit a lot of balls in the air or play a succession of risky shots; his natural ability, quick reflexes and sense of judgement will see him score quickly enough anyway. By playing up to other people's expectations he will only drag himself back to the level of players with less ability and cricketing sense. I'm sure Slats will come to terms with his present situation and return to the top an even better player for going through this soul-searching phase.

DAY 15 — *February 23*
(Australia v Kenya in Visakhapatnam)

AS THE SUN first appeared over the Indian Ocean horizon this morning, I was once again suffering from severe stomach cramps. This was not exactly the preparation I would have preferred for today's game, but it's all part of touring life here, and just a minor hurdle to overcome if I want to be successful.

Today's temperature seemed to be more stifling than in previous days, and we arrived at the ground to see a steady flow of spectators beginning to fill the concrete terraces, shaded by makeshift bamboo and thatched roofs, that had been erected only days before. Shane Lee was named twelfth man for the fifth consecutive time in a one-day international, and must now be desperate for some on-field action. Mind you, he does come under what we jokingly refer to as the 'same pay, no pressure' category.

Just as had been predicted yesterday, the Channel Nine commentators failed to arrive in time, so ace reporter Michael Slater found himself with a microphone in hand giving the millions of viewers back home his pitch assessment, à la Tony Greig. Judging by Slats' professional performance, the Nine boys would be well advised not to make any more mistakes with their travelling arrangements.

After Slats had returned to the commentary box, the Kenyans won the toss and unexpectedly sent us in. Batting first was our preferred option, but before long their decision was looking a wise one. At 2-26 (Taylor 6, Ponting 6), the crowd were ecstatic with proceedings, and perhaps the opposition were having visions of a shock victory to match Zimbabwe's historic 1983 World Cup win over Australia. And the Kenyans' position could have easily been even better. Mark and I played and missed more than once, and looked scratchy early on against what was a highly committed outfit. Their fielding and bowling in the first 15 overs was outstanding, and I had to check twice that their caps weren't red with a palm tree as their emblem.

However, as with most ICC sides, there is a lack of depth to their bowling attack. A few possessed reasonable talent, but the remainder were no more than honest triers, bowling innocuous slow mediums or off spinners that wouldn't turn on a merry-go-round. Mark and I realised the runs would eventually come, once we became accustomed to the slow nature of the wicket, and we gained the ascendancy pretty quickly, to the point where we were regularly taking six or seven runs off each over.

By the halfway stage, our main concern wasn't the opposing bowlers but our health, with yours truly in a fair deal of distress with stomach cramps and Mark complaining that his pads were so hot they felt as if they were on fire. From a potentially disastrous start, the 'Wog' brothers took the score to 233 before Mark departed for 130 entertaining and enterprising runs. In the process, we created a new World Cup partnership record of 207 runs.

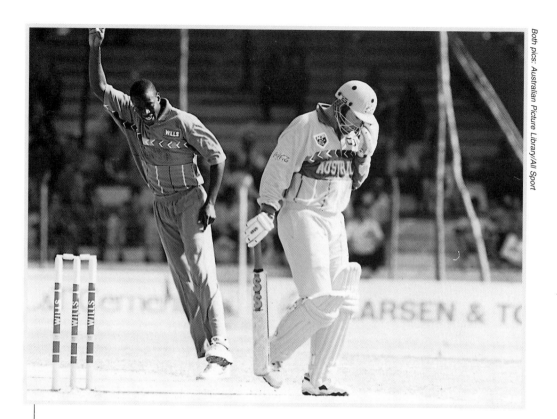

Both pics: Australian Picture Library/All Sport

My time in the middle came to an abrupt end next over, as I fell victim to a sharp caught-and-bowled chance from the Kenyans' impressive opening bowler, Martin Suji, for 82. I'd scored 82 off 88 balls, a stat that was most vital for me, as I've made it a personal goal to try and achieve a 100 per cent strike rate during the competition. But by that point, a big total was assured, and with the help of some innovative cameos from Stuart Law (35) and Ian Healy (17) we passed the magical 300 in a one-dayer and went to our buffet lunch a satisfied group.

Lunches at our matches are generally provided by the hotel we stay at, as we know what we are getting and that the food is of a good quality. A normal menu would consist of soup (either chicken or tomato), a chicken and/or beef dish,

Above: The first Australian wicket to fall in the Cup: Taylor, caught Modi bowled Suji, 6.
Below: Craig McDermott's World Cup ends.

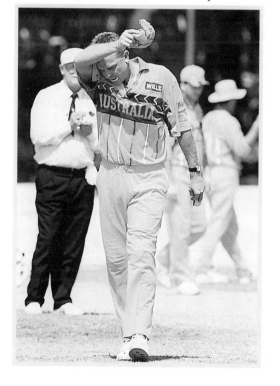

I'm not quite sure which of our reserves this is, but someone is running on to give Mark Taylor some instructions.

vegetables, spring rolls, steamed rice, fried rice, naan bread, and ice cream (if required).

The resumption of the match required our full attention, as we needed to give a good account of ourselves in preparation for the bigger matches ahead. Our initial breakthrough came via a beautifully bowled McDermott outswinger, but was tinged with disappointment as the wingnutted one from Ipswich aggravated his vulnerable right calf muscle. Soon after, Billy was left with no choice but to leave the field, adding to a disastrous run of debilitating injuries he has suffered on overseas tours in recent years.

Sensing what was a somewhat lethargic Australian mood in the field, and the loss of a key bowler, the Kenyans stepped up a gear, and it took a miraculous catch from Punter to put their aspirations on hold. His effort in latching onto a thunderbolt from the flashing blade of the highly respected Steven Tikolo at backward point left our opponents struggling at 2-30, but even so, we sensed the Kenyans would not be going down without a fight.

Normally an incoming batsman likes to acclimatise to the conditions before upping the tempo but not Kenya's captain, Maurice Odumbe. With cat-like reflexes and eyes an assassin would love to possess, he tore off a cover drive, first ball, that Victor Trumper would have applauded. More of the same soon followed, as he and the increasingly confident Kennedy Otieno flailed us to all parts with awesome timing and natural power.

My introduction into the attack was like giving kids fairy bread at a five year old's birthday party — they couldn't get enough, and what they did get they devoured.

Mind you, I wasn't Robinson Crusoe as everyone came in for some harsh treatment. Some of the Kenyans' strokeplay matched the calypso champions at their very best. At the 25-over mark, their run-rate was comparable to ours, but we knew that one wicket would change the course of the match and Michael Bevan, with his deceptively flighted wrist spinners, proved to be the game breaker. Bev claimed Odumbe, caught by Paul Reiffel, for 50 scintillating runs and their skipper was soon joined in the pavilion by Otieno, who succumbed to the strains of keeping wicket and opening the batting and had to retire hurt. This was a great shame, as he was cramping up when on the verge of becoming only the third ICC player to score a century in the history of the World Cup. He was 82 when he limped off, and added only three more after he limped back some overs later.

As we had expected, the Kenyan batting fell away sharply after number four, but they did pass the 200 mark and won much respect and admiration for their carefree and daring approach.

The end result was inevitable, but we did have to work for the win, and in doing so, exhibited both positive signs and a need to do some work in a number of areas, including ground fielding, stemming the early onslaught in the first 15 overs and overcoming a lack of 'hustle' and 'go forward' in all our work. These facets of our game will hopefully come out when the games get tougher and we are forced to switch on completely.

The major negative to come out of today's game was Billy's injury, which was diagnosed after the game as a torn calf muscle. His Cup campaign is definitely over and it will be interesting to see if PILCOM grant us a substitute. The decision is at their discretion.

Possibly the biggest positive to come out of today's game was the manner

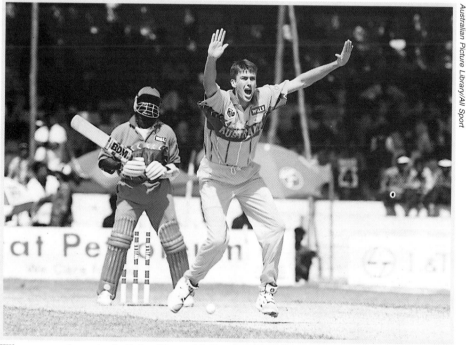

Australian Picture Library/All Sport

Who cares where the ball is. Glenn McGrath appeals unsuccessfully for the wicket of Kennedy Otieno.

in which the two teams, and the umpires, got together back at the hotel for a beer and a chat. A thoroughly enjoyable couple of hours were had by all, with the Kenyans' quest for knowledge insatiable and their desire to improve and gain further experience at this level quite obvious. It was interesting to learn that they had devised individual plans for each of our players, which had been developed after many hours spent watching video footage. I liked their attitude of having a go and not worrying about opposition players' reputations. They were more concerned with trying to establish a name for themselves.

It's amazing these days just where coverage of the Australian domestic season's cricket goes to. We were told that ESPN had shown our recent series against Sri Lanka through all of Kenya. Another interesting piece of information to come out of our conversations was that the Kenyan team was chosen from only 10 sides currently playing in the Nairobi competition. Even more amazing was the news that the Kenyan boys do at least five laps before every training routine and regularly run over 3000 metres in 10 minutes just for fun. This type of 'fun' would definitely see the enforced retirement of many of the current Aussie squad, including Stephen Waugh.

Having seen how keen players like Kennedy Otieno, Steve Tikolo, Maurice Odumbe and Martin Suji were to gain experience, I offered to try and find them a grade cricket club in Sydney, where I'm sure they'd be a huge hit. The evening also provided a chance for me to swap a shirt with their captain and get a photograph of the two sets of brothers in their side (Maurice and Edward Odumbe and Steve and David Tikolo) with Mark and me. The night was a huge success, confirming once again that more mixing between the sides after games can only be beneficial for all concerned.

Three sets of World Cup brothers
— Maurice and Edward Odumbe, Steve
and Mark Waugh, and Steve and David Tikolo.

The World Cup brought together some famous (and not-so-famous) names. On the following eight pages, are photographs of just a few of these cricketers, from the 11 other nations who took part.

Above: Throughout the Cup, India's Sachin Tendulkar (left) and Vinod Kambli promoted the product of the chief rival of the official World Cup soft drink.

Right: Tendulkar's clash with Shane Warne in Bombay was eagerly awaited and when Shane bowled his first ball, the local champion went whack, straight back over the bowler's head for four.

Right: Brian Lara celebrates his century in the quarter-final against South Africa.

Below: England's captain Mike Atherton, typifying his country's ordinary Cup form.

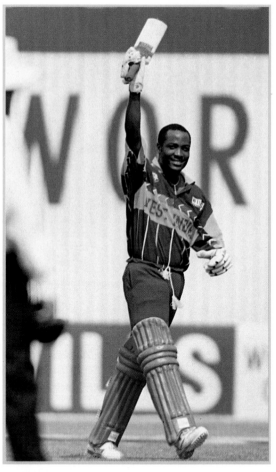

Below: Kenya's Kennedy Otieno, during his marvellous 85 against Australia.

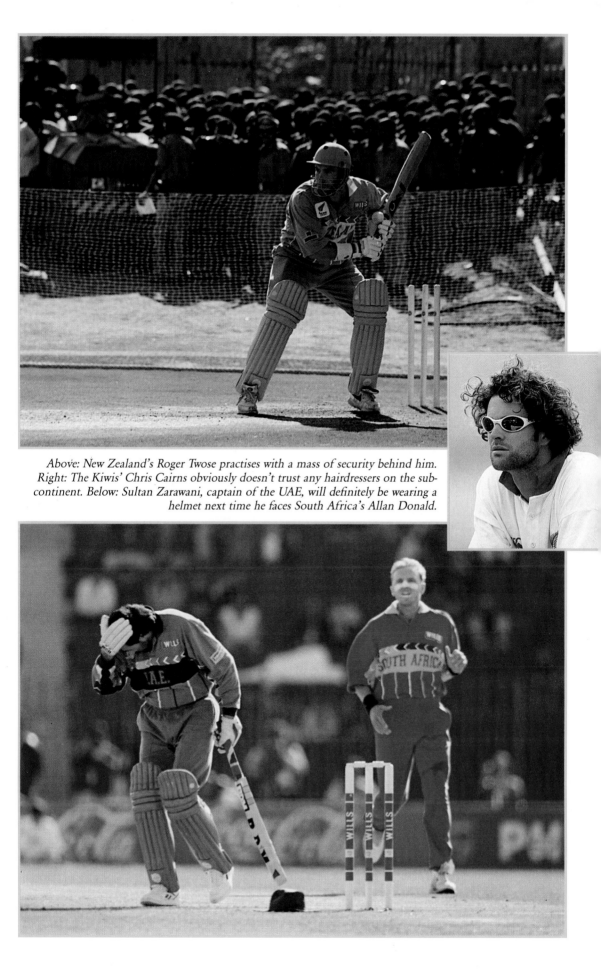

Above: New Zealand's Roger Twose practises with a mass of security behind him. Right: The Kiwis' Chris Cairns obviously doesn't trust any hairdressers on the sub-continent. Below: Sultan Zarawani, captain of the UAE, will definitely be wearing a helmet next time he faces South Africa's Allan Donald.

Holland's Bastiaan Zuiderent (seen here during his innings of 54 against England) was, at just 18, the youngest player in the Cup. His team-mate, 47-year-old West Indies-born Nolan Clarke, was the oldest.

Above: Someone described him as looking like a 'frog in a blender'. Someone else thought he looked as if he was 'trying to change a tyre while the car was still going'. Paul Adams, South Africa's young spinner, is certainly unique. Below left: Pakistan's Javed Miandad, the only man to play in all six World Cups. Below right: South Africa's Fanie de Villiers, cycling though the streets of Faisalabad.

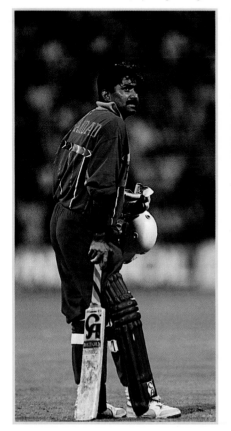

Left: Waqar Younis of Pakistan, the best bowler of yorkers in the world, does it again, this time to Andrew Hudson of South Africa.

Below: Zimbabwe's Andy Waller, a tobacco farmer by trade, takes on the Sheikh of Tweak during the Group A match between Australia and Zimbabwe in Nagpur.

Above: South Africa's ebullient Jonty Rhodes narrowly avoids being run out during the South Africa-West Indies quarter-final in Karachi.

Left: Sanath Jayasuriya, the Sri Lankans' cavalier opening batsman and part-time (but effective) spinner, was named the player of the tournament.
Here he goes over the infield yet again, during his fantastic 82 (from 44 balls) against England in Faisalabad.

Jimmy Adams (left) and Richie Richardson race off the field after the West Indies had beaten South Africa to reach the semi-finals.

DAY 16 — *February 24*
(Visakhapatnam)

TODAY WAS a very quiet one, which was opened by the piercing sound of the phone, which shattered the silence of room 604. We were decidedly weary, after a marathon video session that began after our drink with the Kenyans had petered out, and hadn't ended until *Dumb and Dumber* finished proceedings at 2.30 am.

As well as offering the opportunity for a sleep-in, our morning off also gave me a chance to phone home and catch up on all the news. Distressingly, I had to inform those back in Australia that my diet had had a forced amendment due to my stomach problems. Chicken and corn soup, naan bread and steamed rice are the only options really available, in order for the dreaded 'bug' not to get too strong a hold on me.

This afternoon's training run was preceded by a quick team chat, where we analysed yesterday's game and came up with a few minor problems that need to be addressed. Of concern were our first 15 overs batting, our first 15 overs bowling and a general lack of energy in the field. The consensus was that nothing major is needed to rectify these faults; each player needs to be just a little more focussed.

To change our routine (which is important when we are training just about every day), we enjoyed a centre-wicket session. Slats impressed all with his strokeplay, while Flem was getting his change of pace right. I get the feeling that if Flem can force his way into the side, he could well develop into our trump card — I doubt our opponents are aware of his subtle variations.

Is Kapil Dev fair dinkum?

I was disappointed and more than a little angry to learn that Kapil Dev, the former champion all-rounder who captained India to their only World Cup triumph, in 1983, yesterday called for Australia and West Indies to be banned from international cricket for at least a year for refusing to play their World Cup matches in Sri Lanka.

'Both these teams should not only have been thrown out of the competition, they should also have been barred from playing the game for at least one year,' Kapil wrote in an article in the *Indian Express*.

'I feel that the ICC should have the powers like FIFA have in running international football,' he continued, 'but the ICC, unlike FIFA, is a toothless body and let us leave things at that.'

DAY 17 — *February 25*

(Visakhapatnam to Patna to Calcutta to Bombay)

VIZAG TO BOMBAY should have been a two-hour direct flight, and would have been for any airline bar the 'Official World Cup Airline', Indian Airways. Instead, we faced a ridiculous marathon, via Patna and Calcutta, while the opponents we would face in two days' time, India, calmly practised in Bombay.

The trek began badly, with hot Fantas and Cokes being served for brekky in the airport security lounge, and deteriorated from there. I don't think there has ever been, or ever will be, another specially chartered flight that doesn't actually take you direct to your intended destination. But here we were, on board one! The reason for our stop off at Patna was to drop the Kenyan boys off for their game against Zimbabwe tomorrow (a match I believe they can win). Then things got really absurd. Once the Kenyans had left we had the plane to ourselves, yet we made our way to Calcutta for no apparent reason. The only thing we could think of was that they really were trying to flatten us for our next match. The good news upon reaching Calcutta was the players had the use of the airport hotel for a bit of shut-eye or to watch the South Africa–England match, live from Rawalpindi, on the TV. The bad news was that we were now further away from Bombay than we had been when we left Vizag this morning.

Can someone please explain this rationale to me?

The final leg of our adventure, a two-and-a-half hour flight to Bombay, was typically cramped and uncomfortable, but it did provide us with a decent chicken curry. We couldn't believe the quality — after all, swallowing plane fare on the sub-continent usually threatens to put an end to your tour!

Easily today's most interesting and enlightening experience was the final 75-minute journey from Bombay airport to our hotel. The streets were alive with activity, with street vendors selling their freshly-cooked local delicacies, workmen still performing their back-breaking labours on the roads, hordes of people, with barely a shirt on their backs, sleeping on the footpaths, and animals of all breeds wandering aimlessly wherever they wanted. They, unlike so many of the humans among them, appear to have not a worry in the world.

The country certainly is a bombardment on all of your senses, with unique smells, noises and sights, and exotic spices to tempt the tastebuds. And everywhere you go, there are people.

Amid this story of poverty and hardship lies another world. Bombay is the most cosmopolitan city in India, with a great variety of shops, nightclubs, restaurants, nationalities and business opportunities available. And this fact hasn't been missed by any of the multitudes of companies and individuals currently here trying to cash in on the current boom in this part of Asia. A city that has what is reputed to be the world's biggest slum, Bombay also has more than its fair share of skyscrapers, and boasts some of the highest real estate prices in the world.

Saturday, February 24, 1996

Rs. 10

THE SPORTSTAR

For a ringside view of the world of sport

From the publishers of THE HINDU

MAKING GIANT-KILLING A HABIT

THE BUGLE HAS SOUNDED

STAR POSTER:
CURTLY AMBROSE

The latest edition of Sportstar *came out yesterday, but it wasn't until this morning that I noticed that some idiot had ruined the cover's historic photo of the 12 Cup captains by strolling behind the skippers just as the camera clicked. The men in the shot are (left to right) Mark Taylor (Australia), Mike Atherton (England), Stephen Lubbers (Holland), Maurice Odumbe (Kenya), Arjuna Ranatunga (Sri Lanka), Lee Germon (New Zealand), Sultan Zarawani (UAE), Richie Richardson (West Indies), Wasim Akram (Pakistan), Andy Flower (Zimbabwe), Hansie Cronje (South Africa) and Mohammad Azharuddin (India). Behind them is Steve Waugh (Australia).*

The other two men featured on the cover are Mahesh Bhupathi and Leander Paes, members of the giant-killing Indian Davis Cup team.

DAY 18 — *February 26*
(Bombay)

CRICKET FEVER is certainly the rage in Bombay. Riots occurred this morning after it was revealed that the World Cup ticket organisers had allocated only 7,000 tickets to the general public for tomorrow's Australia–India match. The rest, apparently, have been made available to corporate clients and a very wealthy but very small part of the population. Scalpers are already demanding up to 10,000 rupees for 500-rupee tickets, and the match has become a bonanza for counterfeiters and scalpers alike. To me, the greatest pity is that the region of Bombay, with a population greater than Australia's, has a stadium that can hold no more than 40,000 people, and because of this, a big game such as tomorrow's is priced out of the range of the average cricket fan.

The morning off we were given today came as a welcome relief, as I felt as if I was suffering from jet lag. Recuperation came poolside, soaking up a few rays. The quality of the food, facilities, staff and shops at the Taj are first class and can be best measured by the fact that this Hotel is fully occupied every day of the year.

From the papers, I learned that South Africa had eventually beaten England by 78 runs. Hansie Cronje's side, along with the Pakistanis, look to be the major forces in Group B. Pakistan had begun their Cup campaign in Gujranwala two days back, destroying the UAE by nine wickets, and today they defeated Holland in Lahore by eight wickets, with 20 overs to spare.

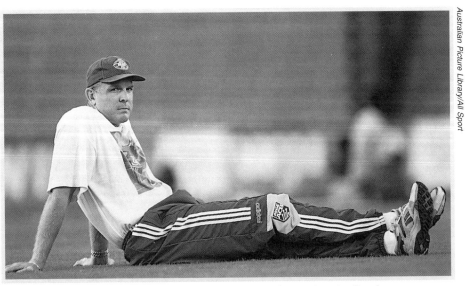

Australian Picture Library/All Sport

A forlorn Craig McDermott, alone during our practice session in Bombay.

How bright are those lights?

I enjoyed an interview Bombay head curator, Sudhir Naik, gave a local journalist today. A veteran of three Tests (against the West Indies and England in 1974) Mr Naik has cut no corners in his efforts to have his baby in perfect order for our game, which will be the first encounter staged under lights in this huge city.

The main activity at the ground over the past three months has been the installation of the expensive new floodlights — no cricket has been played on the ground in that time. And to help ensure a high-quality clash, Mr Naik has prepared the practice wickets, which are situated on the outfield, in exactly the same manner as the game strip. All of them, he says, are bone-hard, with barely a crack and full of runs. He estimates that a score of 270 will be required to win. He also admits that the pitch has been prepared with the local champion, Tendulkar, very much in mind.

Tendulkar versus Warne is the talk of the town, and the stage has been set for a memorable night. 'The lights are so bright,' a member of the groundstaff told reporters proudly, 'the batsmen are going to need goggles.'

This evening's training session made a pleasant change from the normal routine, as we performed under the lights of the Wankede Stadium for two-and-a-half hours. One thing I couldn't help but notice was just how much the ground has improved since my first visit here in 1986. I remember back then that the outfield was as hard as the cat's head, while the wicket was as barren as Kojak's.

Now there is a lush outfield and a pitch that looks like it will give assistance to all types of bowling, not just the spinners. And the lights, while not comparable to Melbourne or Perth, are adequate. However, they are much lower than usual and may cause a bit of trouble for fieldsmen trying to catch balls hit high in the air. All in all, the set-up is very impressive, and I can't wait until game time when the ground will literally come alive.

The practice wickets gave us an insight into how the match wicket might play. Warney was almost unplayable on the clay-based surface, as he spun and deceived all the batsmen with subtle changes of flight aided by the uncertain pace of the track. I believe that he and Damien Fleming (in for Craig McDermott) will be the danger men for the aggressive and highly-talented Indians. Flem's ability to swing the ball and skills at mixing his pace up should never be underrated.

Billy, sadly, will be flying home in the morning. He is being replaced by South Australia's Jason Gillespie, a player whom I've never even met. But from all reports he has improved in leaps and bounds this season and has the impressive stats of 40 Sheffield Shield wickets at 24, largely due, it seems, to deceptive changes in pace and a more than useful outswinger.

His situation takes me back to my first Test match, when I walked out to bat for my first Test innings. My first batting partner was Geoff Marsh, whom I had been introduced to the previous evening, and our conversation had involved maybe half a dozen words. But in this Australian side, making newcomers feel welcome is one of our strengths and I'm sure Jason will feel pretty much settled straightaway.

There may be titles such as 'senior' players, but no-one is more important than anyone else and every player's input is welcomed by all.

DAY 19 — *February 27*
(Australia v India in Bombay)

IT WAS GOOD to see a group of Australian supporters in the foyer of the Taj this morning, over here as part of a Channel Nine supporters' tour. It's always reassuring to see some Aussie flags in the stadium and know you have some support, even when it's among 40,000 partisan home-town fanatics.

Whether our supporters would have remained so loyal had they heard what was emanating out of room 503 this morning, is doubtful. Air pollution is an ongoing problem in Bombay but for us noise pollution was the major concern, as Slats strummed his way through another mediocre medley of music. But perhaps my criticism is too harsh, for he is showing definite signs of progress. Some are even suggesting that *Baa Baa Black Sheep* might soon be conquered, if Slats' rate of improvement continues.

Game time couldn't come quick enough for the boys. The bus that took us to the ground was surrounded by hundreds of well-wishers when we boarded it at the Taj Bombay. They all wanted to catch a glimpse of the lads and yell out either of two phrases that are synonymous with Indian supporters ... 'Wishing you all the best!' or 'Best of luck!' These are two expressions that most countries' sports fans wouldn't say to an opposition team.

Bombay is a ground that has a very special atmosphere when it is full of spectators. The stands are very close to the playing arena and the incline from

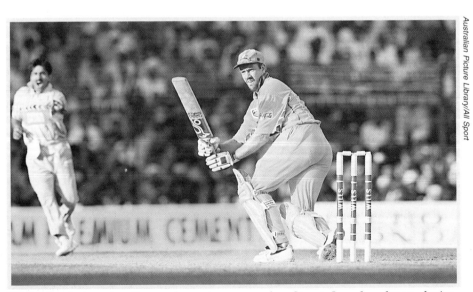

While the shadows lengthen and evening approaches, Stuart Law leg glances during the manic final overs of the Australian innings.

Australian Picture Library/All Sport

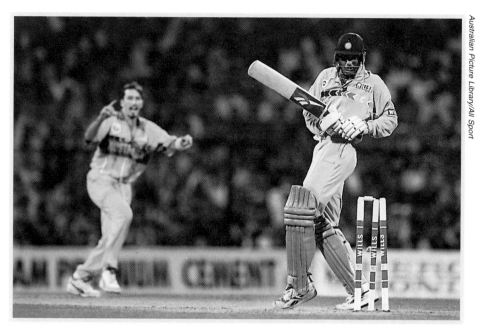

One of the night's most significant moments. Azharuddin, bowled Fleming, 10.

Australian Picture Library/All Sport

back to front in those stands is extraordinarily steep. And the fans are so tightly packed in that they seem almost wedged together. This creates a buzz that produces goose bumps when you're out in the middle of it all. Put simply, it's great to be a part of it.

Pistol hasn't overcome a recurring hamstring strain, so Shane Lee got his chance. Unfortunately for Slats, he again has the task of mixing the Powerade. He must be disappointed — although he may yet play a major part in our campaign, it's hard to see a way into the side for him at the present time.

Mark Taylor won the vital toss in front of an already vocal crowd and had no hesitation in batting on a wicket we believed would suit Shane later on as it slowed down and crumbled a little. The mood was bubbling when the toss was made, but by the start, it had developed into something very special. In fact, the atmosphere in the first 10 overs of our innings was probably the most spine-tingling opening I will ever experience. Each ball caused a collective gasp, or a roar, and when the Indian team appealed, the whole ground went up as one. It was awesome and as close to playing in an FA Cup Final at Wembley as we'll ever get.

Going through the roof

Unfortunately, not everything went to plan for Australia tonight, as one of the Channel Nine cameramen fell through a grandstand roof while covering the action. However, quite miraculously, he became wedged in the asbestos roof, stuck at the armpits, which prevented him from taking a plunge that could have proved fatal not only to himself, but also those wedged tight in the crowd below.

One local paper later added this amusing postscript to its brief report of the incident: 'Prices for tickets for the match had already gone through the roof, here there was somebody going the same way the prices had!'

Taylor's early form was particularly impressive, as he dominated the opening partnership with Mark Waugh, being severe on anything wide. The pair set us up for a 250-plus scoreline, adding 103 in 22 overs before the fragile-looking Raju had our skipper caught in the deep, an event which caused mayhem and madness in the terraces. Soon after, Ricky Ponting fell victim to a superb one-handed catch by Manjreker at backward point and I made my way to the middle, keen to make an impression.

After taking centre, I glanced around the field, checking out exactly where the Indians were, and couldn't help but notice how close the spectators seemed to be. It was as if they were all cardboard cut-outs, joined together with faces everywhere and eyes all looking straight through you. The playing arena seemed almost too small and claustrophobic, and the air had a distinct smell about it, a kind of musty, incense-like aroma. The atmosphere was as thick as pea soup. This, I thought, is what it is all about. As I fended my first ball safely away, I was enjoying every part of the scenario that surrounded me.

Unfortunately, I fell victim to probably the unluckiest way you can ever lose your wicket — run out by the bowler (Raju), who had attempted to field

A Night at the Cricket

by Ray Farrell

We were two Australians heading for the West Stand, our precious tickets grasped tightly in our sweaty fists. It was a humid spring day and the Bombay hustle and bustle seemed even more intense than normal. There was tension and a sense of purpose in the air; taxi drivers, street traders, even the police looked like they had to get their day's work completed within the next two hours.

Cricket was in the air.

The queues extended for about two kilometres and were tightly packed, thanks to the makeshift timber cattle pens that had been erected along the footpath. They reminded me of the old wooden corrals you'd see in a western movie. We shuffled along, like an overcrowded penguin colony, as the police, standing on the barriers, ripped any combustible items (newspapers, programs, posters, placards) from our hands and threw them on the ground. Consequently, we were ankle deep in refuse.

This shuffle, which was punctuated by numerous body searches, continued for about two hours. By this point, the sun was ultra hot and the tension had turned to frustration. If this was a festival it had not yet begun. What struck me about the crowds was what was absent

— there were no program sellers, no t-shirts, caps or flags on offer, no ticket touts, not even merry youths waving obscene banners and singing mindless songs. In Bombay cricket supporters take matters much more seriously. They were going into battle ... and it was nearly time to climb out of the trenches.

Inside the stadium, there was cure for my impatience. The shuffle of the queue had been replaced by a frenzy of pushing and shoving, as we fought our way up the narrow stairs into the stand. The match had already started and no-one wanted to miss a ball. A final search by a policeman discovered my cigarette lighter. Even though there was nothing to burn he wouldn't give it back, and I didn't argue.

We made our way to Block T, Seats 386 and 387. However, the thousand or so seats in Block T were already occupied by what appeared to be about three thousand fanatical Indian supporters. Ever optimistic, we looked for 386 and 387, assuming they would be the only remaining vacant seats in the entire stadium. No such luck. The two seats were occupied by three people who looked like they had been waiting all year for this match and were in no mood to discuss trivialities such as seat allocations. But

the ball but instead deflected it onto the bowler's end stumps. I was backing up, well out of my ground. However, from this point, Mark took control of the game, scoring almost at will. He was aided by a useful contribution from Stuart Law, who played his supporting role to perfection. By the 43rd over, Mark had completed his second century of the tournament and we had taken a firm grip on the match's destiny. He finally fell for a super 126 and received a generous ovation from the knowledgeable crowd.

As so often happens in the last 10 overs of a limited-overs match, wickets fell regularly in the quest for quick runs, and many of the lower order had to sacrifice to get us to a competitive 258, which we felt might be just enough.

As darkness descended and the lights began to illuminate the stadium, we made our way to the middle to face the might of Tendulkar. However, he wasn't the early star. Damien Fleming caught Jadeja and Kambli on the hop, beating both with a mix of pace and swing to stun the at least 10,000-over-capacity crowd. India were 2–7, and this position of superiority could have been enhanced even further had McGrath grabbed hold of a tough caught-and-bowled chance from the batting prodigy.

you have to keep going so, with a lot of bluff and bluster and despite being clearly outnumbered, we wiggled our backsides onto the two square inches of bench that had been left exposed. I am sure someone fell off the end of the bench, but no one noticed.

(We later discovered that the people who had taken our seats in Block T had tickets for Block U. But there were no seats in Block U, because Block U is where they had just installed the stadium's new electronic scoreboard.)

The tension was extraordinary. Australia were batting, and batting well. Conversations were limited to 'good shot'. Before long, the enthusiastic applause which had greeted the first Australian 'good shot' degenerated into nervous moans. There was more than just a cricket match at stake here; this was war with only one survivor. No wonder then that the requirements of cricketing etiquette were wearing thin.

When the home side batted, every Tendulkar boundary was greeted as if it were the winning shot of the World Cup. Spirits were high again. India would win! The ubiquitous Mexican wave whipped around the ground and even the members got involved.

Then Tendulkar fell, and there was a stillness as if someone had requested a minute's silence in respect of the dead. Only as their fallen hero departed into the stands did they begin to applaud. His innings had been only a dream, his dismissal a nightmare. At this point, reality returned and with it the stillness of the night, the humidity, the smell. The war was over. India would lose.

Those who only came to win departed for home with heavy hearts. Only the cricket lovers and the Australians stayed to the death.

Though many had departed early, getting out of the stadium was almost as eventful as getting in. As an ever increasing number of people tried to leave through a two metre-wide lane, the shuffle slowed to a halt. We stood in a pool of mud in pitch darkness, as the crush became intolerable. The air was caked with humidity, while the scent of spices coming from boiling cauldrons of deep fried food nearby reinforced my hunger. All other senses were numb. Eventually, we clambered over loose scaffolding that had been scattered and emerged into the blazing lights of the main street, in pain from bruised shins and a sprained ankle. Somehow, we managed to stop a taxi which took us back to the hotel. So relieved were we to have returned alive that we didn't even haggle over the fare.

— Ray Farrell is an Australian business executive who was in India during the World Cup. He also happens to be my next-door neighbour.

Australian Picture Library/All Sport

In the background, New Zealand umpire Steve Dunne is signalling wide. In the foreground, the Australians (from left: Taylor, keeper Healy, bowler M. Waugh and Bevan) are celebrating Tendulkar's dismissal, stumped for 90. The game has swung dramatically Australia's way.

Then the game turned abruptly on us. Spurred on by a rampaging crowd, Tendulkar took to our bowlers like crocodiles do to chooks. We were massacred by some breathtaking strokeplay and premeditated brutality. While he did have a slice or two of luck during this onslaught, his genius was there for all to see, and he moved the crowd into a state of utter delirium. In one over from McGrath, Tendulkar played a pull shot that defied belief and sent the ball racing past a bemused mid-on, followed by a remarkably improvised hook shot off the front foot to a slower ball which left the crowd screaming and yelling as if they'd already won not just this match but the entire World Cup. A cover drive two balls later nearly lifted the roof of the stadium and even I, an opposition player, had hairs standing up on the back of my neck. Never in my life had I experienced anything quite like it — when you're being slaughtered in this way, are you supposed to feel such an unprecedented adrenalin rush?

Warne came on and Tendulkar, sensing a chance to gain a crucial psychological edge over our main strike weapon, attempted to smash him out of the attack. However, the Indian maestro was lucky to keep his wicket intact, as he skied an attempted six to wide mid-off where Stuart Law dropped a tough chance. This good fortune was, inevitably, met with widespread, sparkling celebrations. But the throng was quietened when India's Muslim captain, Mohammad Azharuddin (or Azhar, for short) became Fleming's third victim, leaving the score at 3–70.

This fall of wicket was merely a minor interruption to the Sachin Tendulkar show. Shots of rare pedigree continued to delight the audience until he somewhat foolishly ran down the wicket to a Mark Waugh wide and got himself stumped. He had made a brilliant 90, but from the moment of his dismissal we knew we wouldn't lose the game. Wickets fell at regular intervals, and we wrapped up their tail with 16 runs to spare, to complete a quite memorable victory for us.

To me, this win had many similarities to our one-run victory against India in the opening match of the 1987 World Cup. That win, like today's, was against the odds. On this occasion, we had McDermott and Reiffel injured, a massive crowd against us, a terrible flight schedule to overcome and only one game under our belts in the past two-and-a-half weeks. Yet we overcame all these hurdles. I believe the spirit and determination we showed will be the catalyst to bigger things; it was impossible to miss the quiet confidence that has already spread through our camp after tonight's outstanding performance.

We decided to try and recreate the mood of the post-match party from 1987 in Madras (after that famous one-run win), so we headed for our hotel's only watering hole. Along the way, we came across a celebrity, the actress Demi Moore, who strolled through the foyer flanked on both sides by bodyguards. 'Had a good game today, guys?' she asked, without so much as breaking stride.

I'm not sure whether we were awestruck or dumb-struck, but a meek 'yeah' was all we could muster.

This unfortunate moment aside, a great night was had by all ... even though the bar shut well before we would have liked it to. Our time together tonight, coming on top of our success, has been enough to convince me that we now know we will be the World Cup winners in three weeks' time.

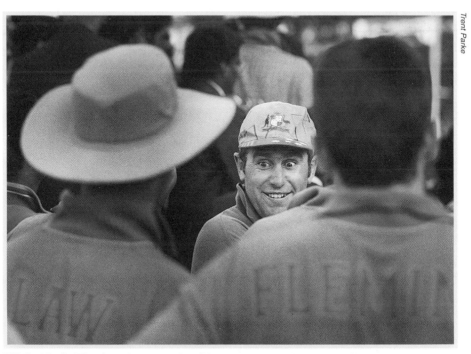

Trent Parke

While Mark Waugh waits to receive his man-of-the-match award, captain Mark Taylor shares a joke with Stuart Law and Damien Fleming.

DAY 20 — *February 28*
(Bombay to Nagpur)

IT'S AMAZING how a couple of rums can make you feel when you haven't touched alcohol for a while — I wasn't in the peak of condition when an 8.15 am phone call reminded me that I was committed to a photo shoot this morning. The photograph was for an IBM ThinkPad promotion I'm involved in. And, if my frail physical condition wasn't enough, the photo concept required me on board a ferry in front of the Gateway to India. The swell was a little choppy, and seemed much, much worse. However, I somehow managed to negotiate the hour and a half needed to get the job completed, before making my way back to the ever-popular Taj to perform every cricketer's least favourite task ... bag packing.

Our joy at re-packing our suitcases was matched only by the thrill we all got from knowing we would be spending more endless hours in an airport lounge. Sure enough, this was exactly where we found ourselves as we began our trek to nearby Nagpur, where we would be facing Zimbabwe.

India's airport lounges are alleged to have private rooms that are supposed to be a safe haven for us. But this is never the case, as we are continually inundated for that most prized possession in these parts — a scribble on a bit of notepaper. Everyone, and I mean everyone, gets into the act, even the police and security. However, without doubt the most interesting approach today came from an Indian Airways pilot, who had specially written a poem in honour of Junior's century yesterday. It was called 'Batsman Beyond Compare' and went as follows:

It was a great sight,
To see you swing your bat left and right,
As you struck the ball far and wide,
Ensuring victory for your side.
Watching it was sheer pleasure,
You are a player great and fine,
And we're just proud to carry you
On our airline.
Best of luck ... Shirali.

The trip to Nagpur left on time, making it unique in the long history of Indian aviation, and arrived as programmed, making it a miracle!

After we reached our hotel, we caught up with the amicable Zimbabweans, who told us of their Sri Lankan fixture. They confirmed that the Sri Lankans had played very well, but what struck me was just how gruelling and unsatisfactory were the impositions placed on the visiting side. It seemed strange that they were not allowed into Colombo (supposedly a safe venue) until just 16 hours before the game. For the two days before that they had been left twiddling their thumbs in Madras.

Australian Picture Library/All Sport

No batsman had managed to score centuries in successive World Cup games until Mark Waugh hit his superb hundred in Bombay, which came after his 130 against Kenya. It seems Mark and Sachin Tendulkar (whose three innings so far have been 127 not out, 70 run out, and 90) are having their own private battle over the 'batsman of the tournament' title.

The worst aspect of this World Cup experience has been the travel arrangements, which would best be described as a shemozzle. The Zimbabweans, for example, finished their game in Colombo against Sri Lanka six days back, and then spent the next day in Madras in transit. Their next game was scheduled for Patna, on February 26, against Kenya, but instead of heading there they flew to Calcutta, where they remained for what you would have thought was a lot longer than they needed to. Their flight to Patna didn't arrive until just 18 hours before the toss. It may have been fortunate that the game was washed out and then replayed the following day. After all, they had been 3-45 after nearly 16 overs in the abandoned fixture. The next day they came out and won comfortably, by five wickets.

Yesterday's other match was between New Zealand and the Sultan's UAE combination in Faisalabad, and ended in an easy win for the Kiwis.

Tonight's meal was without doubt the feed of the tour. We couldn't help but notice the chef proudly looking on as his efforts behind the tandoori oven (an Indian Murg Makhani) hit the right spot with the boys.

DAY 21 — *February 29*
(Nagpur)

SLATS AND I both felt pretty ordinary this morning, as we'd suffered at the hands of pillows only slightly softer than a bag of cement and an air conditioner that spewed out nasties by the truckload. This was not good, especially considering that, because we'd won a toss with the Zimbabwean management, we had first use of the practice facilities ... at 9 am.

The ground in Nagpur is infamous for the collapse of a section of a wall last year, during a one-day international between India and New Zealand. This resulted in the deaths of 13 people, mostly students. We have heard that the issue of compensation to the families of those killed hasn't been resolved as yet, and consequently there is a possibility that there will be some kind of protest outside the ground tomorrow.

Below: Shane Warne attempts a news piece for Channel Nine from the safety and comfort of a rickshaw seat.

Trent Parke

Both pics: Trent Parke

Below: While the
boys ride to school
in comfort, the girls
are obliged to push
the fellas along.

Life on the streets of
Nagpur is vibrant, with
many a strange and
wonderful scene.

Above: A newspaper
vendor is distracted by
the ugly habits of his
pet monkey.

Like so many venues in India, the ground here is small, in this case almost too small for an international fixture. I'm sure, though, that the value we get for our shots will be more than compensated for by what the bowlers will get from the pitch, which looks decidedly under-prepared. Even now, 24 hours before the game is due to begin, the surface is far too dry. It's crumbling already, and will be low and slow in the early section of the game. And then, once the sun and a bit of wear and tear from the bowlers' footmarks have their effect, it will turn square and hold up, making batting extremely difficult. Quite obviously, Warney shapes up as the main danger to Zimbabwe's chances. I can't see any way they'll be able to repel him with any authority.

Unfortunately, training turned out to be a waste of time. The two on-field practice wickets deteriorated with every ball bowled, which left we batsmen with two choices — either to stick it out, work on our technique and take the risk of getting injured, or have a short knock, achieve what we want from the session and then get out of there. I chose the second option, and attempted to loft a few balls over the top. Once that was achieved, I was satisfied.

Most of the lads appear to be in good form and spirits. The only concerns are Pistol's hamstring, which is now almost fully recovered, and Bevo's ailing health (this morning he decorated the outfield with a few heaves during our Aussie rules-style warm-up, which included a kicking-and-handball drill with the 'Sherrin'). As a result, Bev did no more than have a quick net before he retired to the comfort of a cool dressing shed. Having been there and done that, I know how bad it is to be running around in the heat with stomach problems. But over here it is sometimes necessary to push yourself through the pain barrier, if you want to achieve the results you're after.

Our hotel here in Nagpur is comfortable enough, with good showers, beds and eateries — most players' three main considerations. A unique bonus at

Above, right and opposite: Everywhere you go, cricket is a way of life ... and a source of joy and inspiration for every generation.

Both pics: Trent Parke

this hotel is the fact that only cricket players and officials are being allowed to reside here during our stay. No-one else can book into the hotel until we leave Nagpur, and so concerned are the local authorities about security that everyone who enters through the front door has to survive a metal detector search. As a result of this protection (which, in my opinion, is just about bordering on paranoia), we are once again hotel bound, and destined to watch our increasingly important selection of video tapes.

Sticking to my theory of staying with a good safe feed when I come across one, I ventured back to last night's Indian restaurant. Would you believe the Murg Makhani, rice and naan bread were on the table within three minutes of sitting down? This has to be the first time in my life that's it taken less time for the food to be delivered than it has for the bill to arrive after I requested it at the end of the night!

A Day for the Underdogs

After a series of fairly lop-sided encounters during the first two weeks of this World Cup, many sceptics have been calling for the heads of Holland, United Arab Emirates and Kenya to roll. But these same critics are now shaking their very own heads, because the cricketing minnows from Africa today pulled off one of the greatest upsets in sporting history.

They've humbled their heroes from the Caribbean!

If someone had suggested to me that Kenya would bowl out the Windies for 93 in 35.2 overs, when the Windies were pursuing a very modest 167, I would have been very dubious. And if I hadn't watched this entire scenario unfold in front of my very own eyes (I was watching the live television coverage in the comfort of my Nagpur hotel room) I would never have believed it.

I don't think even the Kenyans thought they could win. This came out before the game, when their captain, Maurice Odumbe, was asked 'What do you think about losing the toss?' His refreshingly honest reply was: 'I think we've already lost — the game is over.' His troops, thankfully, had other ideas, and after an ordinary batting performance (all out 166, Ambrose 2–21, Walsh 3–46, Harper 3–15) they began to dismantle the once unbeatable, palm tree-crested calypso kings with a brand of cricket that relied on enthusiasm, energy, teamwork and determination.

These qualities were exemplified by the wicket keeper, Tariq Iqbal. Now Tariq is probably best described as a 'portly' backstop, but today he sentenced his grandchildren to a life of their grandfather fondly recalling the day when he caught out Brian Lara. I can just see him sitting there, perhaps even more portly than he is today, grandkids on his knees and at his feet, explaining thus ...

'I had to move swiftly to my left when I recognised the deflection, and then dive full length to snatch the ball inches from the turf ...

'Boys and girls,' he'll say, with a proud smile across his face, 'it was a miraculous match-winning catch.'

In reality, it was a faint edge that beat the bespectacled-one's gloves and thudded into his ample midriff, However, he managed to clutch the chance as urgently as if he was about to drop a new-born child. But let's never forget, it's not how you look, but what you do that counts. This unlikely dismissal — Lara, caught Tariq Iqbal bowled Rajab Ali 8 — was completed, and the Kenyan team went berserk.

From that point, the Africans lifted and grew in stature. They became unstoppable, forcing the Windies into basic errors; run outs were initiated, bowlers found an extra metre of pace, encouragement was forthcoming from every player, the tempo of the game had been stepped up a gear. The joy on their faces was obvious for all to see. The Kenyans' self-belief grew to a

Craig McDermott's replacement, the ponytailed one, Jason Gillespie, arrived late in the evening, looking fresh and excited at the prospect of being part of the squad. I'm sure 12 months ago he would never have imagined that he would be right where he is now, but that's the beauty of cricket. Now his main concern must be to make the most of this unexpected opportunity.

point where, even from Nagpur, it was clear that they were going to be victorious.

After the last wicket fell, I even had goose bumps as I watched the Kenyans run amok. They showered each other with high fives and bear hugs, in a wild celebration that looked for all the world like some kind of exotic tribal dance. It was great to see this team of innocence carry on their celebrations as if they were the only ones on the face of the earth. It was not for them to care or be aware that their game was being watched not just by a small but ecstatic crowd, but also by millions across the world. A lap of honour followed, with souvenir stumps being held aloft like Olympic torches as they leapt and danced their way around the stadium.

If anyone ever really believed that the World Cup-type events should be only for the so-called elite athletes and countries, inspirational moments such as these should destroy such thoughts for good. Whatever happens in the remainder of this tournament, this occasion will be the highlight ... the game this World Cup is remembered for. And rightly so! As I've explained earlier, this team was picked from a grand total of only 10 sides currently playing in the Kenyan capital, Nairobi. It includes only one player with first-class experience and survives on $66 per day, per player, as remuneration.

This was a day for the underdogs. And it gave further proof to something I've believed for a long time: cricket is predominantly a mind game — you can achieve anything if you want it badly enough.

Don't be surprised if Kenya hold cricket's World Cup aloft in 2008.

DAY 22 — *March 1*
(Australia v Zimbabwe in Nagpur)

A HORROR START to the day — no wake-up call! It was pure luck that I glanced at the bedside table and spotted the hands of my watch showing 7.15 am, which left us only 15 minutes before our departure. This is always a moment of pure panic, but Slats and I managed to overcome this hurdle and even had time to cap off a spirited recovery by throwing down a piece or two of toast.

Unlike our game against India in Bombay, where we faced a packed crowd and traffic problems around the stadium, this morning's short journey to the ground was totally incident-free and almost spectator free. For this match, the Australian XI remained unchanged, after Michael Bevan was deemed healthy enough to take his place in the starting line-up.

The important toss was won by the Africans, who quite correctly opted to have first use of a parched-looking batting surface. Zimbabwe had been disappointing in the Cup so far, especially when you consider that they are now a fully-fledged Test-playing nation, made up almost entirely of full-time professionals. However, some still have jobs, and rather unusual ones at that. Andy Waller is a tobacco farmer, Guy Whittall a hunter and safari guide, and Eddo Brandes a chicken farmer.

Our intensity in the early overs was impressive, typified by Ricky Ponting's full-length dive onto an outfield so hard it was unsafe to have your body come in contact with it. The boundary was saved, and a fair slice of skin lost, but this was just the attitude we needed to get us going.

As expected, Shane Warne dominated proceedings, taking 4–34 and at times turning the ball to an extent that defied the laws of physics. He was well supported by Damien Fleming, who came back well after a slow start, while Glenn McGrath displayed great control on a wicket that was totally unsuitable for his style of bowling. I snuck in for a couple of wickets, in my best spell of

The things you hear and say

There have been a number of memorable quotes from the tour so far. Here are my three favourites to this point.

1. 'Can I have your autograph please — you are my favourite player sir! ... Oh, yes, and what is your name?' — A keen cricket fan, to Mark Waugh.

2. 'Reiffel, you are a very good all-rounder ... you always score 45 runs and chip in with four handy wickets!' — A local expert, doing his best to soothe Pistol's ego.

3. 'Very lucky to be part of the squad.' — The assessment of Damien Fleming in a list of player profiles published by the magazine, *Sportstar*.

Australian Picture Library/All Sport

Ricky Ponting (left) and Mark Waugh discuss the way they chalk their billiards cues, during the match against Zimbabwe in Nagpur.

the tournament to date. Wickets fell at regular intervals, and by halfway through the 45th over the Zimbabweans had been reduced to a meagre 154. Only three-time World Cup veteran (and last-minute replacement in the Cup for the injured David Houghton) Waller, who posted a rearguard 67, showed any resolve.

Chasing a small total can sometimes be dangerous, if you think the game has already been won. However, we reminded ourselves we had to remain positive. Thirty-six overs later, the valuable two points were ours, after Mark Waugh (76 not out), Taylor (34) and Ponting (33) had destroyed a team that appeared to lack direction and self-belief. From a spectator's point of view, this was an average, less-than-entertaining fixture, which can often happen when a one-day game becomes lopsided. But in this case it had been no fault of ours.

While we were batting, as I found myself with plenty of spare time on my hands, I browsed through a local paper. Of course, the Kenyans' fantastic defeat of the West Indies took prominence, and there was also a report of South Africa's outstanding performance against Pakistan in Karachi (Pakistan 6-242 — Aamir Sohail 111, Salim Malik 40; South Africa 5-243 off 44.2 overs — Cullinan 65, Cronje 45 not out, Kirsten 44). But I also read, with a fair helping of disbelief, some more of Arjuna Ranatunga's excuses as to why Sri Lanka didn't win in Australia during their recent tour. I'd like to think he was misquoted, because what he had to say bordered on the absurd. He apparently went as far as to say that it was the neutral umpires who caused them to lose.

I think it's about time he had a look in his own backyard. There he might discover that they were completely outplayed in the Tests (losing 3-0) largely because of an intriguing strategy that involved trying to slow down play whenever possible, abuse the substitute rule from time to time, and play some poor cricket. The sooner Ranatunga realises that these reasons and not his lame ones were the cause of their convincing losses, the better his team will be, because there is no doubt they are a combination with undoubted potential.

Tonight I had my first chance to watch an ultrasound tape of baby Waugh number one, which had been sent over from home. This was an amazing experience, seeing for the first time life from inside the womb, and was one that made me feel both excited and a tinge homesick. More than anything I'm just grateful that modern technology gave me the opportunity to see my own flesh and blood, if only (at this point) on a television screen.

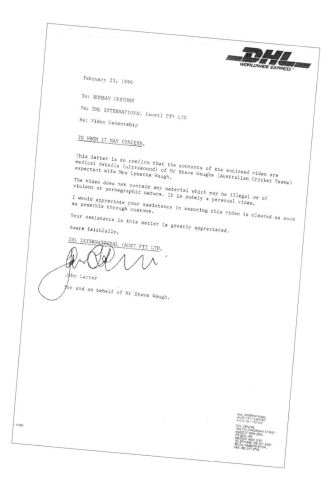

DAY 23 — *March 2*
(Nagpur to Delhi)

I'D HATE TO BE a front rower in rugby league, or any sports person involved in solid body contact for that matter, because I never want to feel any worse than I did first thing this morning. A slight hamstring and glute muscle strain had me hobbling into the bathroom in search of a soothing hot bath and some relief from the pain. Thankfully, training had been called off for the day, because of the poor state of the Nagpur practice wickets.

Some of the lads ventured out of the hotel this morning, only to be mobbed by more of India's ever-inquisitive people. However, the guys' short stay in the streets was time enough for Shane Lee and Ricky Ponting to purchase a couple of mega-sized water pistols, which they instantly put to use. In most countries, a few short, sharp bursts would have discouraged even the keenest autograph hunters. But not here.

We spent the afternoon watching Sri Lanka pull off a superb victory against India in Delhi, after the batting genius of Sachin Tendulkar (137, run out, at exactly a run a ball) had forced them to chase the imposing target of 272. Taking a leaf out of Tendulkar's book, the Sri Lankans' reply was explosive, with the 'Ferrari–Porsche' combination of Ramesh Kaluwitharana and Sanath Jayasuriya tearing 42 runs from the first 18 balls of the innings. This set the tone for the remainder of Sri Lanka's strong batting order. Kaluwitharana fell for 26 (off 16 balls) after an opening stand of 53, then Gurusinha (25) helped Jayasuriya add another 76. Aravinda de Silva managed only 8, and Jayasuriya fell for 79 (off 77 balls), to leave the visitors at 4–141, but no more wickets fell, and there were still eight balls available when the winning run was scored.

India's defeat here could be crucial to the outcome of the tournament. It now appears, after this result and the match in Karachi two days back, that they will play Pakistan in the quarter-finals. If it does turn out this way, one of the hot favourites won't reach the final four.

You'd never have guessed it ... another delayed departure left us languishing in the waiting lounge at Nagpur airport this evening. We're starting to get totally sick of feeling like John Candy and Steve Martin in the movie *Planes, Trains and Automobiles*, always struggling to reach our destinations, with mishaps and mismanagement continually hindering our progress.

By 12.36 am, Glenn McGrath and I arrived at our overnight abode in Delhi, to find the door open. All the locks were broken! Perhaps the local locksmiths were too disappointed by their heroes' defeat to care. By this stage we weren't bothered about security either, and dived straight into bed.

DAY 24 — *March 3*
(Delhi to Jaipur)

A MERE FIVE hours of slumber was certainly not enough, so it was a grumpy and jaded squad of Aussies who boarded the very same bus we'd stumbled off only hours earlier, to catch our flight to the 'Pink City' of Jaipur.

At the airport, I picked up a copy of this morning's paper, which has run a story about Javed Miandad's on-going problems in the Pakistani line-up. Turmoil in their camp is, of course, nothing new; in fact, this spells danger for the other sides, as the Pakistanis have always seemed to thrive on controversy. The dropping, or should I say 'resting', of Miandad for their last game, against South Africa, suggested to the press that some sort of team disharmony existed, especially when both the team captain and the team coach, and player in question, all gave different reasons for his absence. I'm still not sure why Javed came out of a two-year retirement for the Cup, but there are those who say his motivation is more political than sporting. Whatever this might mean! One thing it has done is given Javed the honour of being the only man to

Sadly, cricket is not the only game Indian children know about ...

Tre

... in a land where so many have so little, some images are ghastly and soul destroying.

Trent Parke

appear in all six World Cups, from England in 1975 to India, Pakistan and Sri Lanka in 1996 — a great tribute, not only to his unique talent, but also to his adaptability, durability and persistence.

To arrive in the city of Jaipur is to go back 200 years in time, but in a bizarre way. Camels, cows, donkeys, buffaloes and horses do the heavy work that in a more affluent world is handled by trucks and other forms of sophisticated machinery. But the camel plodding slowly down the poorly-surfaced road is carrying a load of brand new Philips colour TV sets. The camel seems oblivious to all that is happening around it; the whole scene is a movie set, rather than part of the real world.

One thing that always amazes me is how anyone knows who owns which animals. All seem to have the freedom to the city, except for the malnourished camels tied to trees, building sites and telegraph poles. They have barely enough rope to take a step in any direction.

After a couple of weeks in India, you become desensitised to the everyday events of this wondrous place ... the bizarre antics of the rickshaw drivers, always throwing caution to the wind in an attempt to squeeze an extra fare into their 12-hour working days ... humble people squatting on the footpath to relieve themselves — there is nowhere else to go ... wizened women busily thrashing their family's clothes on the footpaths, endeavouring to remove from their lives even some of the grime and dirt ... eager boys imitating Tendulkar in the alleyways, using bats and stumps manufactured from bamboo and bricks ... the hustle and bustle as everyone tries to eke out a living, any way they can.

One only has to drive through the entrance to the Jai Mahal Palace to realise that this city was once a place of grandeur and splendour. Distinctive turrets grace the roofline and glorious gardens encompass the main building. This was once a home for the rich and famous of India, but fortunately for us it is now a hotel. More than any other residence I have ever stayed in, this place gives you the feel of *really* being in India.

Training, of course, is never too far away. This evening's session, for a lot of us, was the first opportunity to have a peek at Jason Gillespie, whom the local press know nothing of at all. He's already been referred to in the media here as 'Julian Gillespie', 'Jason Gilleaspy' and 'Jason Guillispy', but I guess this is fair enough, as we know only fractionally more about him than they do. We're all calling him 'Dizzy', and his first net session went well. He's slotted into the squad nicely, although I know it always takes a little while to feel completely comfortable in such new and, for a young debutante, intimidating surroundings.

The ground in Jaipur is one of the biggest in India, with a reasonably grassed outfield and a rock-hard wicket. Unfortunately for the curator, a heavy storm last night penetrated his sub-standard covers and drenched sections of the match wicket. Fortunately for us, most of the saturated areas are in the middle of the pitch, so they shouldn't affect the game too much. My only concern is that the wicket seems a bit undulating in appearance — exactly what you don't want against quick bowlers. If there are any deficiencies in the track, the Windies quicks will find them. They always have in the past.

'We can't go home!'

The hotel put on a buffet dinner tonight, which gave us a chance to have a chat to the West Indians. The mood within their team was understandably subdued, following their shock loss to the Kenyans, and was best summed up by their batsman, Roland Holder. When I asked him what the reaction to the loss had been from the people back home, he replied quickly: 'We can't go home!'

This type of reaction, when combined with the personal humiliation these cricketers must feel, will inevitably fire them up for a huge effort against us tomorrow. They'll be trying desperately to salvage their pride and respect, two traits they're known for.

Their captain, Richie Richardson, is under immense pressure due to his lack of batting form and doubts over his leadership qualities. But there's one thing we all know about Richie Richardson ...

He'll always give 100 per cent.

Boys on Tour ...
A Cup campaign of a different kind

There are a number of Australian supporters over here, following us as we meander around India. Today at training, a bloke named David McClatchey handed me the story to date of his and five of his mates' World Cup adventures. Where the story goes from here, who knows? But we do appreciate their great commitment to our cause. Unlike the Australian team, there are no five-star hotels, elaborate menus, blanket security arrangements and specially chartered aircraft for these guys. They do it tough, though somehow I don't think they would want it any other way.

The magnificent six, all from suburbs of Sydney, are:
• Dave (aged 27, from Cronulla), a physical education teacher on 12 months leave without pay.
• Woz (23, also from Cronulla), a political science student who's deferred uni for 1996.
• Nathan (21, from Bangor), a porter who quit his job so he could make the tour.
• Andrew (22, from Campsie), a toolmaker who, like Nathan, had to resign so he'd be available for the Cup.
• Chris (21, from Kogarah Bay), a part-time nightfiller with a just-completed science degree.
• James (20, from Glenhaven), a McDonald's Manager who took indefinite leave before heading for the sub-continent.

This is what they've been up to ...

The 'Boys on Tour' 1996 Cup campaign began in Bombay, with the Australia v India game. The day before the match was our initiation to Indian administration — with thousands of desperate Indian supporters, we spent hours waiting outside the stadium until we were finally able to track down an official who had some idea as to how we could obtain tickets. He led us into the 'dungeons' of the Bombay Cricket Association, where we eventually landed our tickets at a cost of 1000 rupees (though you couldn't put enough money on the fact that a healthy portion went into his own pocket).

The boys were in!

That evening, while Indian supporters were abruptly being refused entry, we strolled through the security gates and onto the field to watch the Australians practise. Ricky Ponting, who was last to bat, allowed each of us (plus a few local cricketers, who were clad in their whites) to bowl to him for around 20 minutes.

Match day saw one of the most chaotic crowd scenes outside a stadium you could possibly imagine. There were around 45,000 legitimate ticket holders, truckloads with bogus tickets (exactly how many was impossible to measure but, judging by the number of people who jammed into the aisles and squashed two into every bench inside the stadium, there were more than plenty), and thousands more hoping to stumble on to a ticket by way of divine intervention. And everyone was attempting to enter the ground through just two entrances. Queues were literally two kilometres long, and those attempting to jump these lines were beaten unforgivingly by the hundreds of police officers armed with metre-long wooden batons.

However, amid all the chaos, we were once again able to use our Australian status to enter the ground through the security gates. A friendly nod of the head to the officers on duty, followed by a mumbled 'Australian, Australian', and we were through.

The Indian crowd, despite their obvious fanaticism, were surprisingly friendly towards us and other Aussie supporters in the stands. In fact, a friendly rivalry developed and when the Australians finally won it was as if we had just played the game ourselves; Indian supporters were desperate to shake our hands and congratulate us on 'our' fine victory.

The next match on our itinerary was against Zimbabwe in Nagpur, a bustling little city with as many tourist attractions as the Sahara Desert. The train journey there, on an overnight second-class

Continued over page

Boys on Tour ...

Continued from previous page

sleeper, took 18 hours and was a sweaty, stop-start experience. The 'express' service stopped around a dozen times, and each time an endless procession passed through the carriages — beggars, lepers, shoe-shiners, children sweeping the floor, and the ever annoying sellers of coffee, chy (tea) and omley (omelettes). All the while, these peddlars would cry out at the top of their voices to attract their customers.

Finally we checked into the lovely Shyam Hotel, which came complete with roof-top bar and restaurant (a venue that, no doubt, was responsible for the first bout of 'the belly', experienced by Dave and cost the grand sum of 60 rupees (about $2.10 Australian) per person. Then we made our way up to the ground, where the Australians were training. Once again, it was a case of looking confident, strolling past the three security checkpoints that guarded the tiny stadium, and walking out onto the field for a close-range look at the Australians at work.

We purchased our tickets (150 rupees) at the stadium ticket office, but afterwards we found ourselves surrounded by a number of curious locals who seemed to believe we were players. Here was our 15 minutes worth, and we began signing autographs — Andrew as Damien Fleming, Nathan as Stuart Law, Dave as Ricky Ponting, Chris as Paul Reiffel and James as (believe it or not) Dean Jones. All without a question of doubt!

As we walked from the stadium towards the main street, what had evolved as a small gathering developed into a throng of literally hundreds, all seeking desperately to see or get a signature from their 'heroes'. The chaos was fuelled even further when the children from the local school caught a glimpse of the action and started hurling themselves over the playground fence. It reached the point where traffic was blocked and the local constabulary was required to control the situation. We had created the proverbial monster, so we flagged down some very willing rickshaw drivers who hurried us away from the scene and back to the safety of the Shyam.

The 'all-concrete' Nagpur stadium was sparsely occupied for the Cup match. However, the game gave the Australian supporters an intimate day of cheering for their team and it was here that the 'Boys on Tour' rendition of Hunters and Collectors Throw Your Arms Around Me made its debut. Despite Mark Taylor's mock gestures of blocking his ears, we continued singing of this and many other Aussie classics, until the winning runs were struck in the 42nd over.

The following day another 18-hour epic train journey took us to Agra, for a whirlwind half-hour tour of the Taj Mahal (the light was fading, and visiting hours closed at 7 pm). Then came a quick cab ride into town, to catch the bus ride from hell, to Jaipur. We arrived in that city at 2.30 in the morning and, too tired to care, woke several rickshaw drivers who had been fast asleep but seemed willing enough to earn themselves an easy 20 or so rupees.

This was our first experience of trying to find hotels at a ridiculous hour, but it was to become quite common-place as the tour continued. An hour later, and after several knockbacks from unimpressed nightkeepers, we came across the comparatively upmarket Galaxy Hotel. The owner wanted 85 rupees each per night, a little more than we normally liked to pay, but under the circumstances it seemed a reasonable luxury.

Security at the pre-match day training session at Jaipur was easily the strictest so far. No cameras ... no videos ... no food ... even no bags of any description were allowed into the ground. We tried to reason with the security personnel at the final checkpoint but they were unmoved, so we all walked around a corner and stuffed every item we had on us down our clothing. Cameras, even Dave's video camera went down the front of the shirt. It was all blatantly protruding but not exactly visible, and we were allowed into the ground ...

DAY 25 — *March 4*

(Australia v West Indies in Jaipur)

AT A SHORT pre-match discussion after warming up, Mark Taylor announced that Michael Slater, Shane Lee and Jason Gillespie were the unlucky ones left out of today's fixture. I wouldn't be bowling, because of a slight buttock strain — the quarter finals are only seven days away and we have second place in Group A set in stone, so it wasn't worth the risk.

The skies were clear and the temperatures mild when the game began, but the atmosphere in and around the stadium had a distinctly mosquito repellent tinge to it, which is understandable after yesterday's mass anti-malaria spraying. We were batting, having opted to try and set the Windies a healthy total after winning the toss. However, things didn't look promising early, because one of the world's premier opening attacks (Curtly Ambrose and Courtney Walsh) was making scoring look as difficult as it is to appear co-ordinated at an aerobics workout. After eight intimidating overs, under what were actually pretty difficult batting conditions, Mark Taylor and Mark Waugh had scrounged out a mere nine runs, mostly from edges and mistimed strokes.

As the ball lost its shine, scoring became a little easier, but then we lost brother Mark, caught behind by Courtney Browne off Walsh for 9. Ricky Ponting helped our captain take the score to 84, but boundaries were hard to find (none in the first 15 overs and only nine on the entire innings) and Taylor was stumped off Roger Harper as he tried to boost the run-rate.

Ponting had walked out to bat minus his helmet, a move guaranteed to

Ricky Ponting during his stirring century. Courtney Browne is the keeper.

induce some 'chin music', and Walsh hadn't let him down. But the significance of such a confident and fearless ploy wouldn't have been lost on their pacemen, and a small psychological victory was ours. By the time I reached the middle, in the 25th over, Ricky was looking increasingly confident, and, as the quicks had completed their early assaults, the spin of Harper, Jimmy Adams and Keith Arthurton allowed us to relax and play a more dominating role.

One memorable shot stood out above all others. It came from the flashing blade of Ponting, who charged their fast man, Ian Bishop, and smacked him high over the cover boundary, to stamp his authority on the match and the World Cup. I departed for 57, off 64 balls, happy with my performance and the part I had played in a 110-run partnership, from 114 balls, that swung the match slightly in our favour. Ricky continued on to a memorable 102 (111 balls), only falling in the mayhem of the last half a dozen overs, run out like Bevan and Healy, sacrificing wickets in the quest for quick runs.

I can certainly feel for Michael Bevan, who so far in the tournament has been run out twice and bowled once, all for low scores and all in the final chaotic overs of the innings. Hopefully, he'll get a chance up the order, sooner rather than later, because while no. 6 is a vital spot in the batting line-up of a top one-day side, having no time to play yourself in or build a decent innings doesn't do your technique or self-confidence much good. I know what he's experiencing right now — I batted at no. 6 for well over 100 one-day internationals and reckon it contributed to my demise as a Test-match player in the early 1990s. I couldn't seem to get a decent opportunity in the shortened game, and was continually sacrificing my technique (and often my innings) trying to score as quickly as possible. The limited-overs game really is made for the top three or four batsmen in the order.

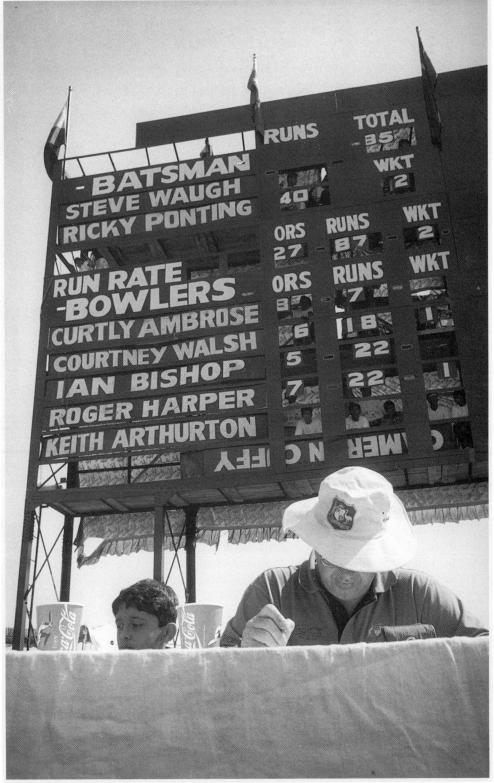

Team scorer Mike Walsh operates in front of the jumbled wooden scoreboard in Jaipur.
At this point, the Ponting-S. Waugh partnership is just three runs old.

The end of one of the best innings of the tournament. Ricky Ponting is run out by Roger Harper for 102.

Our final score of 6-229 was a formidable effort, particularly after our early struggles, but we knew that our chances of success depended on whether we could overcome the genius of Brian Lara.

The Windies changed their batting order, sending out Browne instead of Richardson with regular opener Sherwin Campbell, to try and negate our Victorian opening duo of Fleming and Reiffel. However, their reshuffle misfired (Campbell, c Healy b Fleming, 1, and Browne, run out 10), and at 2-26 we had gained a clear advantage.

Then Lara and Richardson woke the spectators, who had appeared dismayed by the West Indies' mini-collapse, with some dazzling stroke play. It was unusual to play the Windies in India and receive no support, but I guess the underdogs always get generous backing from these fair-minded people. They had certainly been behind us during the 1987 Cup, when few had thought we could win.

The teams we have faced to date have tried to do no more than repel Shane Warne, and not take any risks against him. Then they'll compensate for this conservative tactic by taking on our part-timers. This is, of course, an enormous show of respect for our bowling star, but at the same time very frustrating for him. The same principle has been applied to Lara, as most believe if they can get him, they are well on the way to victory. Perhaps with the champion from Trinidad this approach is a little inappropriate, as I get the impression that after his much-publicised recent disputes with the West Indies Board and the senior figures in the Windies team, he still isn't completely at ease with many of his colleagues. His mind is on other things, so I doubt this World Cup will do his reputation justice.

Even today, when he scored 60 and with his captain fashioned a match-winning partnership, he wasn't as dominating as he can be. We were certainly

Left: Shane Warne's World Cup was hindered to some extent, first by the Sri Lankan controversy and then by a painful spinning finger. He still had his moments of magic, however, especially against India and Zimbabwe in the Group matches and during the final overs of our epic semi-final victory over the West Indies. Here he's in Nagpur, spinning his way through the Zimbabwe batting line-up.

Below: The great Healy-Warne combination at it again ... Zimbabwe captain Andy Flower is stumped for 7, as the Africans struggle on a turning wicket.

Michael Slater (left) and Shane Lee in Jaipur, slowly climbing the mountain on our way to the majestic Amber Fort.

I was involved in two century partnerships during the Cup. The first, with brother Mark, came against Kenya, the second was against the Windies, when Ricky Ponting and I added 110 for the third wicket.

Above: Ricky's innings against the Windies was quite superb — run out for 102 off 113 balls.

Right: I was happy to score 57, and to have had such a good view of the young Tasmanian's brilliant performance.

Above: Brian Lara batting against Australia in Jaipur. Although, by his own high standards, Lara's World Cup was slightly disappointing, he remains just about the most valuable wicket in world cricket.

Below: Richie Richardson's response to the Windies' humiliation against Kenya was to come out and blaze an unbeaten 93 against us, as his side confirmed their spot in the quarter-finals.

The ill-fated 'Mongoose and Cobra Show'. Unfortunately, the brick (far right) that was tied to the mongoose prevented it moving, while the snake preferred the coolness of the basket to the heat of the day.

Top: The Australian cricket team in Bombay, mixing with the locals. Ian Healy and Damien Fleming are interviewing a cabbie, while in the background is the magnificent Taj Hotel.

Above: Many of the things you see in India are distressing, but you cannot dismiss them. They are, sadly, a fact of life. When I saw this beggar in Calcutta, the thing that really haunted me was not his appalling physical condition but the desperate, pleading look on his face.

Right: We discovered this nut and spice seller at the top of the Amber Fort.

Above: Many families in Calcutta have no alternative but to use the filthy water of the Ganges to wash their clothes.

Right: Even worse, some are forced to use the river as their public toilet.

Below: The Gateway to India, as seen from my hotel room in Bombay.

Above: Michael Slater is welcomed to Jaipur.

Below: Press and security, many the victims of the 'Holi day' festivities, being entertained at the Queen of Jaipur's palace. Left to right: Channel Nine reporter Andrew McKinlay, Ryan Mooney (from Nine, who earlier in the tour had fallen through a grandstand roof in Bombay), photographer Trent Parke, Channel 10's James Knight and Manoj, one of our two Group 4 security guys.

below our best, and Richardson and Lara took control as our fielding and bowling fell below expectations. In the final stages we managed something of a fightback, but it was all too late and the Windies went on to win comfortably by four wickets with eight balls to spare. Richardson was still there at the end, 93 not out. His was a gutsy performance and one no-one could feel anything but great admiration for.

The most disappointing aspect of our play today was our inability to recognise quickly enough that we were coasting along and not making things happen. When we finally did, it was all too late. We need to be more pro-active, rather than reactive, if we are to win these close games, and we must think on our feet more effectively. The mood of the dressing room afterwards was one of frustration at losing our winning record, but we are aware that the only game that really matters now is our next one — the quarter final. The knockout stage ... sudden death ... is about to begin.

The preliminary fixtures have clearly shown that the low, slow, flat wickets of both India and Pakistan suit the openers who score quickly and heavily by taking advantage of the hard new ball, coming straight onto the bat, and the quick outfields. Also enjoying success are the spinners, who come into vogue over here as the pitches take turn and the ball, roughened and softened by the abrasive wickets and harsh outfields, becomes more difficult to see late in the innings. This World Cup is not the perfect place for ambitious middle- and late-order batsmen, or for opening bowlers.

After we returned to our hotel, a few beers and a video, *The Shawshank Redemption*, passed the hours away. We had already turned our attention to Madras, our port of call for the quarter finals.

During his slashing unbeaten 93, Richie Richardson was 'caught' in spectacular fashion by Ponting on the leg-side boundary. However, in making this spectacular grab, Ricky stumbled back over the advertising hoarding. So, instead of a wicket falling, the West Indies captain's score increased by six, a fact the spectators in the background were quick to acknowledge.

DAY 26 — *March 5*
(Jaipur)

OUR PLANNED sightseeing tour in and around Jaipur had to be put on hold, as today is 'Holi Day'. This is an extraordinary local celebration that anyone can join, but one that foreigners are advised, for safety reasons, to avoid. It is a time when the law is virtually dismissed, a time for people to vent their angers, show their frustration, have a drink, behave crazily, show more than the usual affections and generally run amok. It is certainly a colourful day, with dyes of all colours being thrown around until everyone is unrecognisable. Put simply, the entire population lets its hair down. Traditionally, the day celebrates the end of the harvest and was conceived as a day to relax. But from what I heard, and the little I observed, there didn't seem to be too much relaxing being done today.

Management organised for us to have lunch at the Rambah Palace and a few drinks with the Queen of Jaipur at her residence, which adjoins the hotel. The Queen is a fascinating woman. She spent about two years in prison, while Indira Gandhi was Prime Minister, but today lives a life that appears comfortable but in no way similar to the grandeur of her predecessors. We were entertained by a unique musical instrument, which is similar in appearance to a violin but is made of local materials and sounds like a sick canary. This music inspired a stirring dance, which featured foot thumping and hip gyrations that had the boys feeling a little uneasy during a stage in the festivities when it seemed we were being serenaded.

Part of the Australian media contingent, Jim Wilson (Channel Seven), Andrew McKinlay (Channel Nine) and James Knight (Channel 10) turned up during lunch, looking as if they'd been just been heavily involved in a massacre. Our three intrepid reporters were covered from head to toe in an assortment of coloured dyes, the result of their early morning street investigations. This was just the latest in a series of problems they have faced to date in the Cup. Pictures back to Australia can only be transmitted from Bombay or Delhi, so the guys have had to wear many long and arduous trips in order to get their stories back to Oz in time. Quite ludicrously, James Knight and his cameraman are still to receive the appropriate media accreditation; technically they can't get into any grounds or training sessions without an identification card. How did they solve this problem? Passport photos were quickly taken, then glued onto a backing board which had the appropriate information printed onto it. This was cut to the right size, covered in a plastic coating and has been successfully passed off as a legitimate press pass in Bombay and Jaipur.

So much for tight security.

Without doubt, though, the biggest news of the day was Richie Richardson's announcement that he will be retiring at the end of this World Cup. I can't help but feel a little sympathy for him. He has looked a worried man for quite

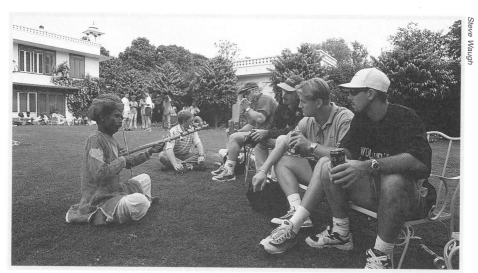

Left to right: Heals (on ground) is deep in conversation with one of the locals, while Slats, Flem, Meadow and Ponts enjoy the musical entertainment at the Queen of Jaipur's Palace.

a while now, and has worn the brunt of abuse the Windies have received since they lost their unofficial world crown. It has also become increasingly evident that his team wasn't 100 per cent behind him, and he has had to battle health problems (in 1994 he had to withdraw from big cricket for a long period while he recovered from the debilitating effects of chronic fatigue syndrome), the personal tragedy of his mother's death and serious injuries his young son suffered when struck by a car. I'm sure all these things have contributed to his decision.

I'm not privy to why his team-mates began to turn against him. But from my perspective, as an opposition player, he has always commanded a lot of respect — you know you're in a tough contest when Richie Richardson is your adversary. The Windies will definitely miss his batting talents, but after the announcements of today (coach Andy Roberts and manager Wes Hall have also been given the axe), they are now looking to a new era, effectively beginning from the end of the World Cup.

An early night was had by Slats and I, with my roomie showing perceptible signs of improvement with the guitar. He even strummed a few lines of the Mellencamp song, *Jack and Diane*, that I recognised, much to his delight. Meanwhile, I worked on my ThinkPad skills, though I didn't last too long as I gave in to the cries of my ailing health, which has been causing a few problems in the last couple of days, and went to bed. Dizzy spells, light-headedness and diarrhoea have meant a change in my diet, to soups, rice and naan bread, which will continue until my stomach returns to normal.

From Rawalpindi came the news that South Africa had completed a perfect run through the Group matches with a demolition of the Dutch. Their openers, Gary Kirsten (83) and Andrew Hudson (161) had added 186 before a wicket fell in the match, and the South Africans had finally totalled 3-328. In reply, Holland got just past halfway towards the target, finishing at 8-168 from their 50 overs. Judging on their results, the South Africans seem in superb form, and will be very hard to beat.

DAY 27 — *March 6*
(Jaipur to Delhi)

AN OPTIONAL sightseeing trip around part of this popular tourist destination, in the area known as Rajastan, was attended by only four players — Reiffel, S. Waugh, Lee and Slater — but this was understandable, as it did involve an 8.30 am start. The highlight of the trip was an elephant ride up to the Amber Fort, which featured around 15 minutes on a steep narrow path up a hillside. The usual long queues associated with this attraction were no problem for us, as security considerations meant we had to go directly to the front of the line. Things sometimes do work both ways!

The elephants were dressed to look like huge test patterns, with a multitude of colours splashed over them to add that little bit of extra mystique to the whole experience. It was unfortunate, though, to look back on the elephants following us up the winding path and see a security police car zipping in and out and in between these mammoth beasts. That took a little away from the occasion.

The mongoose and cobra show at the foot of the Fort was a major let-down. The arch enemy of the cobra found the warm pavement far too alluring and refused to budge a millimetre when the nearby cobra assumed the 'strike' position. No matter how much coaxing the owner tried, the mongoose stayed where he was. This was understandable, because the animal had a brick tied around its neck. Finally, the show ended when the last of the crowd drifted away. The five minutes of nothing Slats and Pistol filmed on their video cameras will, I'm sure, remain among their most valued possessions.

Back to the hotel, another room cleared, bags packed, dash to the bus outside the hotel, and then another delayed

Trent Parke

The mystique of an elephant ride to the top of the Amber Fort was spoiled to some extent by the ever-present police security.

The two Shanes, Warne (left, with back to camera) and Lee, playing chess outside our hotel. The only trouble was they had no idea how to play the game, and the 12 others watching knew even less!

plane trip. This time we found ourselves marooned in the airport lounge for two hours, not bad by World Cup standards. Shane Lee and I had just begun to nod off on a sofa, when a startled Mark Taylor shouted out something like: 'Look out! It's climbing up the wall!!' These words, or, more accurately, the way they were expressed, had us moving quicker than Ben Johnson on steroids. When we settled back down, we were informed that the cause of consternation from our captain was a large rat that had scampered up our sofa, across the top of it and then leapt into a nearby air-conditioner.

Upon our arrival in Delhi, we were ushered to the Ashok Hotel instead of the Taj, where we thought we would be staying. But last-minute changes to flights and accommodation during this World Cup have become commonplace, and almost accepted as being normal. From the television, we learned that the impossible had happened — Tendulkar had failed — but India had still defeated Zimbabwe by 40 runs, at Kanpur, to end the Africans' tournament. In Lahore, Pakistan had, as we had expected, proved too powerful for New Zealand, which set up a Trans-Tasman quarter-final in Madras. And all sorts of records had been broken in Kandy, where Sri Lanka had beaten Kenya by 144 runs. The home team's 5–398 was the biggest total in limited-overs internationals history; the runs scored — 652 — were the most scored in a single one-day game; Aravinda de Silva's 145 was the highest score by a Sri Lankan in one-day cricket and the first century by a Sri Lankan in a World Cup match; and Steven Tikolo's 96 was the highest score by a Kenyan in international cricket.

Tonight we were invited guests at the Australian Embassy, and it was certainly nice to down some good Aussie tucker, see a few friendly faces and sample a few drops of alcohol from back home. From there, we crossed the road and sampled some pommy hospitality at the British Embassy, giving us all the chance to let our hair down a bit and get to know Jason Gillespie a little better.

DAY 28 — *March 7*
(Delhi to Agra to Delhi)

LAST NIGHT'S festivities had seemed a good idea at the time, but as we gathered in the hotel foyer at 5.45 am we began to acknowledge the error of our ways. A four-and-a-half hour trip to the Taj Mahal stared us in the face. To make matters worse, Michael Slater and his increasingly unpopular guitar attempted to entertain us with a crude attempt at *Wild Thing*, which went down like the Titanic. The time was 6.05. In the morning.

The most amazing thing about this country is that you always see people. Not a second goes by when human life isn't before you. We came across an

Damien Fleming is about to complete the first mark ever taken at the Taj Mahal.

Shane Lee entertains the troops on the way back from the Taj. The not-too-comfortable individual behind his left shoulder is S. Waugh.

overturned lorry, which is apparently commonplace on these pot-holed, uneven roads. The lousy surfaces are the main reason for this country's atrocious road toll. Of course, the 'biggest goes first' system doesn't help either, nor does the constant, flagrant abuse of the rules of the road or the sheer numbers of not just vehicles but also animals that try to use the thoroughfares.

When we finally arrived at the front entrance of the Taj Mahal, we got changed into our yellow one-day gear in readiness for a team photo, hopped off the bus and were immediately swamped by hordes of well-wishers and photographers. I guess if we'd wanted to travel incognito, wearing bright yellow outfits with 'Australia' on the front and our own names on the back wasn't a very clever move. However, I'm sure the team photo will look great.

This wonder of the world is very impressive, but for me doesn't rate with the Pyramids of Egypt. Still, the Taj is a truly remarkable sight, and it dazzled us all with its beauty and aura. It was a pity we were ushered through so quickly by our security people, as I, along with the rest of the boys, never actually had a chance to stand back and take it all in.

The return journey was worse than a nightmare, with four stops due to mechanical problems, a succession of bone-jarring bumps (a result of the roads and the lack of suspension in the bus), the failure of the air-conditioner to function and, to cap it all off for me, an accident normally reserved for newborn babies. I was attempting to open a jammed window to try and reduce the soaring temperatures inside the bus, but my exertion was too much for a delicately poised internal system, and the result was too ugly and too obvious for me to go into detail here. The remainder of the journey was, shall we say, an 'uneasy' one, and no-one was more relieved than S. Waugh to see the entrance to the Ashok, after five-and-a-half hours on the road.

I certainly picked a bad day to feel off colour, for Heals had got word that the Colonel was in town. Kentucky Fried Chicken, that is. Despite the security boys' reservations, most of the lads took off on a 20-minute rickshaw ride for an assault on the 11 secret herbs and spices. Meanwhile, Warney found satisfaction in a Pizza Neapolitan at the nearby Hyatt Hotel, to end the near-starvation India's food suppliers have forced upon him.

DAY 29 — *March 8*
(Delhi to Madras)

IT WAS CERTAINLY a feeling of *déjà vu*. Another 5.30 am wake-up call, to begin yet another day of travelling. This time we faced a two-and-a-half hour trip to our quarter-final destination.

As soon as we reached Madras, it was clear that this location was at least five to six degrees warmer than anywhere else we'd been on tour, a fact that should suit us more than the Kiwis. Another bonus for us is that the ground here represents something of a lucky charm for us. It was here we played the famous Tied Test of 1986, a match famous not just for its extraordinary finish but also for Dean Jones' amazing double century — 210 of the bravest and most inspiring runs I've ever seen scored in a cricket match.

Memories of Deano's heroic knock came flooding back as soon as I walked into the change rooms for this afternoon's training session. I can still recall him losing control of his body functions in the latter stages of the innings, as nausea and dehydration took control. He was shaking, urinating in his pants and afterwards couldn't even remember much of what he'd done. His physical appearance had also changed considerably — such was the loss of body fluids, the bones in his face were clearly visible.

It was also here that we defeated India by one run in our opening match of the 1987 World Cup, and where we beat the West Indies in the 1989 Nehru Cup, when the Windies were at their most powerful. However, the outfield has changed greatly since those days, when it was bereft of any type of grass and rock hard in texture. Today it is lush, although the underlying hardness is still there. It remains an impressive stadium, complete with newly-installed lights, and I can't wait to play in front of the expected 40,000 capacity crowd.

A less pleasant memory about this ground that remains today is the putrid smell that hovers in the air. The stench emanates from a slimy green creek that runs around the circumference of the stadium, and takes a while to get used to. I recall that the atmosphere here can become quite stifling if the humidity is high and the temperature hot. This might become another obstacle we must put in the back of our mind if we wish to be successful.

Our training today was excellent. There was no shortage of nets (we used four) and an abundance of net bowlers, and the whole squad went about training in a way that simulated what we'd expect in a match situation. Our approach to practice was no accident, as Simmo had stressed the importance of having three good days of practice at an intensity similar to what we'd experience during the quarter-final.

Tonight's team meeting developed into an open forum in which the emphasis was on how we can improve in the last 10 overs. I suggested that more responsibility should rest on the in-form batsmen who have been getting out around the 40-over mark, at a time when they should really be taking

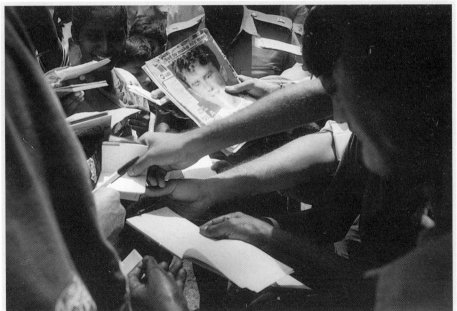

The hand with the pen is mine!

control. It's very hard for middle- and late-order batsmen to come in and score at a run a ball, particularly if the pitch has slowed up, the ball is soft and hard to see off the pitch, and the opposition is employing their best bowlers — as has been the case in every game in this World Cup to date. We'll also be striving to improve our intensity and alertness in the field, and will be concentrating on every ball bowled. One or two careless moments may cost us the match. It was quite a lengthy meeting — around one hour in duration (which I would normally say was by far too long) — but on this occasion it was all constructive and useful.

The business end ...

Tomorrow sees the beginning of the business section of the World Cup. Sri Lanka takes on England, but that match has been completely overshadowed by the first clash between India and Pakistan in India for nine years. Just about every single eye in the two countries will be watching closely. Frankly, I don't really care who wins the England–Sri Lanka encounter, but I'd like to see Pakistan eliminated. I believe they are our biggest dangers, due to the threats of Wasim Akram and Waqar Younis, plus the host of talented strokemakers in their line-up. And we all know that they will be doubly keen to retain the World Cup, seeing as they have been offered the incentives of receiving $US196,000 each, plus a plot of land, from the Pakistan Board of Control and the Pakistani Government if they can pull off the desired result.

Mind you, India are also on huge incentives, though the biggest winners, regardless of who triumphs out on the field, look like being PILCOM. What they will eventually profit by is anyone's guess (though some educated estimates put the figure as high as between $US50 million and $US80 million), but whatever it is, I'm pretty certain it will make the first prize cheque of $US30,000 look obscenely small, and annoying from the players' perspective.

Without us, their profit would be zero.

DAY 30 — *March 9*
(Madras to Fisherman's Cove to Madras)

THE TRAGIC NEWS came through this morning — the vegemite jar is all but empty and the tour could have more than a week to go!

Practice this morning involved well over an hour of solid fielding routines. We began with a team drill and followed up with three separate activities, one of high-ball catching, another of run out opportunities and finally a short-catching exercise. It all seemed very beneficial, until Heals sustained a slight wrist injury attempting a diving catch in a routine designed and run by himself. Hopefully the damage won't be too serious. Warney is the Aussie camp's only other injury concern; he has a hamstring problem and has also suffered a recurrence of the tendonitis that has plagued the ring (or in his case, spinning) finger on his right hand. My buttock strain has responded well to treatment and, if required, I should be able to roll my arm over tomorrow.

As in 1987, our management agreed that an afternoon at Fisherman's Cove (about one hour away from our hotel here) would be a relaxing way to get out of the confines of the hotel. It also offered a chance to catch a few waves, but without doubt the highlight of our excursion was not the beach, but the fare on offer at this resort. Here was our first chance to sample seafood since we left Oz.

The table of Lee, Reiffel, S. Waugh and Bevan nailed four crustaceans, each a different size and different price. Meadow's final bill had the bottom line of 2,400 rupees, around $AUS100, which would buy you a decent seafood platter at Doyle's (one of Sydney's classiest seafood restaurants, at Watson's Bay on the Harbour), and leave you with plenty of spare change as well. That said, we would have each paid twice that if we had to, because there's only so much chicken and sweet corn soup and spaghetti neapolitan one can stomach in four-and-a-half weeks.

After woofing down the local fare, I took a stroll along the beach and caught up with some people from the local fishing village. Inevitably, they all wanted a souvenir to keep or some rupees to help them out, but overall I found them to be extremely friendly people.

Many remembered they had met me on the beach back in 1987, and they all wished me the best of luck ... except, they stressed, if we came up against India. Then they went back to their daily chores; it was fascinating to see them go about their work. I stayed in the background, talking to some of the village children (who spoke excellent English), while women collected whitebait and other small fish that had been left on the beach for the past couple of days to dry. The kids explained that a large basket of dried-out whitebait, which would be sold to chicken farmers as feed, can get them about 50 or 60 rupees.

Images from the beach at Fisherman's Cove, as the local villagers bring in, and then sort through, the day's catch.

Meanwhile, the men of the village were busy dragging in their huge fishing nets in from way out in the ocean. This process took over an hour, before the catch was finally hauled onto the shore. At this point, the entire village congregated on the sand, to see what had been trapped. It seemed to me that their catch was pretty impressive — about four metres by four metres full of fish of different sizes and shapes, including stingrays, pikes and other species whose names I didn't know or didn't understand.

While this was happening, I went berserk with the camera. There was a price to pay for invading their privacy, but the 300 rupee gift, plus a cap and a pair of shorts, had them jumping for joy. I walked away feeling I had short-changed them. To see these marvellous people go about their lives, and make the most of what they have been given, was a remarkable experience. I was privileged that they had shared a part of their day with me.

Not long after the fish had been sorted out, according to their shape and size, in Faisalabad the pommies had also been sorted out, by the rampaging Sri Lankan batting line-up. England managed 8–235 from their 50 overs, a target the Sri Lankans reached with a ridiculous 9.2 overs to spare. From what I saw, the Englishmen were lacklustre and uncompetitive, while the strokeplay of Jayasuriya was exceptional. His 82, off 44 balls, was the type of innings you dream of, but I still get the feeling the Sri Lankans' 'slash-and-burn' tactics in the early overs will backfire on them sooner or later. I just hope we have the opportunity to try and achieve this in the final.

The day's other match, between India and Pakistan in Bangalore, proved to be a match full of excitement, skill and pressure. Eventually the home side got home, largely because of a superb cameo performance with the blade from Ajay Jadeja, who ripped off an amazing 45 from just 25 balls. His whole innings was surreal, especially during an extraordinary episode when he smashed 40 off Waqar Younis' last two overs. Forty!! This was a feat previously thought impossible.

Jadeja's heroics took the home side to 8–287, a target that proved beyond a Pakistani team that was without its injured skipper, Wasim Akram. Stand-in captain Aamir Sohail did manage 55, and the scoreboard at one point reached 4–184, but you always sensed during the Pakistanis' innings that the Indians were in control. Of course, the victory was greeted with joy all over India. At the stadium, fireworks exploded into life and newspapers were rolled up and burned like torches. It is little wonder that all the terraces and stands at Indian grounds are made of concrete, for if they were made of timber, there'd be a huge bonfire after every major local success. And, as cricket history has shown from time to time, there might be the occasional angry outbreak after a major loss as well.

Most of the lads had an early night, in readiness for tomorrow morning's practice session. This probably sounds bizarre, but many of us are feeling a bit jet-lagged from all the recent travel we've had to undertake. And I'm still receiving some ultrasound treatment for my niggling buttock injury. Fingers crossed, it won't affect my match performance.

DAY 31 — *March 10*
(Madras)

CRICKET IS ONE of Australia's great loves. To many back home it is a matter of some importance whether or not the Aussie team wins or loses. Over here, on the sub-continent, it is much, much, much more than that.

This fact was driven home to all this morning, when a report from Islamabad in Pakistan confirmed the following: 'Pakistani cricket fans smashed television sets and one committed suicide amid national gloom over Pakistan's defeat by arch-rivals India in the World Cup quarter-finals. Distraught at the defending champions crashing out of the tournament yesterday, college student Jaffer Khan fired a burst of Kalashnikov bullets into his television screen and then turned the gun on himself.'

A grim feature of the *Frontier Post*, a Pakistani newspaper, was a cartoon showing freshly dug graves and a caption 'a plot for each player'. This was a reference to the incentives of land and cash that had been offered by the Pakistani Prime Minister's husband, Mr Asif Ali Zardari, to his country's cricketers if they retained the Cup. Perhaps the most amazing of all the stories, though, was this one: 'Prime Minister Benazir Bhutto's Government on Sunday offered to inquire into the causes of Pakistan's defeat in the quarter-finals against India, (which is) being mourned in the country as a national disaster.

'Her aide, Iqbal Haider, made the offer in the Senate, as opposition members heaped blame on the Government for the humiliation at the hand of the country's arch rival.'

This fanaticism may seem hard to fathom for anyone who hasn't visited this part of the world. But cricket is the one thing that truly unites the people and gives them something to be proud of. For the people who live on the breadline, cricket provides an escape from the pressures and poverty of everyday life.

This morning was yet another practice session. It almost feels as if we have come to India for a pre-season training camp, with endless amounts of nets, gym work and team meetings, but very little action in the middle.

Calcutta goes Cup crazy

Reports from Calcutta suggest that the city has gone absolutely World Cup crazy. Fans, who had been celebrating long into the night and early morning after India's famous quarter-final triumph, descended on the clubhouse at Eden Gardens this morning, in search of tickets for the semi-final in three day's time. All 94,000 seats for the game have been sold, but officials are apparently having great difficulty in convincing thousands of disappointed ticketless supporters of this fact. In the meantime, prices on the black market have exploded, with tickets usually worth 300 and 450 rupees now fetching many, many times that amount.

Beach cricket, Madras style.

In my opinion, the most important practice session is always the one on the eve of a match, so it was pleasing for me to turn in a good net, with the feet moving well and the confidence on a high. During these sessions, I try to imitate what my game plan will be and stick to it. I want my mind focussed on what I'll be trying to achieve and I also aim to develop good habits, which is vital for success. Bad habits picked up at practice tend to follow you into the match.

Had there been a player of the morning award it would have to have gone to Glenn McGrath, who put in a career-best batting performance. However, he did revert back to his erroneous ways late in his net, when he attempted a huge heave to the leg-side which resulted in nothing more than his bat hurtling through the air a good 30 metres, in the direction of square leg. I guess this lapse of concentration (or temporary loss of brain power) came about because he's never had his batting gloves get sweaty before. Consequently, Pigeon didn't realise that swinging like a rusty gate and an insecure grip is not the mix you're after.

Warney again missed most of the session. After bowling only half a dozen balls, he decided things were too painful to continue. This situation, which has been gradually worsening for a while, is now a major concern for us all. And not just in the short term, but for the remainder of Shane's career. Apparently, the ligaments in his fingers have been stretched due to his knuckle joints loosening up. Our other injury worry, Heals' injured hand, is still tender as well. But I'm sure it won't stop him from taking part in tomorrow's do-or-die fixture.

Driving home, from the ground to the hotel, there are plenty of interesting sights to see and take in. Firstly there is that filthy creek that runs around the ground, and through the hub of a nearby village. There it is obviously used for every purpose; everywhere it gives off a foul-smelling odour. The locals, though, don't seem at all bothered by it and go about their everyday life, selling soft drinks, cooking food in the street stalls, shining shoes, washing clothes and transporting goods by any means they can.

Our trip then takes us along Madras' main beach front, where huts made of buffalo dung, bamboo and thatched roofs litter the water's edges. But the standout feature is the seemingly endless games of beach and street cricket being played. Kids of all ages, with no more kit than three sticks or stumps, one well-worn bat and anything resembling a ball, play as if they are representing their country. From my point of view, it's almost inspiring to see how much these young cricketers love this great game. Every morning while we've been here, the children have seen our bus and immediately their game has come to a halt. They smile, laugh and wave us on, with one thought clearly on their minds ... one day they'll be playing against us.

On most tours, an optional sponsor's team dinner would be dismissed in the blink of an eyelid as a pain in the butt. However, when you've been struggling for entertainment and amusement, it comes almost as a relief. Unfortunately, that relief quickly turned into despair tonight, due to the endless impositions placed upon us by photo takers and autograph hunters. Now, I must stress that I don't mind giving autographs — I remember when I was a kid just how much they meant to me — but at times things can get ridiculous, and this was, after all, supposed to be an opportunity for us to relax on the eve of one of the most important matches of our careers.

Quite absurdly, the allegedly tight net of security was penetrated by a group of Aussie supporters who are over here following the cricket, staying in hostels and other low-budget accommodation and travelling by buses and trains. Shrewdly donning disguises of sandals, shorts and crushed shirts, the boys waltzed into this 'invitation-only' function without so much as a security officer's eyebrow being raised. Once in, they proceeded to tuck into the buffet feed and wash it down with a drop or two of the local brew. They were a good bunch of blokes, and we appreciate the efforts they've gone to support us here, but the fact that they were able to crash tonight's function confirmed for me once again that the enormous amount of security that is supposed to be protecting us is actually more concerned at securing an autograph than securing a building.

Pakistan team's plane diverted to Karachi
Angry fans stone Akram's house, file writ petition

By V. Srivatsa and Agencies

KARACHI, March 12. A shell-shocked Pakistani cricket team arrived here last night after their plane was diverted from Lahore to save them from the "wrath of disgruntled elements."

Distraught fans, yet to get over their disappointment after Pakistan lost to India in the quarter-finals of the Wills World Cup in Bangalore on Saturday, had gathered in large numbers with banners and rotten eggs at Lahore airport.

When they came to know of the change in plans, several angry boys took out a procession, burned an effigy of skipper Wasim Akram and hurled stones and eggs at his house, although he wasn't there at the time.

One fan filed a writ petition against Pakistan's "disappointing" performance.

Admitting the petition for hearing, Justice Munir Shaikh observed that "corruption had derived the game of cricket in Pakistan." Referring to newspaper photographs the judge said: "The

Pakistani players have been shown dancing with girls but when they play the game they feel a crick in their backs."

Another fan, Farooq Omar, tried to file charges in the Lahore High Court against the team, accusing it of deliberately losing the match.

Pakistan cricket board chairman Arif Abbasi dismissed the corruption charges, saying the board won't conduct any investigations. "I am just putting all this down to disappointment," he said.

After arriving in Karachi, the players shut themselves in a hotel for over four hours. No one was allowed in and no phone calls were entertained.

A furious Akram later revealed that he had received death threats. He dismissed allegations that he had bet against his side retaining

its title. One of Akram's neighbours, Khalid Farooq, had accused him of betting against his side.

"I do not deserve this," the all-rounder said at a press conference at Karachi's National Stadium. "I have always played my best for Pakistan. I am ready to swear upon the holy Koran that I am not involved in betting and that I am clean."

Asked manager Intikhab Alam, "Which player or nation deliberately throws the match? It's not the end of the world but we are disappointed at having lost."

The manager was worried about forthcoming Indo-Pak clashes in Singapore and Sharjah. "If the players are not encouraged and are prevented from concentrating on their game, we will be heading for more setbacks."

Both Intikhab and Akram were livid at insinuations that some of the players had not tried their best for reasons other than cricket. "Look at the incentives we would have got had we won the Cup. Could there be more than that?" Intikhab asked.

Rats have a field day in Calcutta's Eden Gardens

CALCUTTA, March 12: Stray rats are causing concern to the organisers of tomorrow's World Cup semi-final between India and Sri Lanka.

The rats have burrowed right under the pitch in Eden Gardens and ground keepers are confused about how to get them out before the day-and-night match begins.

The rats have already chewed up the wire that connects a tiny TV camera placed on the stump and refuse to budge from the pitch area.

The burrows were discovered when a TV crew tried to test the camera that gives a close-up view of the pitch. When it didn't work, the crew checked the wire and found it had been chewed. Further investigation led the ground staff to the burrows.

"The only way out is to seal the burrows with cement or something until the match is over," said one ground worker. (AP)

Two unsuccessful Australian appeals during the long and often frustrating New
Zealand innings in the quarter-final in Madras. Top: Glenn McGrath thinks
century-maker Chris Harris might have edged a catch to Ian Healy. Below: Shane
Warne is convinced he has another lbw victim.

Both pics: Australian Picture Library/All Sport

DAY 32 — *March 11*

(The quarter-final, Australia v New Zealand in Madras)

THE BEST PART of playing a day-night one-day international during this World Cup is that you don't have to get up around 7 am (like you must for the 'all-dayers', which have been beginning at 9 am). Consequently, you have the opportunity to relax in the morning and not be rushed around. However, the later start does provide insatiable sports fans with more time to jam your phone with their best wishes for the day.

(One of the more unusual good luck messages came from a young female fan this morning, who asked: 'Have you got your lucky red hankie for today?' This enquiry shows just how closely the locals scrutinise every little facet and detail of the play.)

This morning was hot. And humid. By 10 o'clock, the sun was spearing its heat into anything that dared to leave the comfort of the air-conditioned hotel rooms. But, while this was a little uncomfortable to begin with, it was something we were prepared for and saw as an advantage rather than a hindrance. We knew we had much greater experience playing under such temperatures than did our opponents. The ugliest aspect of the atmosphere was not the temperature but the stifling air — or, more to the point, the foul odour — that lurked around the stadium.

Our team remained unchanged, with Michael Slater making up the dozen yet again. The New Zealanders, however, had their hand forced when picking their starting XI. Injuries to key bowlers Danny Morrison and Gavin Larsen left them underdone in the bowling department, and this was something we had identified in our team meeting as being a weakness we needed to exploit.

This, unfortunately, was a strategy we were forced to wait a while to implement, after the incorrect side of the coin stared Mark Taylor in the face at the toss. The playing strip was totally devoid of grass, but lacked nothing in hardness, so New Zealand captain Lee Germon had very little to think about. The Kiwis would bat first!

The capacity crowd of around 45,000 roared with delight when the underdogs began with the force of a space shuttle at lift-off. Fifteen runs were ripped from Paul Reiffel's initial over. But then a sense of normality came back into the game, when Damien Fleming wheeled down a wicket maiden (Nathan Astle, caught by Ian Healy, 1). Our enthusiastic audience was steadied a little, as were our nerves.

Fleming has been a bit of a rarity over here — one of the very few successful new-ball bowlers, primarily because he has the rare ability to swing the ball in any conditions. Reiffel, on the other hand, relies more on movement from the pitch, but the wicket he secured in his second over had little to do with any of that; Chris Spearman did well to get some wood on a wide delivery, but was caught by Healy for 12. After three overs, we were very nicely placed, at 2–16.

Ricky Ponting, literally in full flight during the Australian run chase.

However, from this point we began bowling as if our main ambition was to satisfy the after-match highlights. There was plenty of loose stuff from each and every bowler, and the boundaries were too short to contain the onslaught from the flashing blades of Chris Harris and Germon. This pair had come together after Stephen Fleming had hit a Glenn McGrath delivery straight to me, to make the score 3–44, and they weren't separated until the scoreboard had reached 212, in the 34th over. Harris and Germon hadn't featured too heavily on our list of potential dangermen with the bat — names like Fleming, Adam Parore, Astle, Spearman and Chris Cairns had — but such is the lack of predictability in the one-day game that it often provides surprises that catch out even its participants. Harris probably wouldn't have even played, but for the injury to Larsen!

Maybe the fact that we had underestimated the partnership was our problem. Looking back now, we fell for the trap of expecting this run-a-ball stand, which gathered momentum, as snowflakes do, to make an avalanche, to crumble by itself, when we should have been getting stuck in and making things happen. By the time Fleming brilliantly held onto a fence-bound lofted drive from Germon, we were in serious trouble. The Kiwi captain had made 89, and we still hadn't dislodged Harris, whose performance was assuming Fine Cotton status.

(For those less familiar with infamous moments in Australian sporting history, Fine Cotton was a poorly performed racehorse who suddenly emerged in 1984 to land one of the biggest betting plunges in racing history. Only trouble was, the Fine Cotton that raced that day wasn't Fine Cotton, but the much better credentialled, and poorly disguised, Bold Personality. When this was discovered, 'Fine Cotton' was disqualified.)

If only we could have worked out who this 'Chris Harris' really was. Good luck to him, though, and he continued to play the innings of his life until holing out, for an outstanding 130, late in the over count.

Despite Harris' continuing excellence, the dismissal of Germon changed the game. Our effort in containing the Kiwis to 57 runs off their last 10 overs represented a superb comeback after the thrashing we had received. The turning point of the game, in my opinion, was the dismissal of Cairns (c Reiffel b Mark Waugh, 4), because he, like his old man (the former Test all-rounder, Lance) can clear boundaries the way Superman does tall buildings. Had he stayed around for a while, the New Zealanders' total may have been many more than their final 9–286.

Michael Bevan was the bowler primarily responsible for this courageous fightback. Our opponents' middle to late order couldn't quite collar either he or Shane Warne, and though their final total was fairly daunting, it was definitely one we would have accepted midway through their innings.

The mood in the Australian camp at the interval was pensive. But we were very determined and retained a deep confidence in our ability. Unfortunately for myself, the 45-minute break saw me on the physio's table, with ice packs wrapped around both ankles — a result of twisting them on the rock-hard surface they call the field. I can't believe that I went over on not just one ankle, while attempting to back up a throw, but on both. I've never had this type of injury before.

Our run chase got off to a solid, if not spectacular, beginning. However, with the total on 19, Taylor unluckily tickled an attempted leg-glance straight into the keeper's gloves. The ball would have been signalled a wide if Mark hadn't touched it! The crowd's reaction to this dismissal emphasised that, at this point at least, most of them were supporting the underdogs. But this only made us more determined to do well.

Mark Waugh and Ricky Ponting took the score to 50 and beyond, all the while keeping us up to or around the required run rate. As the total moved towards three figures, I briefly mentioned to our vice-captain, Ian Healy, that

Shane Warne is lbw to Nathan Astle, to end the Aussie pinch-hitter's crucial, quickfire 24 that changed the tempo of the quarter-final.

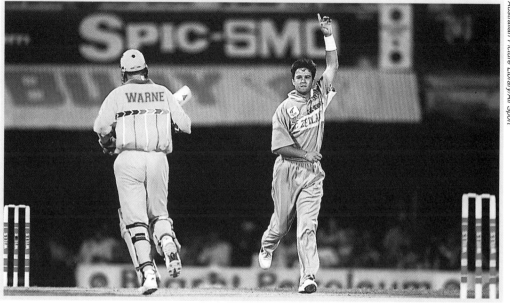

Australian Picture Library/All Sport

Above: (Front, left to right) Shane Warne, Mark Taylor and Jason Gillespie watch anxiously from beyond the boundary, as Stuart Law and I (right, punching Shane Thomson into the covers for another single) steer Australia towards a famous victory.

this would be an ideal time to send in a pinch hitter — someone to try and give us the kick along that would put us in front of the opposition's run rate at the similar point in their innings. The idea of sending in a Warne, a Reiffel or even a Fleming to boost the scoring rate made sense to me, as these normally late-order players more than likely wouldn't have got a hit until at least the last couple of overs. If nothing was gained, nothing would be lost if their attempted hitting didn't come off. And another argument supporting the concept was something we have learned from experience over the years — the only way you can win chasing a large total in one-day cricket is to have quality batsmen at the crease during the last 10 pressure-packed overs. By sending in a pinch hitter, and therefore holding back our top players (at least for a short while), this was going to be more likely.

A quick word was had with our captain, and the idea was agreed to be a worthwhile one. Soon after, Shane Warne made his way to the crease, after Ricky was dismissed with the score on 84, and he proceeded to tilt the balance of power our way by scoring a quickfire 24 off 15 exciting balls. In four-and-a-half overs he added 43 runs with Mark, and gave us just the added impetus the innings needed.

I made my way to the crease full of confidence that we would be able to score the remaining 160 runs from the 25 overs available. It was soon apparent that a little bit of needle was present out in the middle, and a couple of little jibes were thrown my way. But I had to expect this, as I'd given as much in the Kiwis' innings earlier on. I must admit, I love a challenge, even a confrontation in the middle, as it helps me become more focussed on the job at hand and also suggests that the opposition isn't thinking quite the way they should.

I had the supporting role in this fourth-wicket partnership with brother Mark, required to nudge the ones and twos while he began to take boundaries off their attack almost at will. Once I was settled in, we reminded each other it was vital that one or both of us kick on to a big score — it would be difficult for a new batsman to come in and score quickly straightaway, due to the less-than-fantastic lighting, the soft and discoloured ball and the highly-charged atmosphere.

Mark's innings was one of the best of his career, his third century of this World Cup (no-one had ever managed hundreds in one Cup tournament before). He also went past Graham Gooch's record of 471 runs in a single World Cup. When he was finally out, dismissed as much by exhaustion as anything else, he had scored 110, and the remaining six wickets had been left with the task of scoring 76 runs from 70 balls — a target very achievable but also very 'loseable'.

Mark Waugh is man-of-the-match yet again and, having accepted his award, happily accepts the high fives of his delighted team-mates.

Steve Waugh

Ian Healy leads the boys in our victory song. The far-left seat in this photo has a special place in the annals of Australian cricket, for it was there that an exhausted and badly dehydrated Dean Jones sat during breaks in play and after his remarkable innings of 210 in the 1986 Tied Test.

Stuart Law and I stressed to each other the importance of staying level-headed. We remembered also what had been discussed at our pre-game team meeting, about the lack of depth in the New Zealand bowling line-up. We needed to try and score at least a run off every ball, and wait for the odd boundary that would become an inevitability due to loose deliveries and our increasing confidence. On paper, at least, this was a sound plan but in reality it was tougher to achieve, particularly as the stakes both teams were playing for were so high. The losers, after all, were catching the next plane home.

However, it seemed no-one told Stuart Law about all this. Showing maturity that belied his relative inexperience at this level, he made the task look like a stroll in the park, picking off boundaries precisely at the moments we needed them. I just continued on, trying to score a run off each ball. The victory was achieved with 13 balls to spare — a victory that illustrated, above all, how success can be achieved if you stay calm, because this will almost always lead to your opposition becoming frustrated and ruffled.

When we congregated on the ground at the conclusion of the match, our joy was obvious for all to see. At that moment, I remember thinking we have the ability and composure to overcome any hurdle that comes our way. We couldn't wait to reach the haven of our change rooms, to put the feet up, grab a cold Aussie beer and reminisce over the day's events. I think the calm and clinical way we went about our task this evening even surprised most of us, but it was a pleasant discovery, almost as if we have added another dimension to our game. Most certainly, we have dismissed doubts held in some quarters about our ability to chase a large total.

The mood in the rooms was not set by wild out-of-control celebrations, but rather was more sedate; we took great pleasure from a job that had been completed so professionally. The talk was largely about our semi-final, which, surprisingly, will be against the West Indies. Earlier in the day, our arch-rivals, largely on the back of a Brian Lara century, had knocked out the previously unbeaten South Africans, 8–264 to 245.

DAY 33 — *March 12*
(Madras to Delhi)

THE RESULTS of yesterday's two quarter-final matches created an interesting piece of trivia. All the semi-finalists have come from Group A (Australia, West Indies, Sri Lanka and India), while all the semi-finalists from the 1992 World Cup (New Zealand, Pakistan, South Africa and England) have been eliminated. This just goes to show the evenness of most of the Test-playing countries in world cricket, and also underlines the fact that no international side has been able to hold centre stage in the abbreviated game for any length of time. All teams today seem to know not only their own games well, but also how their opponents go about things. Mind you, this isn't surprising when you consider how much one-day cricket is being played.

It will be interesting to see whether or not the World Cup is won by a side using conventional tactics or by improvising and unorthodox methods. Only time will tell!

Breakfast, like many other meals here, is only had out of necessity. My plate was graced once again by scrambled eggs and baked beans, accompanied this time by toast that was so firm and heavy it would probably have been very handy if someone had been constructing a building in the vicinity. The alternatives for breakfast here are fairly limited, a fact brought home to me every time I take a mouthful of baked beans. This is a foodstuff not found in my kitchen cupboard back home, but I must say I've been converted, and Mr Heinz may have found himself a new customer.

My morning was taken up by interviews with media representatives from Channels Seven, Nine and Ten. Easily the most interesting was with the Nine reporter, one Mr Shane Warne. Still clearly excited about his success as a

Introducing Manoj and Negi

Security here was no different from everywhere else, with heavily-armed guards, their bayonets poised, patrolling our third-floor oasis. Meanwhile, our Group 4 security boys, Manoj and Negi, are never out of sight. Now here are two guys with very different make-ups. Manoj is vibrant, loud and more visible, while Negi is the quiet, unassuming customer, always lurking in the background.

Both are very popular with the boys and have fitted in with the squad extremely well. Manoj is a first dan in Tae Kwon Do, Negi is a third dan, and both have the moves to prove their status. Fortunately, the only moves the boys have had to perform so far have revolved around the elbow joints, although the combination of Aussie beer and countless buffet lunches and dinners have seen their belt notches ease out a couple of holes. This appears to be about the most dangerous aspect of the whole tour so far for them.

pinch hitter last night, Warney couldn't help but ask me: 'Do you think I can do it again against the West Indies?'

'That,' I replied, 'would be highly unlikely, as we wouldn't be able to coax you out of the toilet!'

I was, of course, alluding to the difference in pace between the New Zealand pair, Nathan Astle and Shane Thomson, compared to the dynamic Windies duo of Curtly Ambrose and Courtney Walsh, and the state of panic Warney would be in if he was asked to venture out to face the latter two guys.

A mid-afternoon call from manager Col Egar confirmed what we had expected — our flight to Delhi had been delayed — so it was back to watching the Caped Crusaders ward off the likes of the Penguin and company on the satellite TV station.

When we finally arrived at Delhi airport we came across a situation that I, in 12 years of international and domestic travel, had never encountered before. After landing, and then slowly taxiing along the tarmac, we came to an abrupt halt. There followed a brief delay, before the following news crackled over the plane's public address.

'I am sorry,' said the captain, 'we have a small problem. There is no space available in the parking bay. We will be delayed for approximately 10 minutes, or until a space is made available ...

'Thank you.'

Well, it turned out to be a typical Indian 10 minutes — 37 to be precise — so we were obliged to remain in our seats, curse our bad luck and chew on complimentary mango lollies that send cold shivers down the spine.

This unexpected irritation was one that Messrs M. and S. Waugh, Ponting, McGrath and Healy didn't need. We had a press conference scheduled at which we would announce our new partnership with an Indian Marketing Company (Percept), who have agreed to try and market us before and during our tour in September–October 1996. This is a ground-breaking initiative, but the sports business is booming in India — because of the impact of the pay-TV companies, Star TV and ESPN, the fans here know just as much about us as do cricket followers in Australia. Companies in Asia want their products endorsed by sporting personalities, so it seems an ideal time to give such a concept a try.

Marketing of cricketers over here is huge. Sachin Tendulkar seems to be promoting almost

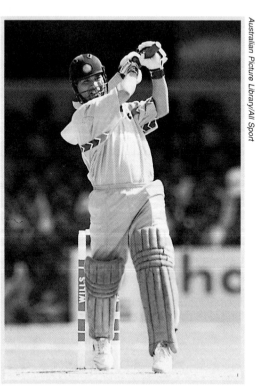

Who knows how many millions Sachin Tendulkar is worth?

The West Indies defeat of South Africa in Karachi was the biggest shock of the quarter-finals. Here Courtney Browne celebrates the wicket of Brian McMillan, lbw to Harper, during the game's final overs.

everything, including Pepsi, Visa Card and Philips electrical gear. He also has a contract with World Tel which will reputedly pay him $US1.5 million per year for the next five years. Everywhere you look, he and Mohammad Azharuddin have their dials plastered across huge billboards, with a Pepsi in hand and the slogan underneath — 'Nothing Official About It'. This line is, of course, a direct slur on Coca-Cola, who won the bid to be the official drink for the World Cup.

It seems there are no rules in this battle for soft drink supremacy in India. Pepsi have continually bought TV space during the games, floated signs carried by helium balloons across the grounds during play and made their presence felt outside the grounds on match days. They have also acquired the services of many overseas players to promote the drink in TV commercials. Warney and I were offered big money to do these, but Shane already had a tie up with Coke and I was unable to be involved because the Australian team was to be sponsored by Coke.

Anyway, back to the press conference, which we felt was at least a reasonable success. As usual, the media were infatuated by the 'twin thing' and asked all the usual questions, including: 'Who's the older? ... 'Do you have ESP?' ... 'Do you get on?' ... 'Do you room together?' And so on and so on.

DAY 34 — *March 13*
(Delhi to Chandigarh)

IT SEEMS that when either India or Pakistan lose a cricket match, the post mortems never end. And there always has to be a finger pointed at someone. The unfortunate accused individual of the moment is Pakistani captain Wasim Akram, who yesterday apparently had a writ filed against him by one of his neighbours. This friendly fellow is alleging that Wasim took 3.7 million rupees to sit out the quarter-final and by doing so let India win. Unfortunately for Wasim, a small but vocal minority will believe this story — already he has had to put on 24-hour security around his home as a safeguard against the lunatic element.

The only consolation we gained from our seven o'clock flight this morning was the majestic sight of the snow-capped Himalayas looming on the horizon as we descended into the peace and prosperity of the Punjab. Chandigarh is a strange choice to host a semi-final of a World Cup, even though the ground here is reputed to be the best on the sub-continent. The major problem revolves around the lack of accommodation — there is only one hotel of any quality, plus maybe a couple more that are in a reasonable state. Inevitably, these hotels have been booked out for over 12 months now, and as a result, none of the Aussie media crews could find a room for the match. Their only option was an awful six-hour drive from Delhi on the day of the game and then a journey back to Delhi after the match, which is hardly satisfactory for such a huge occasion.

Fans relish Jagger's appearance

By Anju Sharma

NEW DELHI, March 12 Oblivious to thousands of western music buffs in the metropolis, the guru of hard rock and founder of the Rolling Stones, Mick Jagger, paid a brief visit to the city. The creator of rock legendary songs like Honky Tonky Woman, Let Us Spend the Night Together and anthem for rock puritans, I Can Get No Satisfaction; was on a personal trip to India.

Contrary to the anti-establishment, wild image that Mick Jagger and his music have been associated with his three-hour stopover in Delhi was a quiet one. In fact, it was difficult to fathom that the idol of the teeny bopper generation in the 60s and 70s and pioneer of the rock revolution was actually in India.

The founder of the longest surviving band in music history, the man who gave the Beatles a run for their fame and glory and for whom thousands of star-struck girls were ready to give their lives despite his not so good looks, checked into the Maurya Sheraton Hotel along with three friends this afternoon.

At 2.00 p.m. the bustling lobby of the hotel almost came to a standstill as people recognised Jagger and

then pinched themselves to feel if it was actually true. The expression on most faces was of disbelief and shock. "It is too good to be true," said a Rolling Stones fan who recognised Jagger immediately. "I even shook hands with him," said

Mick Jagger

the visibly pleased Jagger fan who kept looking at his hand.

Dressed in a white shirt and trousers with a matching polka dot tie, Jagger tried unsuccessfully to hide behind a pair of dark glasses. That he wanted to keep the visit a secret was apparent from the fact

that he did not ask for the usual suites reserved for celebrities. Instead he and his staff checked into an ordinary room.

But his attempt to remain incognito proved to be a futile one as the hotel staff, guests, and the usual luncheon recognised him at the first instance. There was hushed silence in the lobby when he took his room keys and proceeded towards the lift. Another dejected girl, who has been an ardent fan of Rolling Stones since her school days, averred "I was too stunned to even ask for an autograph. Here I come for an ordinary lunch and guess who you run into, your childhood hero, Mick Jagger."

In a chat with this reporter Jagger said that he was on a personal visit to Delhi. Despite repeated questioning he refused to divulge the reason for the trip. His itinerary was kept a closely-guarded secret too. But he is reportedly here for another passion apart from music, cricket. The Wills World Cup has reportedly lured the greatest living rock superstar to the sub-continent. After his brief stopover in Delhi, he is reportedly off to Calcutta to watch the Sri Lankans and Indians battle out at the Eden Gardens.

Ask Jagger if cricket is the purpose of the trip his face breaks

into a big smile and he again insists the trip is "personal". A first look at the reed thin man dressed in white and he will pass off as any ordinary foreigner staying at the hotel. You think he resembles the legendary Mick but immediately you coax yourself for being stupid. But a second look reveals that the slight wrinkle on his face and dark glasses notwithstanding, he is actually the man who pioneered an anti-revolution in music.

In 1963, when Beatles were at their peak and revered for their clean music, Mick Jagger then in early 20s deemed to be different.

The Rolling Stones was set up. They topped the popularity charts immediately in spite of their concerts been wild where the band members would tear off their clothes and disrobe on the stage itself.

But the unassuming rockstar today hardly resembles the Jagger of the 60s — the man who gave the youth a different music — pure rock. In Delhi, Jagger is amused by the attention. In slow monotones he almost whispers "this is not my first trip to India. I have been here before and travelled the country extensively."

Business is slow for Chandigarh's rickshaw drivers, but while most are able to grab some sleep one unlucky individual is obliged to repair a flat tyre.

While we were grateful for being a guest in Chandigarh's number-one establishment, this didn't come without a few hiccups. The first problem surfaced when the room pairing of Slater and Lee arrived in their room only to find only one double bed among the furniture. After a frantic search discovered no alternative bedding arrangements, it was not long before panic began to set in. Both lads were adamant that as they didn't want to risk any sort of bodily contact during the evening, a solution had to be found. A desperate Slats quietly but firmly informed the hotel management that he didn't want his reputation tarnished and demanded a single bed be sent to the room as rapidly as possible.

While the porters were searching the hotel for Slats' bed, Tubby Taylor was experiencing more rat problems. A rodent, obviously put out by the human invasion of his property, scampered across the freshly laid carpet to the safety of a hole that didn't appear to be anywhere. And, as always when trying to catch one of these pesky little blighters, that hole was nowhere to be found when Tubs went looking for it.

It wasn't all smooth sailing for the duet of Waugh and Ponting either, as we failed to locate a fridge. And with good reason. There wasn't one. We also had a problem with the main light switch, which was tougher to find than a clue on an orienteering course. And for a few seconds we thought we faced a Slater/ Lee scenario, as there appeared to be only one double bed among the pre-World War II furniture. But fortunately, there were in fact two single beds lurking underneath the quilt, which brought smiles to both our concerned faces.

We had an evening training session, under lights, on what was a magnificent ground. Equally impressive were the adjoining facilities. One aspect of the ground that does worry us, though, are the 16 light towers, which are much lower than those in Australia and caused plenty of concern for all during the

The scoreboard attendant prepares carefully for Chandigarh's greatest day. However, the 'Rieffel' name plate will have to be redone.

night fielding session. Normally, the glare from the lights is above your hat height, except, of course, when you are looking towards an airborne ball. But here the reflection is permanently under the peak of your cap. We were left wondering why the local cricket association would spend millions on building this ground and then not get something as important as the height of the light towers right. So I asked why. The answer was simple: An army jet base is located close to the ground, and pilots are required to complete low-level flying manoeuvres. It was decided the risk of collision was too high for the light towers to be built any higher!

The team workout was relatively light, while I was restricted to batting and fielding practice as my ankles were still tender as a result of twisting them against the Kiwis. The mood in the camp is one of quiet confidence, but we are well aware that the Windies are capable of beating anyone on their day, particularly with a bowling line-up headed by Courtney Walsh, Curtly Ambrose and Ian Bishop.

Tonight's workout confirmed to all of us that batting under lights tomorrow is going to be tough. The strength of the light is such that shadows are cast off the players — a sure sign that the strength of illumination isn't as powerful as somewhere like Melbourne. As usual over here, the ground staff were a hive of activity, getting the ground and facilities in perfect order. There was the inevitable last-minute painting of buildings, while temporary advertising boards were put in place, pot plants were delivered and placed almost in one movement, and seating arrangements were sorted out for what is expected to be a capacity crowd.

Back at our luxurious residence, a brief team meeting took place. The emphasis was on the need and our desire to back ourselves and believe we are good enough to win, which I'm sure we are. The shortness of this meeting was, I believe, a godsend, as teams can sometimes get carried away with plans and strategies, and neglect the basics (which, nine times out of 10, are why a team wins the game). We all know our jobs as individual players, and talking for the sake of it would serve only as a distraction, rather than being beneficial.

With the team meeting cut short, we opted to watch the second half of the first semi-final, between India and Sri Lanka in front of 100,000 fanatical Indian fans in Calcutta. This was a game of that fluctuated from side to side. Sri Lanka's dynamic opening duo, Jayasuriya and Kaluwitharana, were both unstrapping their pads back in the dressing rooms after a meagre four balls had been bowled in the match. And both had been dismissed in identical fashion — caught at third man after slashing at wide balls in much the same manner as they have all tournament. However, thanks to an astonishing display of bravado from Aravinda de Silva, the tiny island nation posted a highly competitive total of 8–251.

In reply, the hosts looked comfortable as the cool-headed Tendulkar dominated and controlled the innings as a conductor would an orchestra. But the mood of the game, and the nation, changed the moment he was stumped for 65. Suddenly, the wicket was turning square and no Indian batsman was able to come to grips with the deteriorating surface.

The nature of the wicket shouldn't have really been a surprise, particularly as the whole wicket square had been dug up and replaced after the trampling it received at the opening ceremony only six weeks before. Consequently, many people are now finding it difficult to comprehend why Azharuddin didn't

The boys take cover during practice in the early evening, as the stadium is sprayed to keep any malaria-carrying insects away.

Trent Parke

As always in a match involving India, the wicket of Tendulkar was the key. Here, in the first semi-final, in Calcutta, he is stumped by Kaluwitharana off Jayasuriya for 65, and the locals' dream of a place in the World Cup final is gone.

bat first and make use of the wicket before it disintegrated. But then, hindsight is always a great thing.

India's chase quickly became a lost cause, due to a combination of inept batting and unplayable bowling from the normally tame straight breaks off Jayasuriya and de Silva. Such was their turn, it was as if Shane Warne was bowling. Then, with India just about hopeless at 8–120 in the 35th over, sections of the crowd decided they had had enough of proceedings and began to torch sections of the wooden stands in protest. As well, some individuals started hurling projectiles onto the playing surface, which caused a stop to proceedings. Sadly, common sense could not be restored and the game had to be abandoned.

It really was a great pity that these ugly scenes took place, as they not only spoiled what should have been a thoroughly deserved Sri Lankan victory, but also gave Indian people the tag of being bad sports. The truth, of course, is that the vast majority are very fair people who love a clean fair contest.

Sri Lanka's win was a popular one with the Australian team, because we are all very keen to have a crack at them. As I think I've made clear, we haven't been impressed with the 'cry baby' antics that were employed during their summer tour of Australia, where they were given cricketing lessons in all three Tests, but according to their 'butter-wouldn't-melt-in-his-mouth' captain, weren't served at all well by the umpires.

First, though, we must overcome the Windies, who would love to take us down, particularly after we took their 'world champions' crown away from them last year. I drifted off to sleep listening to the tunes of Cold Chisel, as keen as can be to make my second World Cup final a reality tomorrow.

The people of India, both at the ground and watching on television, were stunned by the events at Eden Gardens (above). As the fans slowly departed, and the fires continued to burn (below), a devastated nation went into mourning.

Aravinda de Silva was clearly the man of the match in Calcutta. The fact that he had to be escorted by a Black Cat commando after receiving his reward reflected the ugly way the semi-final ended.

An advertiser's dream turns sour

Hotels, restaurants and bars throughout India have invented exotic dishes and drinks during the World Cup.

For example, at one Delhi pub, you can enjoy a 'Waqar Younis Yorker' or a 'Shane Warne Flipper'. The former sounds flash, but in reality is just a double whisky with soda, while the latter is no more than an elaborately presented brandy and coke. Meanwhile, patrons at one of Delhi's finest restaurants are being offered as a starter a 'Courtney's away swinger', which (apparently, I haven't tried it) is a delightful tomato soup, laced with basil, and named after the Windies paceman, Courtney Walsh. A Donald's sizzling tenderloin steak or a de Silva duck oriental are two of the main courses on offer, while the desserts include a 'long leg' banana split or a 'silly short leg' apple strudel with vanilla ice-cream.

Another group to do very well out of the Cup has been India's mobile phone industry. Business, as they say, has been booming, as cricket fanatics struggle to keep up with the latest scores. One company tempted potential customers by transmitting the latest scores on pagers, free of cost, while others are preying on the consciences of business executives who don't want to leave their television sets, for fear of missing a crucial wicket, yet still have to manage their companies.

Sadly, a pen company's attempt at cashing in on Cup fever came unstuck to some extent. In a newspaper advertisement on the eve of the India v Sri Lanka semi-final in Calcutta, they wished the Indian team luck and suggested that the home-team cricketers: 'set Eden Gardens on fire with a performance that will do every Indian proud.'

Unfortunately, it was the fires that angry fans lit in the grandstands that the occasion will be most remembered for.

Above: Nathan Astle, caught Healy bowled Fleming, in the second over of our quarter-final against New Zealand in Madras.

Below: Chris Harris celebrates his amazing hundred. But for injuries to two of his team-mates, Harris may well have been watching in the stands. Instead he smashed 130 from 124 balls.

Above: Mark Waugh, as imperious as ever against the Kiwis, on the way to his third century of the tournament.

Below: When Mark was dismissed, for 110, the quarter-final was delicately poised. However, Stuart Law handled the pressure of the concluding overs perfectly and the match was won with 13 balls to spare.

Aravinda de Silva was one of the stars of the Cup. After hitting the best ever one-day international score by a Sri Lankan, 145 against Kenya, he was man of the match in both the first semi-final and the final.

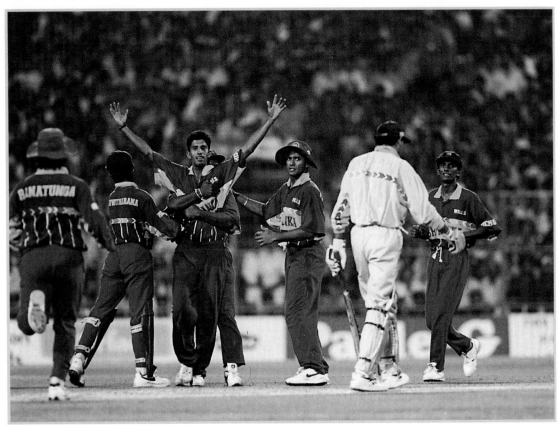

Above: In Calcutta, during the first semi-final, Sri Lanka's Kumara Dharmasena celebrates the dismissal of Mohammad Azharuddin, as India's chase for a Cup final place begins to disintegrate.

Below: Police and security guards try to quell the crowd's fury at India's poor display. Soon after, the match was abandoned.

Michael Bevan in Chandigarh, during his superb partnership with Stuart Law which turned our dreadful start into a respectable score.

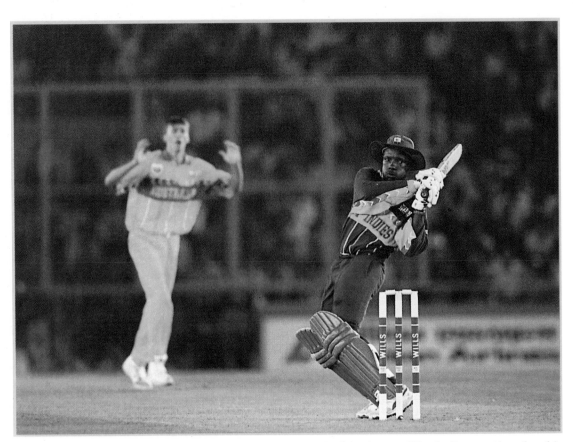

Above: Richie Richardson, in what would prove to be his final innings as West Indies captain, plays his favourite hook shot off Glenn McGrath during the exciting final overs of the second semi-final.

Below: The 49th over ... Shane Warne celebrates the fall of Ian Bishop and the West Indies are 8-194. Fourteen runs are still needed. The odds, for the first time in the match, now favour the Australians.

Above: Damien Fleming — the new 'iceman' bowls Courtney Walsh, to give Australia our great victory. And we all went crazy ...

Below: Damien charged through the ruck to Ian Healy, in an embrace that quickly involved the entire team (including reserves). Left to right: Mark Waugh, Steve Waugh, Fleming, Healy and Mark Taylor.

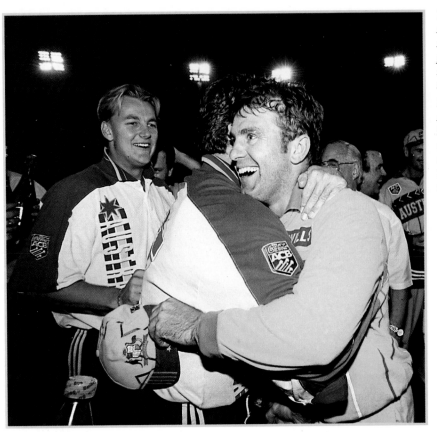

The support we received from our non-playing personnel was a major reason for all we achieved.

Left: Physio Errol Alcott congratulates Mark Taylor after our amazing semi-final win, while Shane Lee (left) grins in the background.

Below: Michael Slater (left), in the process of capturing the post-semi-final festivities on his video, asks the Australian wicketkeeper for a comment.

DAY 35 — *March 14*

(The semi-final, Australia v West Indies in Chandigarh)

EVEN GETTING to the breakfast room proved to be a difficult proposition. A swarm of well wishers and autograph hunters had congregated in the foyer adjoining the eatery, and virtually demanded we stop and give them a piece of our time. I'm sure every Indian gets an autograph book and a camera for their first birthday!

My pre-game meal was more brunch than brekky, as it was just after 10 am by the time I made it to the table. So I settled for an orange juice (in reality, more mandarin-flavoured than orange), toast covered in vegemite (gee, that re-supply was handy!), baked beans, fried eggs on toast, and a couple of pancakes and honey. It was a feed that was as good as it gets over here.

During our trip to the ground, we felt as if we were extras in a remake of the movie, *Speed*. Our driver was keen to accelerate into the roundabouts, which often left at least half the bus airborne. Some critics rated it the drive of the tour. Not so, our captain, though, who gave 'Keanu Reeves' a bit of a dressing down when we landed at the stadium. Tubby explained to the driver that he believed there were advantages in arriving at an important match with the pulse below 180.

Once we'd arrived and regained our composure, we had 30 or so minutes, before warm-ups, to relax and take in the atmosphere of the ground. Most notable were the huge dressing rooms, which have enough space in them to stage a basketball fixture. This feature made all the lads happy, as there is nothing more frustrating (or provocative) for players such as Craig McDermott and Ian Healy as when their piece of immaculate 'turf' is intruded upon by messier types such as S. Warne, S. Waugh and D. Fleming.

A brief inspection of the wicket revealed a cream-coloured strip that was

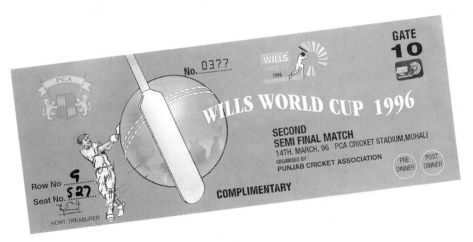

The worst possible start. In his five previous innings in the Cup,
Mark Waugh had scored 472 runs at an average of 118, including three magnificent
centuries. Now, he was lbw, second ball of the semi-final, to Curtly Ambrose ... for a duck.

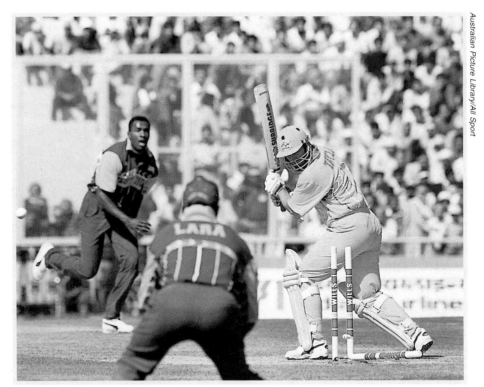

Mark Taylor, bowled by Ian Bishop for 1, one of four Australian wickets to fall (for 15 runs) in the semi-final's first 10 overs.

bereft of grass. The surface was rock hard in some places, but softer in others, which suggested we would be playing on a wicket that would be 'up and down' a little. It looked a good toss to win, and then bat first before the wear and tear of 50 overs took its toll on the uneven surface. A big crowd was building up, under a cloudless sky which was dotted by huge hovering eagles, and they gave both teams a good ovation as we went about our stretching routines. We followed our fitness work with a 10-minute fielding drill and, finally, with a bat or a bowl depending on our individual needs. Meanwhile, Mark Taylor got the better of Richie Richardson at the toss.

When batting at No.4, I usually sit back and watch the first few overs before I bother to get my gear out or even put my half spikes on. But not today, as Mark Waugh was out, second ball of the match, to the deadly assassin, Curtly Ambrose. The mode of dismissal was leg before wicket, to a ball that was typically spot on target at a time when a batsman is inevitably at his most vulnerable. Consequently, my gear was being tossed out of my kit and all over the place, in the desperate search for the items needed to keep at bay those five-and-a-quarter ounces of leather.

By the fourth over I was in the middle, after Taylor edged an Ian Bishop delivery back into his stumps. It was immediately evident that the Windies had discovered some common ground of late, as the on-field talk so typical of previous years was showing itself again. Ricky Ponting and I desperately wanted to begin a stabilising partnership, but it proved beyond us, as an Ambrose thunderbolt beat the talented one for pace. Three for 8. I was next to go, bowled by Bishop off the inside edge attempting to break the shackles the Carribean

163

Stuart Law came to the crease with the score at 3–8, and didn't depart until he was the fifth wicket to fall, run out for 72 when the total was 153.

pacemen had applied. My idea was right but the execution poor, as it wasn't really a ball to be aggressive to; that, combined with a lack of patience and concentration, saw me perish, leaving us in more trouble than a one-armed accordion player. Four for 15, off 9.1 overs — a score card that would have looked more at place in an under-10 game.

It was now salvage time, with anything over 150 an acceptable score in the circumstances. Fortunately, Michael Bevan and Stuart Law played the situation superbly, reverting back to a virtual Test-match style of batting. The good balls were left well alone, ones and twos 'milked' where possible in the hope of putting away the very occasional loose ball for four. Risks were ignored. Slowly the total built to 43, at which point came what might have been the turning point of the whole game ... Law was caught ... off a no-ball. Another wicket here, and the road back might have been too long and treacherous to negotiate.

These two very proficient one-day cricketers clawed their and Australia's way back into the game, adding 138 marvellous runs before Stuart was run out trying to lift our run-rate still further. The game was back on pretty much an even keel now, and with Ian Healy once again playing a crucial cameo at the end, scoring at better than a run a ball, we squeezed past the 200 mark, to 8–207. Such a total had appeared impossible just a couple of hours before.

At this point, we honestly believed we had better than 50-50 chance of winning. I'm sure most teams in this situation wouldn't have been anywhere near as positive, considering scores of 270 and more have been chased and overtaken in this World Cup. But this positive attitude is one of the main reasons we have been so dominant in world cricket over the past eighteen months. So pumped up were we, in anticipation of achieving a memorable comeback victory, that a good 10 minutes before we were due back out in the middle, the entire team was up and ready to go. Gum was chewed just that little bit harder, an extra stretch was completed, and plenty of encouragement was shouted around the big room in order to keep the atmosphere hyped up. And once the umpires had waltzed out onto the ground, we burst from the dressing room door like Spanish bulls in search of their first victim.

However, the early signs weren't all that encouraging, with the first eight overs offering no rewards. The important thing, though, was that our attitude didn't change and we continued to give it everything we had. Then luck, destiny, skill, whatever you might call it, produced our first wicket. Our skipper called Shane Warne to the bowling crease, and although Shane's first delivery wasn't his best, it did the trick, as he took a smart return catch to dismiss Courtney Browne for 10.

This wicket reminded me of one of Ian Botham's most valuable traits. Like Shane Warne, 'Both' had that rare and precious ability to conjure something from nothing, and by doing so, turn the tide of a game. Browne's departure brought to centre stage the genius of Lara, to immediately face the unparalleled

The magician gets us on track with his very first ball. Makeshift Windies opener Courtney Browne is caught and bowled for 10.

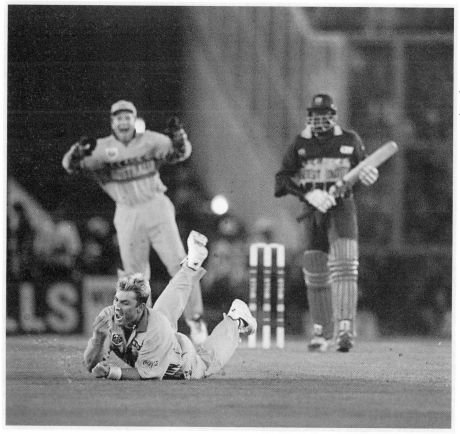

class of Warne ... a match that no doubt had the commentary teams frothing at the mouth. But the contest lasted only a couple of intriguing overs, before our trump card was put away to be saved for the later overs, where he has so often proved as hard as anyone to score from. The trouble with this policy was that Lara quickly began to look in ominous touch, spanking arrogant drives and cuts to the boundary. Such was the power of a couple of these blows that they smashed into the fence, even though boundary fieldsmen were located in the immediate vicinity. Even more annoyingly, they were smashed off my bowling!

By the 23rd over, the Windies had moved to 1-93. Lara was 45, Chanderpaul 35, and I was in the middle of my bowling stint. I felt I was bowling a tidy spell, without any rewards, so I dug deep and produced my best delivery of the tournament, which clipped the top of the West Indies champion's off stump and kept us in the hunt. To be honest, I don't know who was more surprised at the delivery, which was angled in to the left hander and tailed away after hitting the pitch. It was certainly not a pre-meditated thing, but I guess the extra effort did the damage. Whatever, with Lara gone our spirits lifted noticeably, as we believed the rest of their batting order was more than a little brittle.

Unfortunately, it seemed the fact that a defeat would mean that this would be the West Indian captain's last game had compelled him to give it his all. While the stubborn Chanderpaul dug in and didn't look like being dismissed, Richie Richardson set about steering his side into the final, and soon the bookies' pre-game outsiders were on target for a comprehensive victory. The total reached 2-165, just 43 from victory with 8.5 overs remaining, when Chanderpaul suddenly played the rash shot we wished he'd attempted many hours earlier. He tried to loft Glenn McGrath, but was caught by Damien Fleming. The game was on again!

McGrath was in the middle of one of the bowling spells of the tournament. He would finish with 2-30, having stemmed the flow of West Indian runs at a crucial stage and bowled us back into the game. His was a courageous performance, considering he had run into some lean times in previous games in this series.

In the overs before Chanderpaul's dismissal, as Glenn charged gallantly in and even though our World Cup dream appeared to be slipping away, the boys had remained pumped up. Now, this small piece of encouragement was just what we needed. In a somewhat surprising move, the Windies sent all-rounder Roger Harper to the wicket, with the apparent intention of wrapping up the game with some lusty hitting. Here was a man who looked as if he meant business, his eyes cold, hard and focussed. But his temperament, thankfully, didn't match his looks, and he soon became our fourth victim, lbw to McGrath, playing across the line. The tempo of the game had clearly begun to change ... we were setting the scene now ... and so had the mood within the stadium. The crowd sensed that this game was going to have the far from dull and lifeless finale they yearned for after all.

Warne, of course, was our big trump card, so back he came for his final spell. Almost immediately, Otis Gibson was caught behind and our opponents moved into panic mode. Jimmy Adams made his way out to the middle, but it was soon apparent that this normally calm left hander was flustered, as he played at balls almost before they were delivered. Like Harper and Gibson, he was soon back in the pavilion, lbw Warne, and the momentum had swung even further our way.

*The magic moment.
Courtney Walsh is
bowled (above) and the
celebrations (left) begin.*

Even so, the West Indies needed only 25, with four wickets in hand and 21 balls remaining. But four runs later, as the marooned Richardson watched helplessly from the bowler's end, an out-of-sorts Keith Arthurton continued his disastrous tournament by slogging wildly at Fleming when a cool head was needed. He was caught behind, to add another 0 to his previous scores in this World Cup of 1, 0, 0, and 1, and surely ensure him some more time to play in the Red Stripe competition back home next season. Having batted in the often sacrificial no. 6 or 7 positions many times in one-day cricket, I can feel some sympathy for him, but tonight he had his chance and he didn't take it.

As each wicket fell, our self-belief became stronger, as did our desire to pull off one of the greatest-ever wins in one-day cricket. Our only danger

The calm before the after-match party. Jason Gillespie (left), Ricky Ponting (centre) and the rest of the lads try to take in what we'd just achieved.

now appeared to be Richie Richardson, who was attempting, with mixed success, to sustain the required scoring rate, which had climbed to more than six runs an over.

As I write this tonight, the last few overs from Shane and Damien are almost a blur. I think we all overdosed on adrenalin in the search for that something extra to ensure victory. A diving boundary save in the third last over by Ricky Ponting defied belief and, more importantly, rescued a run for our cause. Bishop was lbw to Warne early in the 49th over — 8–194 — but Richardson and Ambrose managed four more before the over was completed. With six balls remaining, the scenario was this: 10 runs to win, two wickets to fall.

When Richardson hoicked the first ball of the 50th over to the mid-wicket boundary, the odds had moved once again, this time slightly in the Windies' favour. The crowd at this point was making as much noise as any 'impartial' crowd could ever have done — who they were cheering for no-one in the middle could tell. As Fleming moved in for the over's second delivery, everyone — fans, bowler, batsmen, umpires, fieldsmen, and, I imagine, the TV viewers back home — took a deep breath. Any mistake would probably cost your team the match. My only negative thought was that of having to try and catch a steepling catch in the glare of the lights, but I tried to dismiss that concept and instead focus on a positive — such as completing a run out or taking a match-winning catch.

It was the Windies who took the wrong option. A Richardson slash took a bottom edge, and trickled through to Healy. As the batsmen set off for a desperate single, our trusty keeper scooped up the ball and threw down the stumps (in much the same way he does thousands of times at practice) ... and big Curtly was short of the line. Or so we thought. However, the verdict in our favour wasn't confirmed until we'd been obliged to wait for the video replay. That wait, I can tell you, took a very, very long time.

The Windies were nine down, six runs from victory, and had their in-form captain 49 not out and at the non-striker's end. On centre stage, we tried to settle down in a huddle and focus on finishing the job. A brief discussion took place among the 11-man brains trust, and we came up with the perfect plan for the next delivery. A searing yorker!

Courtney Walsh came to the middle. We all went back to our places, and Fleming went back to his mark. Then, with ball in hand and agreed strategy in mind, Damien approached the wicket, a whole nation's hopes upon his shoulders.

At the moment he delivered the ball it was, for me, as if everything had gone into slow motion. The crowd was there, but not an issue — they were like cardboard cut-outs, apart from the drama. The ball landed just short of the intended mark, on a good length rather than the popping crease, and Walsh looked to win the game with one lusty blow. He swung wildly, throwing the textbook out the window and, in doing so, throwing away his side's dream of victory. The familiar 'death rattle' of the stumps shook me back into normal speed, and we went berserk, chasing after Fleming as if he'd just pickpocketed us.

Ian Healy was first to try and arrest the rampaging Victorian, but Damien was out of control, much like the rest of us. Finally we all caught up with each other, to form a swarming circle, yelling and screaming, as we released all the tension of the previous 50 overs. It was an emotional couple of minutes.

An award for one of the most amazing efforts of the night must go to Shane Lee who, after me, was fourth man into the huddle! A fair effort considering he came from the viewing area, beyond the boundary. But it was that sort of win, where everyone in the squad — physio, coach, reserves and management included — was overcome with the emotion of the moment. We continued to celebrate on the pitch, backslapping each other, embracing one

This was an impossible victory — the best one-day experience I have been involved in. The emotion in our victory song reflected this fact.

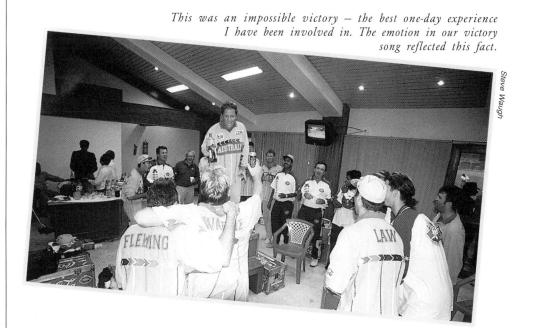

Steve Waugh

another and marvelling at our extraordinary comeback. For a moment or two we felt great sympathy for Richie Richardson, left stranded in what *was* his farewell game, but then we bounded back to the dressing rooms to carry on like good sorts for the following two hours.

There was one highly unusual thing that occurred out on the field immediately after the match. As the two teams shook hands ... Curtly spoke! It was something like: 'Well played, don't wast' it now, mon. Go all the way.' A simple 'thanks' was all we could muster in reply, more due to shock than anything. It was, though, a gesture we all appreciated.

To say we enjoyed our victory is like saying the boys like a pizza with a beer on a big night out. We were all still high on emotion as we sat down in the sanctuary of our rooms, almost unable to comprehend what had just happened to us. Flem couldn't recall his last two overs. I couldn't remember the crowd's reaction at the end. And others struggled to put together their own private memories of the match. Perhaps it will all come back to us in time. Heals, following the retirement of David Boon, now has the distinction of getting up and leading us in our victory chorus, *Under the Southern Cross*, and, boy, tonight was it a beauty, up with the best of my time.

We expected a quiet reception back at the hotel, seeing as it was after midnight, but instead it was overcrowded and very boisterous, with plenty of Aussie flags and supporters amid the throng. Our party continued back in the room of our manager, Mr Egar, who clearly hadn't planned on such an event, for the beer stocks were low. So, instead of downing a few celebratory ales, Slats stepped up and produced his tortured guitar, backed by the much more gifted Shane Lee. As if typifying this crazy night, Slats stole the show with a highly-charged and raw rendition of *Wild Thing* that shook the rafters and forever destroyed the rumour-mongers among us who had dismissed him as a man of little or no musical ability.

Before we knew it, the wee hours of the morning had arrived. Considering the final is now only two days away, we opted to call it stumps, putting to an end perhaps Australia's finest-ever day as a one-day international outfit!

Sorrow, anger and ... joy

While reaction to the ugly finish to Calcutta's semi-final has been universally gloomy in India (there has been at least one reported suicide, and a number of demonstrations involving the burning of effigies, firing of warning shots by police, and so on), in Pakistan, people have celebrated in the streets and started up impromptu street parties.

Reports from Lahore tell of chanting crowds blocking traffic and letting off crackers in the city's main thoroughfare, while motorcycle gangs have raced through the streets flying Pakistani flags and shouting anti-Hindu messages. And the English-language Muslim newspaper protested at the way local television covered the fateful final minutes at Eden Gardens.

'When millions of emotional people were all for seeing India being humiliated by the Lankans,' the paper editorialised, 'PTV (the government-backed station) started showing irritating commercials.'

DAY 36 — *March 15*
(Chandigarh to Lahore)

HAVING PREDICTABLY been carried away with proceedings late last evening, I was aghast to receive a 7.15 am phone call to remind me of my obligations this morning — a photo shoot with Mark for an Indian clothing company. Can't wait to see the end results!

My next and more pressing duty for the day was to gather, collect, find or discover my wardrobe from all over the room. Bags had to be ready and packed by quarter past 10. Even though our flight wasn't scheduled until nearly five hours from then, it is always an absolute must in this part of the world to get the baggage, particularly the colossal amount we lug around, to the airport as quickly as possible. In most cases so far on this trip, our bags have either been sent on other flights to disperse the load or sent to the next destination by road. On this occasion time was especially vital, as our flight was an international one and customs checks in the North of India are understandably, given the often fragile relationship between India and Pakistan, as strict as any in the world.

To expect a smooth passage through customs was indeed wishful thinking, as organisation is never the Indians' strong point. Our arrival at the terminal was chaos free, as was our passage through the first metal detector for the afternoon. Upon reaching the other side of that detector, a very bureaucratic and intrusive government official made doubly sure of our good intentions by giving us the once over with a hand-held device, poking and prodding each person like a meat inspector examining a carcass. It was not long after this process that we realised we were in for the long haul, as someone pointed to our bags, which were strewn across the terminal floor with no tags attached to them. Sure enough, we had to identify each piece and a customs tag was then placed on each and every item.

Next came the distribution of boarding passes, which were then stamped at a checkpoint on the way to our specially chartered aircraft. Believe it or not, but a mere 10 metres on from that checkpoint we had to not only hand over our passports, boarding passes and plane tickets (which I guess was fair enough), but also locate our bags and identify them, which was tough as they were still lying back on the terminal floor where we'd located and identified them just a few minutes previously.

Once this was achieved, we then came upon yet another checkpoint, possibly international customs clearance. Here we had the metal detector treatment once again, and on this occasion I, for one, wouldn't have minded wearing a protector, as a heavy-handed official went about his work. This hurdle cleared, another stamp was placed on our by now well-worn boarding passes, while our personal luggage came under the scrutiny of an x-ray machine. Unluckily, either the machine was broken or the security guys just loved doing things for the sake of it, because everyone had to open their bags and explain what everything in their bags did and what was inside everything in their bags.

This inspection caused enormous grief for Errol Alcott, who has a wide and varied collection of gadgets at his disposal. Our physio did, however, get his revenge on one unsuspecting uniformed individual who demanded a demonstration of the capabilities of Errol's electromagnetic pulse machine. Seconds later, two electrodes had been placed at each end of the inspector's palm, and with a flick of the switch, an electric pulse sent his hand into a small-scale spasm and provided enough evidence to reassure the guy it was purely a 'therapeutic' device.

Other items to be scrutinised included electric razors, adaptors and walkmans, which apparently haven't been seen too often before in these parts. Many of the lads were forced to hit the play button on their walkmans, and then hand over the earphones to confirm the nature of the beast. Then, just when we thought we had passed all the tests and cut through the many metres of red tape, we were informed that baggage identification was a duty we all needed to attend to. Hadn't we done that before? Boarding passes were stamped once more, we made our way onto the tarmac and spotted and confirmed our valuables once again, and then we returned to the waiting lounge until our VIP specially chartered flight was called.

Many hours later, we touched down in Lahore, all keen to begin preparations for one of the biggest games of our lives. The World Cup final! Once again, I was paired with Pigeon, this time at the comfortable Pearl InterContinental Hotel. More than half of us are familiar with the place, as it was home for a while not long ago, during our 1994 tour of Pakistan. The hotel staff treated us like long-lost friends, although we quickly learned that the receptionists' expertise hadn't improved in the past 12 months. When I tried to locate physio Errol Alcott for some treatment on my dodgy ankles, I was politely informed that the Australian team hadn't checked in yet.

Tonight's feed was a long-awaited treat, courtesy of the American Club in Lahore. The T-bone steaks didn't touch the sides, while Warney found himself in heaven, devouring plate after plate of cheese-coated Nachos.

Sri Lankans are on a good wicket

The Sri Lankan government has revealed that their cricketers are going to do extremely well out of this World Cup. Following some pretty amazing donations and promises from a number of Sri Lankan companies and wealthy supporters, cars, cash and holidays will be given to our opponents, regardless of the result of the final.

Arjuna Ranatunga is soon to be the owner of a brand new vehicle. A similar prize awaits the man of the match in the final, if he's wearing a Sri Lankan shirt.

Their players have been promised 1,000 rupees (around $A20) for every run they score, 300,000 rupees for hitting a half-century and one million rupees if they manage a century.

A wicket will earn the bowler 20,000 rupees, with catches and run outs worth similar amounts.

And a rich businessman from The Maldives wants to award each player $US1,000 and treat them and their families to an all-expenses-paid holiday at a tourist resort in his country.

DAY 37 — *March 16*
(Lahore)

BY THE TIME I ventured down to the foyer this morning, the hotel was teeming with journalists and media, all here to cover one of the biggest sporting events of the year. As a measure of the final's significance, we have been informed that the match will be televised to over 800 million people. As a player, you can't dwell on such a statistic, as it may make you overawed by the whole deal. It had already been stressed that we should just concentrate on our own and the team's preparation and performance.

We read in the papers that our good buddy, Arjuna, was at it again, sprouting his wisdom by saying words to the effect that Warney is an overrated bowler and easy to handle. He also claims that the Waugh brothers have been given far too much good press of late. All I can assume from these alleged remarks is that the Sri Lankan captain is either suffering from amnesia or trying to unsettle us by getting under our skin. But the latter isn't possible any more, as it happened three months ago!

Street life in Lahore.

Trent Parke

Training was a bit of a botch-up, as both teams turned up within half an hour of each other, which led to us only having one net each to use. This is always a poor substitute for having two or three nets available, because the session goes for twice as long and the bowlers become a bit jaded. Fortunately, we had a couple of keen local net bowlers to help us out, but from a personal point of view it wasn't one of my better net sessions. But, even despite this minor irritation, I'm still going into the match full of confidence and in pretty good form.

The most noticeable feature of the ground here is how far the crowd will be from the boundaries. It would have to be around 30 metres. This is fairly unusual for Pakistani and Indian venues, where the spectators are normally right on top of the players, creating a special and exhilarating atmosphere. The 1987 World Cup Final, at Eden Gardens in Calcutta, was one such memorable experience, with a huge capacity crowd giving off a buzz and air of excitement that was truly memorable. Hopefully, tomorrow's atmosphere will be similar, but we might lose at least a little of the sense of occasion because the crowd is being kept at a distance.

My afternoon was designed to be as relaxing as possible, a trend I like to follow before big matches. Room service consisted of my 50th bowl of chicken and sweet corn soup for the tour and my 20th serving of Spaghetti Neapolitan. Final eve was certainly no time to be experimenting with food types and menus I wasn't accustomed to — food poisoning would be a terrible reason to miss out on a game of this magnitude. While I ate, I admired the handmade carpet I had been presented with earlier in the day. A carpet-makers' convention is being held in the hotel, and the participants decided to present each of us with an example of their merchandise.

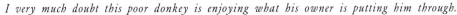

I very much doubt this poor donkey is enjoying what his owner is putting him through.

Trent Parke

A tale of two cultures. The great Richie Benaud delivers his pre-World Cup message to the world, through the latest Channel Nine technology (right) and the more antiquated equipment of a local news service.

Being a high-profile sporting identity does provide the occasional bonus.

An afternoon massage was next on the agenda, followed by a spot of television. But the TV soon got the flick, because of a combination of poor choices and the editing out of any scene that involved a male touching a female (from holding hands on), which leaves viewers with the task of imagining the missing pictures. As much as 50 per cent of a show can be replaced by a blank screen. This policy, of course, is due to Pakistan's strict religious and moral beliefs (the country is 97 per cent Muslim).

Our usual pre-game team meeting was held in Col Egar's room, which isn't exactly spacious, and players were obliged to sit on coffee tables, TV stands, or stretch out on the floor. Having played against these guys so often in the past six months, inevitably we did little more than go over old ground, but we did pay extra attention to certain individuals in their line-up.

For example, we've decided to bowl a full length to Kaluwitharana and a tight line to their other opener, Jayasuriya. If we do this, we believe we can upset their rhythm and therefore get the entire batting order off balance. Most of their batsmen relish any width, so it was stressed to all of us that we must keep the ball in and around off stump, to prevent them from freeing their arms and flailing at the ball in the manner they love. We also concluded that slower balls and the constant use of changes of pace would be effective weapons, as would a prolonged and blatant intensity in our fielding — along similar lines to our fantastic semi-final effort, something which had previously been missing from our displays.

Batting-wise, the tactics would be pretty much the same as always. We'd

Aussies are favourites ...
but don't tell anyone!

Illegal bookmakers here in Pakistan are allegedly doing pretty big business on the Cup final. One report quoted Lahore stock exchange brokers suggesting that bets worth 25 million rupees ($US720,000) have already been accepted, in a country where gambling is officially forbidden.

The extent of betting on cricket in India and Pakistan really is quite mind-boggling. My mind goes back to one report I read after the India-Pakistan quarter-final. Although officially it is illegal to bet on cricket in India, that match apparently attracted one billion rupees worth of bets in Bombay alone.

The final is a sell-out, though many tickets are apparently still available on the black market (and, I noticed this morning while reading a local newspaper, in the classifieds). We're told the best price available for the cheapest tickets is the equivalent of around $A40, which is twice their face value.

be aiming for a solid start, before gathering momentum in the middle of the innings and then cashing in during the final 10 overs, when we'd hopefully still have plenty of wickets in hand. In our opinion, the bowlers we need to counter are Chaminda Vaas and Muralitharan, as the effectiveness of the Sri Lankans' whole attack usually revolves around their performances.

We all left the meeting in a buoyant mood, confident of our abilities and the fact that our methods had been successful under pressure before. In contrast, Sri Lanka haven't really come through under championship conditions too often in the past. I really believed we would win tomorrow, but was also aware that the Sri Lankans were desperate to have a crack at us after our boycott of Colombo and the thrashings they received from us in Australia. The final will be a game with a tough competitive edge to it, exacerbated by an underlying animosity that still lurks, just below the surface.

Late this afternoon, our management was informed that an official World Cup dinner was to be held tonight in the gardens adjoining the hotel, with the President of Pakistan, Sardar Farooq Ahmad Khan Leghari, as a guest speaker. Disappointingly, the function turned out to be an absolute shambles from go to whoa, right from the point when we arrived at what we had been told was the right time but was actually 30 minutes before anyone else showed up. This wouldn't have been so bad, but do you think anyone could locate any sort of beverage? A full 54 minutes after we first arrived, a coke was offered to us by a previously unseen waiter. But then it took at least another quarter of an hour before he came good with his promises.

The seating arrangements were disgraceful. Both the Sri Lankan and Australian teams were many metres away from the official stage, which we couldn't see because a couple of large trees blocked our view. Then, as our patience dwindled, the speeches lengthened and our hunger intensified. We were finally let loose on the buffet at 9.45 pm — this was not exactly the quiet relaxing pre-match evening we were all looking for.

Above: Aussie fans, led by some of the 'Boys on Tour' (in Australian rugby jumpers), enjoy their team's fightback during the afternoon session of the semi-final in Chandigarh.

Below: In the foreground is the ever-present security; in the background Michael Bevan rehearses his spinners during our first pre-final workout in Lahore.

Above: The boys at play in Lahore ... odds on the mark was spilt.

Below: The Australian team lines up while the national anthems are played before the World Cup final. Unfortunately for the Sri Lankans, their anthem wasn't played — they were forced to listen to someone else's instead. Left to right: Fleming, Slater, Ponting, Law, S. Waugh, Gillespie, M. Waugh.

Right: Since he became Australian captain, Mark Taylor has adopted an aggressive attitude to opening the innings in one-day cricket. This shot, during the Cup final, typifies his approach.

Below: Ricky Ponting is bowled by Aravinda de Silva in the final. The loss of Taylor (74) and Ponting (45) in the middle overs of the innings changed the game. While they were there, a huge Australian score seemed likely.

Although the Australians' pre-dinner innings is still to be completed, the lights in Lahore are already shining on the 1996 World Cup final.

Three images from the Sri Lankan innings in the final. Above: Jayasuriya is run out, thanks to a brilliant Healy pick-up. Left: De Silva becomes part of Sri Lankan folklore. Below: Gurusinha slams Reiffel to the sightscreen.

Above: Mark Taylor offered his hand to Pakistan's Prime Minister, Benazir Bhutto, at the post-match presentation. However, he was quickly told that it is incorrect protocol to touch a female in public.

Below: Officials struggled to keep the Sri Lankan supporters and cricketers apart in the post-match festivities, which led to Arjuna Ranatunga and the Cup trophy taking an undignified tumble.

The Australian dressing room after the final was as quiet as any I have ever been in. We took great pride in the fact we had given it everything we could, but were desperately disappointed that on the day we had performed below our best.

DAY 38 — *March 17*

(The final, Australia v Sri Lanka in Lahore)

CUP FINAL DAY. The first thing I did, after receiving our wake-up call, was separate the curtains and see what was happening outside. Amid this daze that most call early morning, I recalled that my night's sleep had been interrupted more than once by the sound of heavy rain outside, and I know just how poorly some of the grounds here respond to storms. Perhaps we'd have to wait until the reserve day to have a crack at the Lankans? However, the outlook was better than I had envisaged — sure, the sky was overcast, but there was no sign of threatening clouds. That said, the puddles all over the streets and pathways betrayed just how much rain had fallen through the night.

We had a couple of hours spare, before our scheduled departure for the ground, so Glenn McGrath and I made the short trip down to the carpet expo. Interestingly, no-one wanted to know us today, perhaps because there were no cameras around, or media exposure to be had, so our lap of the joint took no time at all and we quickly headed back for our room. The toughest part was the scamper through the hotel lobby, but fortunately we reached the lift before any of the hordes of autograph collectors could spot us. Had we stopped to give one signature, we might never have made it to the ground.

Col Egar, Mark Taylor and Bob Simpson decided to go down to the ground early, as the word was that we probably wouldn't be starting on time, because the outfield was saturated. Such was the strength of that rumour, the rest of us settled back onto our beds to catch a bit of TV — we didn't expect anything positive to happen for a while, if at all. But within half an hour, we'd each received the call ...

Get ready, the game will be starting on time!

The 15-minute trip to the stadium was made by two buses, half the side in

My innings in the Cup final is over, caught by de Silva off Dharmasena for 13, as the mood of the game begins to shift towards the Sri Lankans.

each. Where I was, the mood was relatively quiet, even pensive, but then it's always a bit like this on match day, as each player mentally goes through how they'd like the day to pan out. Always in the back of your mind is that little bit of doubt and some nervousness, which I guess is really a good thing, because it ensures you don't get over-confident, and helps you stay totally focussed on the job at hand.

Our warm-ups were conducted in front of a crowd which was steadily building up towards the expected 50,000 full house. The people already there greeted our arrival in subdued fashion; in fact, it appeared as if half owned Sri Lankan flags. This, I guess, was to be expected, given the location, the favourable press our opponents had been getting, and the 'underdog' thing that everyone seems to love.

The toss was of interest only to the statisticians, because Sri Lanka were always going to bowl first. They consider themselves better equipped to chase a total, while we would usually prefer to bat first and post an intimidating score. Our line-up was as expected, with the unlucky Slater again watching from the sidelines along, with the impressive Gillespie and the tremendously talented Lee. Although they must be disappointed, these guys have been superb in handling the needs and requests of the playing XI, and this support continues to be a major reason why Australia is so strong in world cricket.

We started okay, but with the total on 36, Mark Waugh flicked a ball from Chaminda Vaas straight to Jayasuriya at square leg. This, however, was a minor scare, for Taylor and Ponting began to dominate, finding the ropes regularly. After 25 overs, we couldn't have been better placed, cruising at 1–134 and looking set to score anything up to around 280.

Unfortunately for us, we had peaked at this precise moment. From this point, we began to hand the ascendancy back to the Sri Lankans. Both Taylor and Ponting fell to the spin of Aravinda de Silva (Mark for 74, Ricky for 45), just as they looked set to kick on and post really big scores. This left us with two new batsmen at the crease for the beginning of the final 20 overs. This normally isn't such a bad scenario, but with the added pressure of the Final, the softness of the ball and a wicket that was beginning to turn a little, we proceeded to dig ourselves into a hole that in the end we couldn't escape from. As the tempo of the match changed, the Sri Lankans picked up their fielding and began scampering between wickets at the end of every over. It was as if they were hustling us at our own game.

With the score on 156, I fell to what I'd call a 'nothing' shot. The plan was to chip the ball over the infield, but I only succeeded in catching a leading edge and the ball ballooned to deep mid-on. There are few worse experiences for a batsman in a big game than to see a ball in the air and know you're about to be caught.

I still believed that with the remaining batting at our disposal, especially Law, Bevan and Healy, we could make at least 250 to 260. But, unfortunately for Australia, everyone seemed to be having an off day, and instead of charging to a match-winning score, we stumbled and stuttered our way to 7–241. Our total was, of course, still respectable, but we considered it disappointing, especially after our excellent start. Mind you, had it not been for the skill of Michael Bevan, who fashioned 36 runs from 50 balls without ever looking comfortable, we would have finished with even less.

The extent of our frustration at the apparent lack of timing and confidence in the latter half of our innings is reflected in our almost inconceivable statistic: we didn't manage a single boundary between the 19th and the 43rd overs.

Not even the genius of Michael Bevan could get us going.

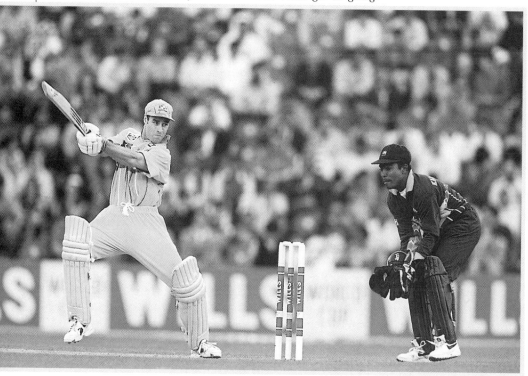

A rare moment of joy — Asanka Gurusinha is about to lose his off-bail to Paul Reiffel.

However, I must also say that the Sri Lankan spinners bowled exceedingly well, while their fielding was outstanding.

The only consolation in our total was that it was 34 more than we'd managed in the semi-final against the Windies. However, the Sri Lankan batting order had been in superlative form, so to have a chance, early wickets were imperative, and the standard of our fielding needed to be top class.

Both teams' preparations were thrown into chaos 15 minutes before the scheduled re-start, when the lights blacked out owing to a power shortage. This possibility had been a concern in many venues in the past six weeks, to the extent that some cities had been asking their citizens to ease up on the electricity when they were hosting a day/night game. I'm not sure whether either team benefitted from this interruption, but it certainly wasn't welcomed by the Australian camp, as we had just started to prepare ourselves and talk it up in the rooms when the despairing moans of the crowd filtered through to the dressing room.

Thankfully, a major embarrassment was averted when the lights came back to life. The first thing I noticed was that the stadium was now filled to absolute capacity, which it certainly hadn't been for at least most of the Australian innings. The second thing was that the outfield was now noticeably damp, apparently because of a heavy dew. This hadn't happened in any of the other day/night fixtures we'd played in the Cup, but then these had all been in India. But this gave the batting side a considerable advantage. One, it meant that the ball was going to get wet, slippery and hard to hold. Two, the ball would swell up as its leather soaked up the moisture, leaving the seam soft and not as abrasive as before, and resulting in a lack of movement off the seam. Three, a wet ball is particularly difficult for spinners to grip and give it a rip, which leads to lack of turn. And four, the bottom of your boots become soaked, which leaves a bowler with little or no confidence when landing at the crease, for fear of slipping or falling down.

But these factors were more frustrating than game-turning, and certainly didn't influence the outcome of the game. That, as things turned out, was the result of the skill of our opponents. After 5.1 overs, we were looking the goods, having run out Jayasuriya by the barest possible margin and dismissed the talented but at this stage overrated Kaluwitharana for just 23.

These early inroads were crucial, but the balance of the game was now down to whether or not we could separate the steady and experienced duo of Gurusinha and de Silva before a partnership could develop. Unfortunately for us, the Sri Lankans began to dominate, through courageous strokeplay, while we crumbled in the field. Catches were put down and some fielding mistakes made us look like a novice outfit. It was as if the life that had so buoyed the team was now slowly being squeezed out of us, through a combination of their excellent play and our self-inflicted mediocrity. The harder we tried, the worse things became — it was a display that reminded me of the Australian sides in the mid 1980s.

Shane Warne couldn't grip the ball with any certainty and, as a result, we lost our main strike bowler, but we have a well-rounded attack, and normally someone would have put their hand up and become the man for the occasion. Not tonight, though; our intensity was down and we just couldn't get out of neutral. Why? I'm not sure. Perhaps we were tired after having played three high-powered games and endured endless hours of travel over the past six days. Maybe the emotion of our semi-final triumph took more from us than we had imagined. Whatever, we were no match for the rampaging and very hungry Sri Lankans, who didn't lose their third wicket until they were 94 runs from home.

Gurusinha's dismissal, bowled by Paul Reiffel, gave us a brief respite, but any hopes we might have had of another famous comeback were snuffed out by those two very good one-day players, de Silva and Ranatunga. De Silva went on to a superb century, which will ensure his name becomes part of the folklore of one-day cricket and also set him up financially for life in his own country.

If one moment symbolised our struggle, it was a flipper that slipped out of Shane's hand. Ranatunga smashed it over the fence and then poked his tongue out at the bowler to further rub salt into our gaping wounds. Our misery was finally over after 46.2 overs, at which point the Sri Lankan team invaded the ground, claiming a prize that the whole nation will no doubt rejoice in for a long time to come. I was disappointed we saved our worst display of the year for the most important game, but we were outbatted, outbowled and outfielded by a better team on the day. Importantly, we all knew we'd given it 100 per cent, which is always a source of comfort in a loss, even though it doesn't make it any easier to handle.

In keeping with the organisation of most of the tournament, the presentation ceremony was a complete shambles, largely due to the enormous security contingent required to protect the Pakistani Prime Minister, Benazir Bhutto. It was Mrs Bhutto's job to present the World Cup to the winners, but so diligent were her security staff that they even kept the players outside the roped-off area until they realised we were needed for the presentation. One pleasant change was that the players shook hands and exchanged pleasantries, so unlike the

The end of the 1996 World Cup.

Australian Picture Library/A▶

Trent Parke

What to say?

'boycott' the Sri Lankans put on in Sydney after the World Series one-day finals. Less attractive was the victors' attempt at a proud and well-deserved lap of honour. Unfortunately, a swarming media contingent made it impossible — I'm sure the guys will rue this missed opportunity in years to come.

Mark Taylor had an unusual experience when he went up to the dais to receive the runners-up trophy and cheque from Mrs Bhutto. Keen to do the right thing, our leader attempted to shake hands, but he was quickly informed that it was incorrect protocol to touch a female in public. So he had to be content with a brief chat.

The losing dressing room was, as always, a very sombre place. There was little or no chat, but plenty of head shaking and heads in hands. What we wanted most was to be able to turn back the clock and start again. At times such as these, words are of little or no comfort and it's best to let players work the regrets out of their system. Everyone from the coach to the room attendant was devastated, but in time you do come to your senses and realise the sun will still come up tomorrow and plenty of worse things will happen in your life.

Some of the lads — mostly the bowlers as they wouldn't have eaten too much during the tea interval for fear of feeling bloated — had a feed on some leftover, reheated spaghetti. Others made token attempts to sort through their gear (of which about two thirds was left to the locals, who couldn't believe their luck). Then the post mortems began in earnest, with the overwhelming consensus being that we just weren't good enough on the day. One important point someone made is that we must try to learn something and improve from today, rather than become downcast at one loss. After all, we have enjoyed a period of enormous success over the past 18 months.

DAY 39 — *March 18*
(Lahore)

I FINALLY nodded off last night about 2 am, after playing another 100 overs in my head. Unfortunately, the result of this mind game didn't count for anything, for when I picked up the morning's paper that had been shoved under the door, the headlines screamed: 'SRI LANKA WIN!'

Today was a day of packing, post mortems, postponements, panic, provocation and pleasure.

Assembling six weeks' worth of gear and trying to squeeze it into the same bags you came with is generally a nightmare, but as most of the locals are sporting new wardrobes, this normally onerous task became a five-minute affair. Some concern swept across my brow when I couldn't locate my passport, cash and valuables sachet first time around, but this was soon sorted out, and then I went downstairs to find out which of our flights had been aborted.

Sure enough, our first flight out of Lahore was cancelled, but alternative arrangements were engineered by our industrious management. We were to board a flight to Delhi, our overnight destination, before flying to Hong Kong for a six-hour stopover, then on to Melbourne, and finally to my home port, Sydney. Touchdown on Australian terra firma is always a wonderfully secure feeling. You know instantly you are home and back where you belong.

We were most annoyed, and downright angry, to discover today that PILCOM have decided in their wisdom to award an additional $US100,000 to Sri Lanka

Such is life

Although they are in the middle of a civil war, Sri Lankans have apparently celebrated their Cup victory long and very enthusiastically. Reports from Colombo indicate that although today was supposed to be a working Monday, a great many factories and offices are at least near-deserted.

Cricket fans hugged each other, exploded firecrackers and danced in the streets. But nowhere was Sri Lankan pride greater than at one Colombo wedding. The bride and groom had made the foolish mistake of scheduling their betrothal for the same day as the Cup final, but had placated disappointed guests and relatives by installing two gigantic TV screens at the reception hall to ensure no-one missed the big game.

Sadly, these reports also indicated there was one cloud on the festivities. This, inevitably, was provided by the Tamil Tigers, who on the same Sunday night that their country's cricketers were performing so grandly, attacked an army observation post, killing two soldiers. Earlier, a spokesman for the rebel guerrillas had admitted they were a little unsure whether they should be supporting the Sri Lankans in the World Cup final, or their opponents.

Such is life in that corner of the world.

for winning the Cup. We're still waiting for our runners-up bonus, and I'm pretty certain we wouldn't have been $US100,000 richer if we'd been holding the winners' trophy aloft.

We shouldn't be too disappointed with our overall performance, considering the events that led to us begin the tournament as outcasts back in early February. I feel proud to have been part of a side that put aside so many hurdles and went on and played some great cricket, most notably in the quarter-final and semi-final. This was a tour that demonstrated we are a tough team to beat, in any conditions and in any form of cricket.

In my opinion, even though we are not returning home with the World Cup, we have further enhanced our reputation as the number-one all-round cricket team in the world.

Until next time ...

by James Knight

We had just arrived in Calcutta, at the beginning of our World Cup adventure, and must have looked like clowns leading a clumsy circus as we struggled through the airport, chased by a gleeful line of porters who were tripping over each other as they raced to be first to offer their services. Most were careful, but some launched into our luggage as if they were plugging a broken river bank with sandbags!

Out on the streets, four run-down taxis laboured under the weight of 330 kilograms of luggage. As we wound through still populated thoroughfares at one o'clock in the morning, our television equipment rolled above us on rusty roofracks with little more than gravity for support. This, we already knew, was going to be a challenging tour ... and so it proved. During our six-week stay we were ruled by Murphy's Law; what could go wrong, certainly did!

It took little time for Ron Meyer (Channel 10's cameraman) to add a crease to his forehead. After battling regular power blackouts in Vizag, he finally managed to set up editing equipment which would be shared by Channels 10, Nine and Seven. However, when he flicked the switch for the gear's unveiling, an unfamiliar whirr introduced an unfamiliar cloud of smoke. Rob promptly uttered what would become the most familiar expression of the tour:

"#*&^%$ hell!!!'

Getting media accreditation wasn't easy. While Coca-Cola was the official drink of the World Cup, their arch-rival, Pepsi, provided a fitting counter. Throughout the tournament, advertisements carried the slogan: 'Pepsi, Nothing Official About It!'

Some members of the media could have launched a sister campaign following their battles to acquire official accreditation. Despite endless hours of phone calls, meetings and arguments, some luckless few were left stranded without passes. So, it was decided unofficial means were needed and Xerox colour copiers are now strongly endorsed by the 'Pepsi Journalists'!

This wasn't the only tactic used. One reporter wore an official pass that actually belonged to an officially accredited colleague who had withdrawn from the tour. Despite the all-too-obvious differences in names and photo profiles, the reporter waltzed through the toughest security checks untouched! By the end of the tour, he could even convince himself that he wasn't who he thought he was!

Communication with the outside world was also a concern. After reaching any ground or hotel, there was always an anxious inspection of facilities. 'Can we get out?' was the question everyone wanted answered. Press writers and photographers needed unbroken power and clear phone lines to send their material to Australia. But this wasn't always possible and when there were problems, the sound of frantic rushes out of the media box warned all to stay clear.

Tim Gilbert, of Sydney radio station 2UE, had another concern. He continually puzzled hotel staff with his passionate pleas for rooms with 'south-west aspects'. This angle enabled him to set up his satellite phone with direct access to a specific 'bird' in the sky. Throughout the tour, Tim's inseparable travelling companion was a compass!

The television crews became the tour's 'journeymen'. Bombay and Delhi were the only two places in India where we could gain access to our satellite. When we were away from these cities, our frequent flyer points ticked over more quickly than Mark Waugh's run rate. In Madras, a bemused Canadian couple who were heading to Delhi acted as couriers for us ... they knew nothing about cricket, but still clutched our tapes excitedly. This, they decided after hearing our pleas, was a real-life adventure. Only the cold war spies were missing.

The most enduring race back to find our satellite occurred on the night of Australia's semi-final win over the West Indies at Chandigarh. Such was the shortage of accommodation in that city, Channels 10 and Seven had been obliged to drive from Delhi on the morning of the game. This was a five-hour, 250-kilometre obstacle course that had us dodging goats, camels, cows and even overloaded buses that swayed according to the bias of their human rooftops. Then, after the match, we turned around and drove back. It was nearly midnight, but our two taxi drivers often turned their lights off, not only to conserve their batteries but also to shorten our life expectancies. It was a frightening trip ... we passed at least 20 overturned vehicles that hadn't been there the previous morning, and when we finally made it, shaken but alive, we had less than an hour before our stories went back to Australia.

Throughout the tour, driving was an excursion into the unknown. Indian taxi drivers use their bumper bars as brakes and their brakes as a footrests, while slowing down at intersections is simply an afterthought! And it didn't take long for the inevitable to happen ...

We were trying to get to the ground in Vizag, for the Australia–Kenya match. Our driver (aged no more than 20) had taken us to the airport by mistake and was clearly anxious to make up for lost time. Ignoring our pleas to slow down, he hurried through back streets no broader than the width of a cricket pitch but when the streets widened his luck ran out, and he ploughed into a mo-ped rider, who bounced off our minivan's windscreen. Glass covered Andrew McKinlay (Channel Nine), while Tim Gilbert and I were badly shaken.

We went over to the mo-ped rider, who was lying in the street. Already a large group had gathered, and people were gently slapping his face and throwing water at him. However, before we could ascertain whether he was okay or otherwise, a member of the cricket club (which, thankfully, was close by) ushered us away. He warned us that if we lingered, some of the onlookers would blame us for the accident and possibly vent their anger. So we continued on to the ground; as we drove away we looked back to see the victim being lifted into an auto-rickshaw.

I don't know whether he survived. I rang a hospital that night but it was like searching for the proverbial needle; accidents, sadly, are an all too frequent part of Indian life. But I can still picture the injured mo-ped rider's face ... it was the most depressing moment of the tour.

Despite all the frustrations and desperate images I recall, my lasting memories of this World Cup are of the Indian and Pakistani people. Unlike the Australian players we were here to cover, we walked the streets unhindered. In Jaipur, we joined in 'Holi' festival, where locals dusted our faces with paint dye to celebrate friendship and the coming of spring. Unfortunately, a colourful day turned into a painful week as we scrubbed our faces clean, but it was worth all the lost skin.

Our most rewarding experience occurred in Nagpur, where Jim Wilson (Channel Seven) and I were invited to roll our arms over in a schoolyard cricket match. With the sun setting behind us, a match that began with only 10 players ended in darkness with at least 100 keen locals involved. The following evening, many 'loyal' faces waited outside our hotel, so another match was launched, which this time featured at least an extra 10 media ring-ins.

After we pulled stumps for the final time, our friends disappeared. But they soon returned, with a 10-rupee block of chocolate as a gift. We all shared it, then they left again, but only after promising to wait on the same cricket field for the Australians' return later this year.

James Knight covered the 1996 World Cup for Australia's Channel 10

STATISTICS
The Matches

FEBRUARY 14   England v New Zealand, in Ahmedabad, India (Group B, match 1)

New Zealand	
CM Spearman c & b Cork	5
NJ Astle c Hick b Martin	101
SP Fleming c Thorpe b Hick	28
RG Twose c Thorpe b Hick	17
CL Cairns c Cork b Illingworth	36
CZ Harris run out	10
SA Thomson not out	17
*+LK Germon not out	13
Extras (4b, 2lb, 4w, 2nb)	12
Total (6 wickets, 50 overs)	**239**

Did not bat: GR Larsen, DJ Nash, DK Morrison
Fall of wicket: 12, 108, 141, 196, 204, 212
Bowling: Cork 10-1-36-1; Martin 6-0-37-1; Gough 10-0-63-0; Illingworth 10-1-31-1; Hick 9-0-45-2; White 5-0-21-0

#England	
*MA Atherton b Nash	1
AJ Stewart c & b Harris	34
GA Hick run out	85
GP Thorpe b Larsen	9
NH Fairbrother b Morrison	36
+RC Russell c Morrison b Larsen	2
C White c Cairns b Thomson	13
DG Cork c Germon b Nash	19
D Gough not out	15
PJ Martin c Cairns b Nash	3
RK Illingworth not out	3
Extras (1b, 4lb, 1w, 2nb)	8
Total (9 wickets, 50 overs)	**228**

Fall of wicket: 1, 100, 123, 144, 151, 180, 185, 210, 222
Bowling: Morrison 8-0-38-1; Nash 7-1-27-3; Cairns 4-0-24-0; Larsen 10-1-32-2; Thomson 10-0-51-1; Harris 9-0-45-1; Astle 2-0-6-0

NEW ZEALAND WON BY 11 RUNS

FEBRUARY 16   South Africa v UAE in Rawalpindi, Pakistan (Group B, match 2)

South Africa	
AC Hudson b Samarasekera	27
G Kirsten not out	188
*WJ Cronje st Abbasi b Zarawani	57
DJ Cullinan not out	41
Extras (1b, 1lb, 3w, 3nb)	8
Total (2 wickets, 50 overs, 210 min)	**321**

Did not bat: JN Rhodes, JH Kallis, BM McMillan, +SJ Palframan, SM Pollock, CR Matthews, AA Donald
Fall of wicket: 60, 176
Bowling: Zarawani 10-0-69-1; Altaf 3-0-22-0; Dukanwala 10-0-64-0; Saeed 7-0-41-0; Hussain 5-0-32-0; Samarasekera 9-2-39-1; Laeeq 6-0-52-0

#United Arab Emirates	
S Azhar Saeed c McMillan b Pollock	11
G Mylvaganam c Palframan b Donald	23
M Hussain b Donald	14
V Mehra run out	2
M Aslam b McMillan	9
A Laeeq not out	43
JA Samarasekera c Hudson b Donald	4
*SM Zarawani c Cronje b McMillan	0
+I Abbasi c Palframan b McMillan	1
S Dukanwala not out	40
Extras (3w, 2nb)	5
Total (8 wickets, 50 overs)	**152**

Did not bat: SA Altaf
Fall of wicket: 24, 42, 46, 60, 62, 68, 70, 72
Bowling: Pollock 9-2-28-1; Donald 10-0-21-3; Kallis 6-0-27-0; Kirsten 3-1-9-0; Cronje 4-0-17-0; McMillan 8-1-11-3; Matthews 10-0-39-0

SOUTH AFRICA WON BY 169 RUNS

Note:
 # indicates team that won toss
* indicates captain
+ indicates wicketkeeper
Two Group A games — Sri Lanka v Australia (match 2) and Sri Lanka v West Indies (match 7) — were abandoned. In both cases, the matches were awarded to Sri Lanka on forfeit.

FEBRUARY 16 Zimbabwe v West Indies, in Hyderabad, India (Group A, match 1)

⁺Zimbabwe

*A Flower c Browne b Ambrose	3
⁺GW Flower c & b Gibson	31
GJ Whittall run out	14
ADR Campbell run out	0
AC Waller st Browne b Harper	21
CN Evans c Browne b Ambrose	21
SG Davies run out	9
HH Streak lbw Walsh	7
PA Strang not out	22
EA Brandes c Chanderpaul b Ambrose	7
APC Lock not out	1
Extras (10lb, 4w, 1nb)	15
Total (9 wickets, 50 overs)	**151**

Fall of wicket: 11, 53, 56, 59, 91, 103, 115, 125, 142

Bowling: Ambrose 10-4-28-3; Walsh 10-3-27-1; Gibson 9-1-27-1; Bishop 10-3-18-0; Harper 10-1-30-1; Arthurton 1-0-11-0

West Indies

SL Campbell b Strang	47
*RB Richardson c Campbell b Strang	32
BC Lara not out	43
S Chanderpaul b Strang	8
KLT Arthurton c Campbell b Strang	1
RA Harper not out	5
Extras (5b, 3lb, 10w, 1nb)	19
Total (4 wickets, 29.3 overs)	**155**

Fall of wicket: 78, 115, 123, 136

Bowling: Streak 7-0-34-0; Lock 6-0-23-0; Brandes 7-0-42-0; Whittall 2-0-8-0; Strang 7.3-1-40-4

WEST INDIES WON BY 6 WICKETS

FEBRUARY 17 New Zealand v Holland, in Baroda, India (Group B, match 3)

⁺New Zealand

CM Spearman c Zuiderent b Lubbers	68
NJ Astle run out	0
SP Fleming c Zuiderent b Lubbers	66
RG Twose st Schewe b Lubbers	25
CL Cairns b Cantrell	52
AC Parore c Clarke b Aponso	55
CZ Harris c Schewe b Bakker	8
*⁺LK Germon not out	14
DN Patel c Schewe b Bakker	11
DK Morrison not out	0
Extras (7lb, 1w)	8
Total (8 wickets, 50 overs)	**307**

Did not bat: RJ Kennedy
Fall of wicket: 1, 119, 155, 165, 253, 279, 292, 306
Bowling: Lefebvre 10-0-48-0; Bakker 10-0-51-2; de Leede 7-0-58-0; Aponso 10-0-60-1; Lubbers 9-0-48-3; Cantrell 4-0-35-1

Holland

NE Clarke b Kennedy	14
PE Cantrell c Astle b Harris	45
GJAF Aponso c Astle b Harris	11
*SW Lubbers run out	5
RP Lefebvre b Kennedy	45
TBM de Leede lbw b Harris	1
KJ van Noortwijk not out	36
⁺M Schewe st Germon b Fleming	12
B Zuiderent not out	1
Extras (3b, 5lb, 8w, 2nb)	18
Total (7 wickets, 50 overs)	**188**

Did not bat: E Gouka, PJ Bakker
Fall of wicket: 18, 52, 66, 100, 102, 147, 181
Bowling: Morrison 4-1-11-0; Kennedy 10-2-36-2; Cairns 7-1-24-0; Harris 10-1-24-3; Patel 10-0-42-0; Astle 5-0-19-0; Fleming 2-0-8-1; Twose 2-0-16-0

NEW ZEALAND WON BY 119 RUNS

FEBRUARY 18 India v Kenya, Cuttack, India (Group A, match 3)

Kenya

D Chudasama c Mongia b Prasad	29
⁺K Otieno c Mongia b Raju	27
S Tikolo c Kumble b Raju	65
*M Odumbe st Mongia b Kumble	26
H Modi a Jadeja b Kumble	2
T Odoyo c Prabhakar b Kumlole	8
E Odumbe not out	15
AV Karim not out	6
Extras (2b, 11lb, 7w, 1nb)	21
Total (6 wickets, 50 overs)	**199**

Did not bat: M Suji, R Ali, D Tikolo
Fall of wicket: 41, 65, 161, 161, 165, 184
Bowling: Prabhakar 5-1-19-0; Srinath 10-0-38-0; Prasad 10-0-41-1; Kumble 10-0-28-3; Raju 10-2-34-2; Tendulkar 5-0-26-0

⁺India

AD Jadeja c Ali b Karim	53
SR Tendulkar not out	127
NS Sidhu c Suji b S Tikolo	1
VG Kambli c D Tikolo b M Odumbe	2
⁺NR Mongia not out	8
Extras (5lb, 6w, 1nb)	12
Total (3 wickets, 41.5 overs)	**203**

Did not bat: *M Azharuddin, M Prabhakar, J Srinath, SL Venkatapathy Raju, AR Kumble, V Prasad
Fall of Wicket: 163, 167, 182
Bowling: Ali 5-0-25-0; E Odumbe 3-0-18-0; Suji 5-0-20-0; Odoyo 3-0-22-0; Karim 10-1-27-1; D Tikolo 3-0-21-0; M Odumbe 9.5-1-39-1; S Tikolo 3-0-26-1

INDIA WON BY 7 WICKETS

FEBRUARY 18   England v United Arab Emirates, in Peshawar, Pakistan (Group B, match 4)

⁺United Arab Emirates	
S Azhar Saeed lbw deFreitas	9
G Mylvaganam c Fairbrother b deFreitas	0
M Hussain b Smith	33
V Mehra c Russell b Smith	1
M Aslam b Gough	23
A Laeeq b Smith	0
S Raza b Cork	10
JA Samarasekera run out	29
*SM Zarawani b Cork	2
S Dukanwala lbw Illingworth	15
⁺I Abbasi not out	1
Extras (4b, 4lb, 4w, 1nb)	13
Total (48.3 overs)	**136**

Fall of wicket: 3, 32, 48, 49, 49, 80, 88, 100, 135, 136

Bowling: Cork 10-1-33-2; de Freitas 9.3-3-16-2; Gough 8-3-23-1; White 1.3-1-2-0; Smith 9.3-2-29-3; Illingworth 10-2-25-1

England	
AJ Stewart c Myhaganamb b Laeeq	23
NMK Smith retired hurt	27
GP Thorpe not out	44
*MA Atherton b Saeed	20
NH Fairbrother not out	12
Extras (4b, 2lb, 2w, 6nb)	14
Total (2 wickets, 35 overs)	**140**

Did not bat: ⁺RC Russell, DG Cork, C White, PAJ de Freitas, D Gough, RK Illingworh
Fall of wicket: 52, 109
Bowling: Samarasekera 7-1-35-0; Laeeq 7-0-25-1; Raza 5-1-20-0; Saeed 10-1-26-1; Zarawani 6-0-28-0

ENGLAND WON BY 8 WICKETS

FEBRUARY 20   New Zealand v South Africa, in Faisalabad, Pakistan (Group B, match 5)

⁺New Zealand	
CM Spearman c Palframan b Matthews	14
NJ Astle run out	1
SP Fleming b McMillan	33
RG Twose c McMillan b Pollock	13
CL Cairns b Donald	9
AC Parore run out	27
CZ Harris run out	8
SA Thomson c Cronje b Donald	28
*⁺LK Germon not out	31
GR Larsen c Cullinan b Donald	1
DK Morrison not out	5
Extras (5lb, 2nb)	7
Total (9 wickets, 50 overs)	**177**

Fall of wicket: 7, 17, 36, 54, 85, 103, 116, 158, 165
Bowling: Pollock 10-1-45-1; Matthews 10-2-30-1; Donald 10-0-34-3; Cronje 3-0-13-0; Symcox 10-1-25-0; McMillan 7-1-26-1

South Africa	
G Kirsten lbw Harris	35
⁺SJ Palframan b Morrison	16
*WJ Cronje c Fleming b Astle	78
DJ Cullinan c Thomson b Astle	27
JH Kallis not out	11
JN Rhodes c & b Larson	9
BM McMillan not out	2
Total (5 wickets, 37.3 overs)	**178**

Did not bat: SM Pollock, CR Matthews, PL Smycox, AA Donald
Fall of wicket: 41, 87, 146, 159, 170
Bowling: Morrison 8-0-44-1; Cairns 6-0-24-0; Larsen 8-1-41-1; Harris 4-0-25-1; Thomson 8.3-0-34-0; Astle 3-1-10-2

SOUTH AFRICA WON BY 5 WICKETS

FEBRUARY 21   Sri Lanka v Zimbabwe, in (SSC) Colombo, Sri Lanka (Group A, match 4)

⁺Zimbabwe	
*A Flower run out	8
⁺GW Flower run out	15
GJ Whittall c Jayasuriya b Muralitharan	35
ADR Campbell c Muralitharan b Vaas	75
AC Waller b Jayasuriya	19
CN Evans not out	39
HH Streak c de Silva b Vaas	15
PA Strang not out	0
Extras (16lb, 4w, 1nb)	22
Total (6 wickets, 50 overs)	**228**

Did not bat: EA Brandes, SG Peall, C Lock
Fall of wicket: 19, 51, 92, 160, 194, 227
Bowling: Ranatunga 2-0-14-0; Dharmasena 10-1-51-0; Jayasuriya 10-0-44-1; Muralitharan 10-0-37-1; Wickremasinghe 8-0-36-0; Vaas 10-0-30-2

Sri Lanka	
ST Jayasuriya b Streak	6
⁺RS Kaluwitharana c Peall b Streak	0
AP Gurusinha run out	87
PA de Silva lbw Streak	91
*A Ranatunga not out	13
HP Tillekeratne not out	7
Extras (5lb, 17w, 3nb)	25
Total (4 wickets, 37 overs)	**229**

Did not bat: RS Mahanama, WPUJC Vaas, HDPK Dharmasena, GP Wickremasinghe, M Muralitharan
Fall of wicket: 5, 23, 195, 209
Bowling: Streak 10-0-60-3; Lock 4-0-17-0; Brandes 8-0-35-0; Peall 3-0-23-0; Strang 5-0-43-0; Whittal 2-0-20-0; GW Flower 5-1-26-0

SRI LANKA WON BY 6 WICKETS

FEBRUARY 21   India v West Indies, in Gwalior, India (Group A, match 5)

⁺West Indies

SL Campbell b Srinath	5
*RB Richarson c Kambli b Prabhakar	47
BC Lara c Mongia b Srinath	2
S Chanderpaul c Azharuddin b Kapoor	38
RIC Holder b Kumble	0
RA Harper b Kumble	23
⁺CO Browne b Prabhaker	18
OD Gibson b Kumble	6
IR Bishop run out	9
CEL Ambrose c Kumble b Prabhakar	8
CA Walsh not out	9
Extras (2lb, 5w, 1nb)	8
Total (50 overs)	**173**

Fall of wicket: 16, 24, 91, 99, 99, 141, 141, 149, 162, 173.

Bowling: Prabhakar 10-0-39-3; Srinath 10-0-22-2; Kumble 10-0-35-3; Prasad 10-0-34-0; Kapoor 10-2-41-1.

India

AD Jadeja b Ambrose	1
SR Tendulkar run out	70
NS Sidhu b Ambrose	1
*M Azharuddin c Walsh b Harper	32
VG Kambli not out	33
M Prabhakar c & b Harper	1
⁺NR Mongia not out	24
Extras (3lb, 1w, 8nb)	12
Total (5 wickets, 39.4 overs)	**174**

Did not bat: J Srinath, AR Kumble, V Prasad, AR Kapoor.

Fall of wicket: 2, 15, 94, 125, 127.

Bowling: Ambrose 8-1-41-2; Walsh 9-3-18-0; Bishop 5-0-28-0; Gibson 8.4-0-50-0; Harper 9-1-34-2.

INDIA WON BY 5 WICKETS

FEBRUARY 22   England v Holland, in Peshawar, Pakistan (Group B, match 6)

⁺England

NMK Smith c Clarke b Jansen	31
AJ Stewart b Bakker	5
GA Hick not out	104
GP Thorpe lbw Lefebvre	89
*MA Atherton b Lubbers	10
NH Fairbrother not out	24
Extras (12lb, 4w)	16
Total (4 wickets, 50 overs)	**279**

Did not bat: ⁺RC Russell, DG Cork, PAJ de Freitas, D Gough, PJ Martin

Fall of wicket: 11, 42, 185, 212

Bowling: Lefebvre 10-1-40-1; Jansen 7-0-40-1; Aponso 8-0-55-0; Bakker 8-0-46-1; de Leede 2-0-9-0; Lubbers 10-0-51-1; Cantrell 5-0-26-0

Holland

NE Clarke lbw Cork	0
PE Cantrell lbw de Freitas	28
TBM de Leede lbw de Freitas	41
*SW Lubbers c Russell b de Freitas	9
KJ van Noortwijk c Gough b Martin	64
B Zuiderent c Thorpe b Martin	54
RP Lefebvre not out	11
⁺M Schewe not out	11
Extras (4lb, 6w, 2nb)	12
Total (6 wickets, 50 overs)	**230**

Did not bat: GJAF Aponso, PJ Bakker, F Jansen

Fall of wicket: 1, 46, 70, 81, 195, 208

Bowling: Cork 8-0-52-1; de Freitas 10-3-31-3; Smith 8-0-27-0; Gough 3-0-23-0; Martin 10-1-42-2; Thorpe 6-0-28-0; Hick 5-0-23-0

ENGLAND WON BY 49 RUNS

FEBRUARY 23   Australia v Kenya, in Visakhapatnam (Group A, match 6)

Australia

*MA Taylor c Modi b Suji	6
ME Waugh c Suji b Ali	130
RT Ponting c Otieno b Ali	6
SR Waugh c & b Suji	82
SG Law run out	35
MG Bevan b Ali	12
⁺IA Healy c E Odumbe b Karim	17
PR Reiffel not out	3
SK Warne not out	0
Extras (1b, 10w, 2nb)	13
Total (7 wickets, 50 overs, 214 min)	**304**

Did not bat: CJ McDermott, GD McGrath

Fall of wicket: 10, 26, 233, 237, 261, 301, 301

Bowling: Suji 10-1-55-2; Ali 10-0-45-3; Odoyo 8-0-58-0; E Odumbe 4-0-21-0; Karim 10-1-54-1; M Odumbe 4-0-35-0; D Tikolo 3-0-21-0; S Tikolo 1-0-14-0

⁺Kenya

⁺K Otieno b McGrath	85
D Chudasama c Healy b McDermott	5
S Tikolo c Ponting b Reiffel	6
*M Odumbe c Reiffel b Bevan	50
H Modi b Bevan	10
E Odumbo c Bevan b Reiffel	14
D Tikolo not out	11
T Odoyo st Healy b Warne	10
M Suji not out	1
Extras (7lb, 6w, 2nb)	15
Total (7 wickets, 50 overs, 215 min)	**207**

Did not bat: AV Karim, R Ali

Fall of wicket: 12, 30, 132, 167, 188, 195, 206

Bowling: McDermott 3-0-12-1; Reiffel 7-1-18-2; McGrath 10-0-44-1; SR Waugh 7-0-43-0; Warne 10-1-25-1; Bevan 8-0-35-2; ME Waugh 5-0-23-0

AUSTRALIA WON BY 97 RUNS

Through the following eight pages are photographs featuring all the members of the 1996 Australian World Cup squad.

Above: The team photo taken at the Taj Mahal. Standing (left to right): Ian McDonald (media manager), Michael Slater, Damien Fleming, Shane Lee, Glenn McGrath, Jason Gillespie, Paul Reiffel, Stuart Law, Ricky Ponting, Mike Walsh (scorer). Front: Shane Warne, Steve Waugh, Mark Taylor, Col Egar (manager), Ian Healy (vice captain), Mark Waugh, Bob Simpson (coach). Absent: Michael Bevan (who was too ill to travel to the Taj) and Craig McDermott (who had returned to Australia).

Right: Mark Taylor (left) and Michael Bevan congratulate me on taking the wicket of Sanjay Manjrekar during our match against India.

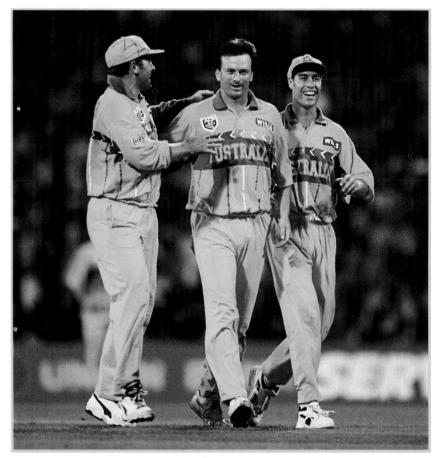

Above: Captain Mark Taylor is deep in thought as the top-order West Indies batsmen take control in the semi-final in Chandigarh.

Left: Mark Waugh, the dominant Australian batsman of the competition, during his century against Kenya in Visakhapatnam.

Above: Ian Healy takes time out to tutor a young cricketer at the Gymkhana club in Bombay during the early days of our World Cup adventure.

Below: The immensely talented Shane Lee in Agra, having taken in the magnificence of the Taj Mahal, strides back to the team bus.

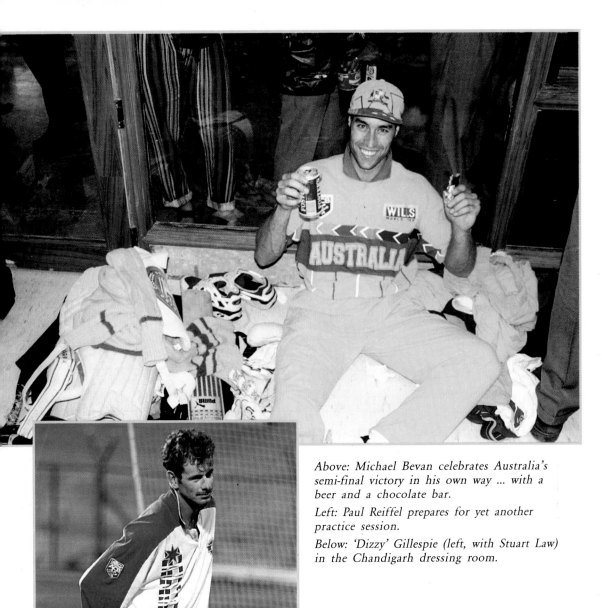

Above: Michael Bevan celebrates Australia's semi-final victory in his own way ... with a beer and a chocolate bar.

Left: Paul Reiffel prepares for yet another practice session.

Below: 'Dizzy' Gillespie (left, with Stuart Law) in the Chandigarh dressing room.

Right: Craig McDermott in the pool in Calcutta during the early days of the tour.

Below: No, it's not Merlin the Magician, it's Damien Fleming, Australia's leading wicket-taker (equal with Shane Warne) in the World Cup.

Left: The unlucky Michael Slater attempts a change of sports.

Below: Stuart Law (second from left) and friends (Lee, Fleming, McGrath and Reiffel) celebrating after the Windies win. Note the dressing room attendants in the background.

Above: The greatest spin bowler in the world, Shane Warne, in a relaxed mood before training at the Gymkhana club in Bombay.

Below: Ricky Ponting takes it easy during our practice match in Bombay before the start of the World Cup.

Above: With two security guards to keep him company, Glenn McGrath tries to avoid the autograph hunters by adopting an 'Arnold Schwarzenegger' disguise. Although Glenn's bowling spells in some of the early games were slightly below his best, in the semi-final he produced probably the finest display of his one-day career, and with Shane Warne and Damien Fleming bowled us to an impossible victory.

Left: Bob Simpson with the Queen of Jaipur. By Cup final time, with Craig McDermott having gone home early, Simmo and I were the only survivors from the 1987 World Cup-winning team.

FEBRUARY 24   Pakistan v UAE, in Gujranwala, Pakistan (Group B, match 7)

UAE

G Mylvaganam b Mushtaq	13
S Raza c Miundad b Aaqib	22
A Saeed run out	1
M Hussain c Waqar b Mushtaq	7
M Aslam b Mushtaq	5
I Mahammad b Wasim	12
A Laeeq c Ijaz b Aaqib	9
JA Samaresekera b Waqar	10
S Dukanwala not out	1
*SM Zarawani b Wasim	1
+I Abbasi not out	0
Extras (1lb, 5w, 2nb)	8
Total (9 wickets, 33 overs)	**109**

Fall of wickets: 27, 40, 47, 53, 54, 70, 80, 108, 109

Bowling: Wasim 7-1-25-2; Waqar 7-0-33-1; Aaqib 6-0-18-2; Mushtaq 7-0-16-3; Aamir 6-1-16-0

Pakistan

Aamir Sohail b Samarasekera	5
Saeed Anwar not out	40
Ijaz Ahmed not out	50
Extras (1lb, 12w, 4nb)	17
Total (1 wicket, 18 overs)	**112**

Did not bat: Salim Malik, Inzamam-ul-Haq, Javed Miandad, *Wasim Akram, +Rashid Latif, Mushtaq Ahmed, Waqar Younis, Aaqib Javed.

Fall of wickets: 7

Bowling: Samarasekera 3-0-17-1; Laeeq 4-0-24-0; Dukanwala 3-1-14-0; Raza 3-0-17-0; Zarawani 3-0-23-0; Saeed 2-0-16-0

PAKISTAN WON BY 9 WICKETS

FEBRUARY 25   England v South Africa, in Rawalpindi, Pakistan (Group B, match 8)

+South Africa

G Kirsten run out	38
+SJ Palframan c Russell b Martin	28
*WJ Cronje c Russell b Gough	15
DJ Cullinan b deFreitos	34
JH Kallis c Russell b Cork	26
JN Rhodes b Martin	37
BM McMillan b Smith	11
SM Pollock c Fairbrother b Cork	12
PL Symcox c Thorpe b Martin	1
CR Matthews not out	9
PS de Villiers c Smith b Gough	12
Extras (1lb, 5w, 1nb)	7
Total (50 overs)	**230**

Fall of wickets: 56, 85, 88, 137, 163, 195, 199, 202, 213, 230

Bowling: de Freitas 10-0-55-1; Cork 10-0-36-2; Gough 10-0-48-2; Martin 10-0-33-3; Smith 8-0-40-1; Thorpe 2-0-17-0

England

*MA Atherton c Palframan b Pollock	0
NMK Smith b de Villiers	11
GA Hick c McMillan b de Villiers	14
GP Thorpe c Palframan b Symcox	46
AJ Stewart run out	7
NH Fairbrother c Palframan b Symcox	3
+RC Russell c Rhodes b Pollock	12
DG Cork b Matthews	17
PAJ de Freitas run out	22
D Gough b Matthews	11
PJ Martin not out	1
Extras (7lb, 1w)	8
Total (44.3 overs)	**152**

Fall of wickets: 0, 22, 33, 52, 62, 97, 97, 139, 141, 152

Bowling: Pollock 8-1-16-2; de Villiers 7-1-27-2; Matthews 9.3-0-30-2; McMillan 6-0-17-0; Symcox 10-0-38-2; Cronje 4-0-17-0

SOUTH AFRICA WON BY 78 RUNS

FEBRUARY 26   Pakistan v Holland, in Lahore, Pakistan (Group B, match 9)

+Holland

NE Clarke c Rashid b Aaqib	4
PE Cantrell c Ijaz b Waqar	17
TBM de Leede c Rashid b Waqar	0
KJ van Noortwijk c Mushtaq b Aaqib	33
GJAF Aponso b Waqar	58
*RP Lefebvre b Waqar	10
B Zuiderent run out	6
E Gouka not out	0
Extras (7lb, 4w, 6nb)	17
Total (7 wickets, 50 overs)	**145**

Did not bat: +M Schewe, PJ Bakker, F Jansen

Fall of wickets: 16, 28, 29, 102, 130, 143, 145

Bowling: Wasim 10-1-30-0; Waqar 10-0-26-4; Aaqib 9-2-25-0; Mushtaq 10-2-27-0; Aamir 9-0-21-0; Salim 2-0-9-0

Pakistan

Aamir Sohail c Jansen b Lefebvre	9
Saeed Anwar not out	83
Ijaz Ahmed c Lefebvre b Cantrell	39
Inzamam-ul-Huq not out	18
Extras (1lb, 1w)	2
Total (2 wickets, 30.4 overs)	**151**

Did not bat: Salim Malik, Javed Miandad, *Wasim Akram, +Rashid Latif, Mushtaq Ahmed, Waqar Younis, Aaqib Javed

Fall of wickets: 10, 104

Bowling: Lefebvre 7-1-20-1; Bakker 7-1-13-0; Jansen 2-0-22-0; de Leede 4-0-20-0; Aponso 5-0-38-0; Cantrell 4-0-18-1; Gouka 1.4-0-19-0

PAKISTAN WON BY 8 WICKETS

FEBRUARY 27   Kenya v Zimbabwe, in Patna, India (Group A, match 8)

Kenya

D Chudasama run out	34
Tariq Iqbal b Lock	1
+K Otieno b Peall	19
S Tikolo st A Flower b B Strang	0
*M Odumbe c B Strang b PA Strang	30
H Modi b B Strang	3
E Odumbe c Campbell b PA Strang	20
T Odoyo c GW Flower b PA Strang	0
AV Karim lbw PA Strang	0
M Suji c GW Flower b PA Strang	15
R Ali not out	0
Extras (3lb, 8w, 1nb)	12
Total (49.4 overs)	**134**

Fall of wickets: 7, 60, 61, 63, 67, 109, 109, 109, 134, 134

Bowling: Streak 7-2-23-0; Lock 8-2-19-1; Whittall 5-0-21-0; Peall 10-1-23-1; B Strang 10-0-24-2; PA Strang 9.4-1-21-5

+Zimbabwe

AC Waller c S Tikolo b M Odumbe	30
+GW Flower b Ali	45
ADR Campbell c S Tikolo b M Odumbe	6
GJ Whittall c E Odumbe b Ali	6
*A Flower lbw Ali	5
CN Evans not out	8
HH Streak not out	15
Extras (3b, 4lb, 12w, 3nb)	22
Total (5 wickets, 42.2 overs)	**137**

Did not bat: PA Strang, B Strang, SG Peall, C Lock

Fall of wickets: 59, 29, 104, 108, 113

Bowling: Suji 9.2-0-37-0; Ali 8-1-22-3; E Odumbe 2-0-14-0; Odoyo 2-0-7-0; Karim 10-2-21-0; M Odumbe 10-2-24-2; S Tikolo 1-0-5-0

ZIMBABWE WON BY 5 WICKETS

FEBRUARY 27   New Zealand v UAE, in Faisalabad, Pakistan (Group B, match 10)

New Zealand

CM Spearman b Raza	78
NJ Astle b Samarasekera	2
SP Fleming c & b Dukanwala	16
RG Twose c Mazhor b Saeed	92
CL Cairns c Abbasi b Zarawani	6
AC Parore c Saeed b Zarawani	15
SA Thomson not out	31
*+LK Germon b Saeed	3
DJ Nash lbw Saeed	8
DK Morrison not out	10
Extras (2b, 12lb, 1nb)	15
Total (8 wickets, 47 overs)	**276**

Did not bat: RJ Kennedy

Fall of wickets: 11, 42, 162, 173, 210, 228, 239, 266

Bowling: Samarasekera 6-0-30-1; Laeeq 2-0-16-0; Dukanwala 10-0-46-1; Zarawani 10-0-49-2; Raza 9-0-48-1; Saeed 7-0-45-3; Mazhar 3-0-28-0

+UAE

A Saeed c Fleming b Nash	5
S Raza c Kennedy b Morrison	21
Mazhar Hussain c Cairns b Thomson	29
V Mehra c Cairns b Thomson	12
Mishaq c Fleming b Kennedy	8
M Aslam c Twose b Thomson	1
S Dukanwala c & b Cairns	8
A Laeeq run out	14
JA Samarasekera not out	47
*SM Zarawani c Thomson b Nash	13
+I Abbasi not out	2
Extras (2lb, 2nb, 3w)	7
Total (9 wickets, 47 overs)	**167**

Fall of wkts: 23, 29, 63, 70, 81, 88, 92, 124, 162

Bowling: Morrison 7-0-37-1; Nash 9-1-34-2; Cairns 10-2-31-1; Kennedy 6-0-20-1; Thomson 10-2-20-3; Astle 5-0-23-0

NEW ZEALAND WON BY 109 RUNS

FEBRUARY 27   India v Australia, in Bombay, India (Group A, match 9)

+Australia

ME Waugh run out	126
*MA Taylor c Srinath b Raju	59
RT Ponting c Manjrekar b Raju	12
SR Waugh run out	7
SG Law c & b Kumble	21
MG Bevan run out	6
S Lee run out	9
+IA Healy c Kumble b Prasad	6
SK Warne c Azharuddin b Prasad	0
DW Fleming run out	0
GD McGrath not out	0
Extras (8lb, 2nb, 2w)	12
Total (50 overs)	**258**

Fall of wickets: 103, 140, 157, 232, 237, 244, 258, 258, 258, 258

Bowling: Prabhakar 10-0-55-0; Srinath 10-1-51-0; Prasad 10-0-49-2; Kumble 10-1-47-1; Raju 10-0-48-2

India

AD Jadeja lbw Fleming	1
SR Tendulkar st Healy b ME Waugh	90
VG Kambli b Fleming	0
*M Azharuddin b Fleming	10
SV Manjrekar c Healy b SR Waugh	62
M Prabhakar run out	3
+NR Mongia c Taylor b Warne	27
AR Kumble b Fleming	17
J Srinath c Lee b Fleming	7
V Prasad c Bevan b SR Waugh	0
SLV Raju not out	3
Extras (5b, 8lb, 1nb, 8w)	22
Total (48 overs)	**242**

Fall of wickets: 7, 7, 70, 143, 147, 201, 205, 224, 231, 242

Bowling: McGrath 8-3-48-0; Fleming 9-0-36-5; Warne 10-1-28-1; Lee 3-0-23-0; ME Waugh 10-0-44-1; Bevan 5-0-28-0; SR Waugh 3-0-22-2

AUSTRALIA WON BY 16 RUNS

FEBRUARY 29   Kenya v West Indies, in Pune, India (Group A, match 10)

Kenya

D Chudasama c Lara b Walsh	8
*Tariq Iqbal c Cuffy b Walsh	16
K Otieno c Adams b Walsh	2
S Tikolo c Adams b Harper	29
*M Odumbe hit wkt b Bishop	6
H Modi c Adams b Ambrose	28
M Suji c Lara b Harper	0
T Odoyo st Adams b Harper	24
E Odumbe b Cuffy	1
AV Karim c Adams b Ambrose	11
R Ali not out	6
Extras (8lb, 14w, 13nb)	35
Total (49.3 overs)	**166**

Fall of wickets: 15, 19, 45, 72, 77, 81, 125, 126, 155, 166

Bowling: Ambrose 8.3-1-21-2; Walsh 9-0-46-3; Bishop 10-2-30-1; Cuffy 8-0-31-1; Harper 10-4-15-3; Arthurton 4-0-15-0

*West Indies

SL Campbell b Suji	4
*RB Richardson b Ali	5
BC Lara c Iqbal b Ali	8
S Chanderpaul c Tikolo b M Odumbe	19
KLT Arthurton run out	0
*JC Adams c Modi b M Odumbe	9
RA Harper c Iqbal b M Odumbe	17
IR Bishop not out	6
CEL Ambrose run out	3
CA Walsh c Chudasama b Karim	4
CE Cuffy b Ali	1
Extras (5b, 6lb, 4w, 2nb)	17
Total (35.2 overs)	**93**

Fall of wickets: 18, 22, 33, 35, 55, 65, 78, 83, 89, 93

Bowling: Suji 7-2-16-1; Ali 7.2-2-17-3; Karim 8-1-19-1; M Odumbe 10-3-15-3; Odoyo 3-0-15-0

KENYA WON BY 73 RUNS

FEBRUARY 29   Pakistan v South Africa, in Karachi, Pakistan (Group B, match 11)

Pakistan

Aamir Sohail c Cronje b Pollock	111
Saeed Anwar c McMillan b Cronje	25
Ijaz Ahmed lbw Cronje	0
Inzamam-ul-Haq run out	23
Salim Malik c Palframan b Adams	40
*Wasim Akram not out	32
*Rashid Latif lbw Pollock	0
Rameez Raja not out	2
Extras (1b, 2lb, 4w, 2nb)	9
Total (6 wickets, 50 overs)	**242**

Did not bat: Mushtaq Ahmed, Waqar Younis, Saqlain Mushtaq

Fall of wickets: 52, 52, 112, 189, 233, 235

Bowling: Cronje 5-0-20-2; Matthews 10-0-47-0; Donald 8-0-50-0; Adams 10-0-42-1; McMillan 8-0-31-0; Pollock 9-0-49-2

South Africa

AC Hudson b Waqar	33
G Kirsten b Saqlain	44
BM McMillan lbw Waqar	1
DJ Cullinan b Waqar	65
JH Kallis c & b Soqlain	9
*WJ Cronje not out	45
SM Pollock not out	20
Extras (8b, 4lb, 6w, 8nb)	26
Total (5 wickets, 44.2 overs)	**243**

Did not bat: *SJ Palframan, CR Matthews, AA Donald, P Adams

Fall of wickets: 51, 53, 111, 125, 203

Bowling: Waqar 8-0-50-3; Wasim 9.2-0-49-0; Saqlain 10-1-38-2; Aamir 6-0-35-0; Mushtaq 10-0-54-0; Salim 1-0-5-0

SOUTH AFRICA WON BY 5 WICKETS

MARCH 1   Australia v Zimbabwe, in Nagpur, India (Group A, match 11)

*Zimbabwe

AC Waller run out	67
*GW Flower b McGrath	4
GJ Whittall c & b SR Waugh	6
ADR Campbell c ME Waugh b SR Waugh	5
*A Flower st Healy b Warne	7
CN Evans c Healy b Warne	18
HH Streak c SR Waugh b Fleming	13
PA Strang not out	16
B Strang b Fleming	0
SG Peall c Healy b Warne	0
C Lock b Warne	5
Extras (8lb, 3w, 2nb)	13
Total (45.3 overs)	**154**

Fall of wickets: 21, 41, 55, 68, 105, 126, 140, 140, 145, 154

Bowling: McGrath 8-2-12-1; Fleming 9-1-30-2; Lee 4-2-8-0; SR Waugh 7-2-22-2; Warne 9.3-1-34-4; ME Waugh 5-0-30-0; Law 3-0-10-0

Australia

*MA Taylor c B Strang b PA Strang	34
ME Waugh not out	76
RT Ponting c & b PA Strang	33
SR Waugh not out	5
Extras (6b, 2lb, 1w, 1nb)	10
Total (2 wickets, 36 overs)	**158**

Did not bat: SG Law, MG Bevan, S Lee, *IA Healy, SK Warne, DW Fleming, GD McGrath

Fall of wickets: 92, 150

Bowling: Streak 10-3-29-0; Lock 4-0-25-0; B Strang 3-0-20-0; Whittall 2-0-11-0; PA Strang 10-2-33-2; Peall 4-0-20-0; GW Flower 3-0-12-0

AUSTRALIA WON BY 8 WICKETS

MARCH 1   Holland v UAE, in Lahore, Pakistan (Group B, match 12)

Holland

NE Clarke c Mehra b Altaf	0
PE Cantrell c Abbasi b Saeed	47
GJAF Aponso c & b Dukanwala	45
TBM de Leede c & b Saeed	36
KJ van Noortwijk c Zarawani b Dukanwala	26
*SW Lubbers c Saffar b Zarawani	8
RP Lefebvre c Ishaq b Dukanwala	12
B Zuiderent st Abbasi b Dukanwala	3
⁺M Schewe b Dukanwala	6
R Oosteram not out	2
PJ Bakker not out	0
Extras (5b, 15lb, 11w)	31
Total (9 wickets, 50 overs)	**216**

Fall of wickets: 3, 77, 148, 153, 168, 200, 200, 209, 210

Bowling: Altaf 10-3-15-1; Samarasekera 9-1-35-0; Saffar 3-0-25-0; Dukanwala 10-0-29-5; Zarawani 8-0-40-1; Raza 5-0-23-0; Saeed 5-0-29-2

⁺UAE

A Saeed run out	32
S Raza c Zuiderent b Lubbers	84
M Hussain c Clarke b Lefebvre	16
V Mehro not out	29
Ishaq Mohammad not out	51
Extras (4lb, 3b, 1w)	8
Total (3 wickets, 44.2 overs)	**220**

Did not bat: JA Samarasekera, Sal-Saffar, S Dukanwala, *SM Zarawani, S Altaf, ⁺I Abbasi

Fall of wickets: 117, 135, 138

Bowling: Bakker 8-0-41-0; Lefebvre 8-0-24-1; Lubbers 9-0-38-1; Cantrell 8-0-30-0; Aponso 7.2-0-47-0; de Leede 4-0-33-0

UAE WON BY 7 WICKETS

MARCH 2   India v Sri Lanka, in New Delhi (Group A, match 12)

India

M Prabhakar c Gurusinha b Pushpakumara	7
SR Tendulkar run out	137
SV Manjrekar c Kaluwitharana b Dharmasena	32
*M Azharuddin not out	72
VG Kambli not out	1
Extras (4b, 7lb, 11w)	22
Total (3 wickets, 50 overs)	**271**

Did not bat: AD Jadeja, ⁺NR Mongia, AR Kumble, J Srinath, V Prasad, SA Ankola

Fall of wickets: 27, 93, 268

Bowling: Vaas 9-3-37-0; Pushpakumara 8-0-53-1; Muralitharan 10-1-42-0; Dharmasena 9-0-53-1; Jayasuriya 10-0-52-0; Ranatunga 4-0-23-0

⁺Sri Lanka

ST Jayasuriya c Prabhakar b Kumble	79
⁺RS Kaluwitharana c Kumble b Prasad	26
AP Gurusinha run out	25
PA de Silva st Mongia b Kumble	8
*A Ranatunga not out	46
HP Tillekeratne not out	70
Extras (4b, 9lb, 3w, 2nb)	18
Total (4 wickets, 48.4 overs)	**272**

Did not bat: RS Mahanama, HPDK Dharmasena, WPUJC Vaas, KR Pushpakumara, M Muralitharan

Fall of wickets: 53, 129, 137, 141

Bowling: Prabhakar 4-0-47-0; Srinath 9.4-0-51-0; Prasad 10-1-53-1; Ankola 5-0-28-0; Kumble 10-1-39-2; Tendulkar 10-0-41-0

SRI LANKA WON BY 6 WICKETS

MARCH 3   Pakistan v England, in Karachi, Pakistan (Group B, match 13)

⁺England

RA Smith c Waqar b Salim	75
*MA Atherton b Aamir	66
GA Hick st Rashid b Aamir	1
GP Thorpe not out	52
NH Fairbrother c Wasim b Mushtaq	13
⁺RC Russell c & b Mushtaq	4
DA Reeve b Mushtaq	3
DG Cork lbw Waqar	0
D Gough b Wasim	14
PJ Martin run out	2
RK Illingworth not out	1
Extras (11lb, 4w, 3nb)	18
Total (9 wickets, 50 overs)	**249**

Fall of wickets: 147, 151, 156, 194, 204, 212, 217, 241, 247

Bowling: Wasim 7-1-31-1; Waqar 10-1-45-1; Aaqib 7-0-34-0; Mushtaq 10-0-53-3; Aamir 10-0-48-2; Salim 6-1-27-1

Pakistan

Aamir Sohail c Thorpe b Illingworth	42
Saeed Anwar c Russell b Cork	71
Ijaz Ahmed c Russell b Cork	70
Inzamam-ul-Haq not out	53
Javed Miandad not out	11
Extras (1lb, 2w)	3
Total (3 wickets, 47.4 overs)	**250**

Did not bat: Salim Malik, *Wasim Akram, ⁺Rashid Latif, Mushtaq Ahmed, Waqar Younis, Aaqib Javed

Fall of wickets: 81, 139, 214

Bowling: Cork 10-0-59-2; Martin 9-0-45-0; Gough 10-0-45-0; Illingworth 10-0-46-1; Reeve 6.4-0-37-0; Hick 2-0-17-0

PAKISTAN WON BY 7 WICKETS

MARCH 4   Australia v West Indies, in Jaipur, India (Group A, match 13)

⁺Australia

ME Waugh st Browne b Harper	30
*MA Taylor c Browne b Walsh	9
RT Ponting run out	102
SR Waugh b Walsh	57
MG Bevan run out	2
SG Law not out	12
⁺IA Healy run out	3
PR Reiffel not out	4
Extras (3lb, 6w, 1nb)	10
Total (6 wickets, 50 overs)	**229**

Did not bat: SK Warne, DW Fleming, GD McGrath

Fall of wickets: 22, 84, 194, 200, 216, 224

Bowling: Ambrose 10-4-25-0; Walsh 9-2-35-2; Bishop 9-0-52-0; Harper 10-0-46-1; Arthurton 9-0-53-0; Adams 3-0-15-0

West Indies

SL Campbell c Healy b Fleming	1
⁺CO Browne run out	10
BC Lara c McGrath b ME Waugh	60
*RB Richardson not out	93
S Chanderpaul b ME Waugh	10
RA Harper lbw Reiffel	22
KLT Arthurton lbw ME Waugh	0
JC Adams not out	17
Extras (12lb, 5w, 2nb)	19
Total (6 wickets, 48.5 overs)	**232**

Did not bat: IR Bishop, CEL Ambrose, CA Walsh

Fall of wickets: 1, 26, 113, 146, 194, 196

Bowling: Reiffel 10-2-45-1; Fleming 7.5-1-44-1; McGrath 9-0-46-0; Warne 10-1-30-0; ME Waugh 10-1-38-3; Bevan 2-0-17-0

WEST INDIES WON BY 4 WICKETS

MARCH 5   Holland v South Africa, in Rawalpini, Pakistan (Group B, match 14)

⁺South Africa

G Kirsten c Zuiderent b Aponso	83
AC Hudson c van Ooosterom b Gouka	161
*WJ Cronje c Lubbers b Cantrell	41
DJ Cullinan not out	19
JH Kallis not out	17
Extras (5lb, 2w)	7
Total (3 wickets, 50 overs)	**328**

Did not bat: BM McMillan, *SJ Palframan, SM Pollock, CR Matthews, PL Symcox, AA Donald

Fall of wickets: 186, 274, 301

Bowling: Bakker 10-1-64-0; Lubbers 8-0-50-0; de Leede 10-0-59-0; Aponso 10-0-57-1; Cantrell 10-0-61-1; Gouka 2-0-32-1

Holland

NE Clarke c Pollock b Donald	32
PE Cantrell c & b Matthews	23
TBM de Leede b Donald	12
KJ van Noortwijk c Palframan b Symcox	9
GJAF Aponso c Kirsten b Symcox	6
B Zuiderent run out	27
⁺M Schewe b Matthews	20
E Gouka c Kallis b Pollock	19
R van Oosterom not out	5
*SW Lubbers not out	2
Extras (7lb, 5w, 1nb)	13
Total (8 wickets, 50 overs)	**168**

Did not bat: PJ Bakker

Fall of wickets: 56, 70, 81, 86, 97, 126, 158, 163

Bowling: Donald 6-0-21-2; Pollock 8-0-35-1; Symcox 10-1-22-2; Cronje 3-1-3-0; Matthews 10-0-38-2; McMillan 4-2-5-0; Kallis 7-0-30-0; Cullinan 2-0-7-0

SOUTH AFRICA WON BY 160 RUNS

MARCH 6   Sri Lanka v Kenya, in Kandy, Sri Lanka (Group A, match 14)

Sri Lanka

ST Jayasuriya c D Tikolo b E Odumbe	44
⁺RS Kaluwitharana b E Odumbe	33
AP Gurusinha c Onyano b Karim	84
PA de Silva c Modi b Suji	145
*A Ranatunga not out	75
HP Tillekeratne run out	0
RS Mahanama not out	0
Extras (1b, 5lb, 11w)	17
Total (5 wickets, 50 overs)	**398**

Did not bat: WPUJC Vaas, HPDK Dharmasena, M Muralitharan, KR Pushpakumara

Fall of wickets: 83, 88, 272, 378, 384

Bowling: Suji 9-0-85-1; Ali 6-0-67-0; Onyango 4-0-31-0; E Odumbe 5-0-34-2; Karim 10-0-50-1; D Tikolo 2-0-13-0; M Odumbe 9-0-74-0; S Tikolo 5-0-38-0

⁺Kenya

D Chudasama b Muralitharan	27
⁺K Otieno b Vaas	14
S Tikolo b Dharmasena	96
*M Odumbe c Kaluwitharana b Muralitharan	0
H Modi run out	41
D Tikolo not out	25
E Odumbe c Muralitharan b Ranatunga	4
L Onyango c sub b Ranatunga	23
M Suji not out	2
Extras (1b, 9lb, 7w, 5nb)	22
Total (7 wickets, 50 overs)	**254**

Did not bat: AV Karim, R Ali

Fall of wickets: 47, 51, 51, 188, 196, 215, 246

Bowling: Vaas 10-0-44-1; Muralitharan 10-1-40-2; Pushpakumara 7-0-46-0; Ranatunga 5-0-31-2; Dharmasena 10-0-45-1; Jayasuriya 7-0-34-0; Tillekeratne 1-0-4-0

SRI LANKA WON BY 144 RUNS

MARCH 6   India v Zimbabwe, in Kanpur, India (Group A, match 15)

India

SR Tendulkar b Streak	3
NS Sidhu c Streak b PA Strang	80
SV Manjrekar c Campbell b Lock	2
*M Azharuddin c Campbell b B Strang	2
VG Kambli c GW Flower b Lock	106
AD Jadeja not out	44
+NR Mongia not out	6
Extras (1lb, 3w)	4
Total (5 wickets, 50 overs)	**247**

Did not bat: J Srinath, SL Venkatapathy Raju, AR Kumble, V Prasad

Fall of wickets: 5, 25, 32, 174, 219

Bowling: Streak 10-3-29-1; Lock 10-1-57-2; B Strang 5-1-22-1; PA Strang 10-0-55-1; Peall 6-0-35-0; Whittall 3-0-19-0; GW Flower 3-0-16-0; Campbell 3-0-13-0

#Zimbabwe

AC Waller c Tendulkar b Kumble	22
GW Flower c Azharuddin b Raju	30
GJ Whittall run out	10
ADR Campbell c & b Jadeja	28
*+A Flower b Raju	26
CN Evans c Srinath b Jadeja	6
HH Streak lbw Raju	30
PA Strang b Srinath	14
B Strang lbw Srinath	3
SG Peall c Rajub Kumble	9
C Lock not out	2
Extras (4b, 11lb, 11w, 1nb)	27
Total (49.4 overs)	**207**

Fall of wickets: 59, 59, 96, 99, 106, 168, 173, 193, 195, 207

Bowling: Srinath 10-1-36-2; Prasad 7-0-40-0; Kumble 9.4-1-32-2; Raju 10-2-30-3; Tendulkar 6-0-23-0; Jadeja 7-0-31-2

INDIA WON BY 40 RUNS

MARCH 6   Pakistan v New Zealand, in Lahore, Pakistan (Group B, match 15)

Pakistan

Aamir Sohail c Thomson b Kennedy	50
Saeed Anwar run out	62
Ijaz Ahmed c Spearman b Cairns	26
Inzamam-ul-Haq run out	39
Javed Miandad run out	5
Salim Malik not out	55
*Wasim Akram not out	28
Extras (5lb, 5w, 6nb)	16
Total (5 wickets, 50 overs)	**281**

Did not bat: +Rashid Latif, Mushtaq Ahmed, Waqar Younis, Aaqib Javed

Fall of wickets: 70, 139, 155, 173, 201

Bowling: Astle 9-0-50-0; Cairns 10-1-53-1; Kennedy 5-0-32-1; Morrison 2-0-17-0; Nash 10-1-49-0; Thomson 6-0-35-0; Twose 8-0-40-0

#New Zealand

CM Spearman c Rashid b Aaqib	14
NJ Astle c Rashid b Waqar	6
*+LK Germon c sub (Afa-ur-Rehman) b Mushtaq	41
SP Fleming st Rashid b Salim	42
RG Twose c Salim b Mushtaq	24
CL Cairns c Rashid b Aamir	32
AC Parore c Mushtaq b Salim	36
SA Thomson c Rashid b Waqar	13
DJ Nash not out	5
RJ Kennedy b Aaqib	2
Extras (4b, 9lb, 6w, 1nb)	20
Total (9 wickets, all out, 47.3 overs)	**235**

Did not bat: DK Morrison (absent hurt)

Fall of wickets: 23, 23, 83, 132, 138, 182, 221, 228, 235

Bowling: Waqar 9-2-32-2; Aaqib 7.3-0-45-2; Mushtaq 10-0-32-2; Salim 7-0-41-2; Ijaz 4-0-21-0; Aamir 10-0-51-1

PAKISTAN WON BY 46 RUNS

FINAL TABLES

Group A	Played	Won	Lost	Points	R/R
Sri Lanka	3**	3	0	10	0.87
Australia	4*	3	1	6	0.88
India	5	3	2	6	0.40
West Indies	4*	2	2	4	-0.12
Kenya	5+	1	4	2	-0.49
Zimbabwe	5+	1	4	2	-0.96

Group B	Played	Won	Lost	Points	R/R
South Africa	5	5	0	10	2.06
Pakistan	5	4	1	8	0.99
New Zealand	5	3	2	6	0.93
England	5	2	3	4	0.06
UAE	5	1	4	2	-1.82
Holland	5	0	5	0	-1.95

13 matches, 5 won by team batting first
5475 runs, 174 wickets, average 31.46
** Sri Lanka won v Australia and v West Indies on forfeit
* lost v Sri Lanka on forfeit
+ abandoned match on February 26 (replayed on February 27) is not included in this table

15 matches, 8 won by team batting first
6349 runs, 192 wickets, average 33.06

Note: R/R indicates net run rate

FACTS AND TRIVIA FROM THE GROUP MATCHES

England v New Zealand (Ahmedabad):
Astle was the seventh player to score a century on his World Cup debut. The feat had previously been achieved by DL Amiss and GM Turner in 1975, AJ Lamb and TM Chappell in 1983, GR Marsh in 1987 and A Flower in 1992.

South Africa v UAE (Rawalpindi):
This match was originally scheduled for February 15, but was delayed because of rain. UAE became the 12th team to play in a World Cup match (the two teams who had competed in previous Cups but were not playing in 1996 were East Africa, who failed to win a game in 1975, and Canada, who lost their three matches in 1979). Kirsten's 188 not out was the highest score in Cup history, beating IVA Richards' 181 v Sri Lanka in Karachi in 1987. This was the first century in a World Cup match by a South African, beating the previous highest - 90 by half-brother PN Kirsten v New Zealand in Auckland in 1992. Kirsten was the eighth player to score a century on his Cup debut.

New Zealand v Holland (Baroda):
Holland became the 13th team to compete in the World Cup. Clarke, at 47 the oldest player in the tournament, had played for Barbados between 1969-70 and 1976-77. Cantrell had played for Queensland between 1988-89 and 1990-91.

India v Kenya (Cuttack):
Kenya became the 14th team to compete in the World Cup. This was Azharuddin's 200th one-day international – he became the seventh player to reach this mark, after AR Border, DL Haynes, Javed Miandad, Kapil Dev, RB Richardson and Salim Malik.

England v UAE (Peshawar):
White suffered a torn intercostal muscle during his second over and took no further part in the tournament. DA Reeve replaced him in the England squad. Smith retired ill at 1-57.

South Africa v New Zealand (Faisalabad):
Cronje reached 50 off 36 balls.

Sri Lanka v Zimbabwe (Colombo SSC):
This was the first World Cup match played in Sri Lanka. Gurusinha and de Silva added 172 for the third wicket, the highest partnership for Sri Lanka in one-day internationals. Gurusinha's six sixes equalled the World Cup record shared by Kapil Dev (175 not out v Zimbabwe in 1983) and IVA Richards (181 v Sri Lanka in 1987).

Australia v Kenya (Visakhapatnam):
The Waugh brothers added 207 for the third wicket - a World Cup record for any wicket. ME Waugh's 130 was Australia's highest World Cup score. McDermott suffered a calf injury after bowling three overs and took no further part in the tournament. JN Gillespie replaced him in the Australian squad. Otieno retired hurt (leg cramps) when 82 at 3-166 and resumed at 5-188.

Pakistan v UAE (Gujranwala):
Javed Miandad, at age 38, became the only player to appear in all six World Cup tournaments. Overnight rain reduced the match to 33 overs per innings.

Zimbabwe v Kenya (Patna):
This was the first World Cup match to be replayed - rain after 15.5 overs had caused the February 26 match to be abandoned. Teams and umpires were the same on both days. Performances on

February 26 are not counted in tournament records. PA Strang's 5-21 is Zimbabwe's best bowling in one-day internationals.

New Zealand v UAE (Faisalabad):
Morning mist reduced the match to a maximum 47 overs per innings. Cairns' four catches was a new Cup record for catches by a fielder in an innings.

Australia v India (Bombay):
ME Waugh became the first player to score consecutive World Cup centuries. Fleming took five wickets on his Cup debut, becoming the fourth player to achieve this feat (DK Lillee and GJ Gilmour, in 1975, and WW Davis, in 1983, are the others).

Kenya v West Indies (Pune):
Adams' five dismissals equalled the Cup record for most dismissals by a keeper held by SMH Kirmani (India v Zimbabwe, 1983). Kenya's victory was the fourth in World Cup history by a non-Test playing team against a Test playing team, after Sri Lanka's 47-runs defeat of India in 1979 and Zimbabwe's defeats of Australia (by 13 runs in 1983) and England (by nine runs in 1992). West Indies' innings total was their lowest in World Cup matches, and the equal fourth lowest in Cup history.

Australia v Zimbabwe (Nagpur):
ME Waugh's third innings of the 1996 Cup took his tournament aggregate to 332, at 166.

UAE v Holland (Lahore):
Dukanwala's 5-29 is the best bowling for UAE in one-day internationals. Salim Raza's 84 took 68 balls and included six sixes (equalling the World Cup record).

Sri Lanka v India (Delhi):
Jayasuriya and Kaluwitharana scored the first 50 runs of the Sri Lankan innings in 4.4 overs. Jayasuriya required only 36 balls to reach his half-century.

Pakistan v England (Karachi):
Fairbrother injured a hamstring while fielding and took no further part in the tournament. MR Ramprakash replaced him in the England squad.

South Africa v Holland (Rawalpindi):
Hudson and Kirsten added 186 for the first wicket, breaking the Cup opening partnership record of 182 by RB McCosker and A Turner (Australia v Sri Lanka in 1975). South Africa's total was their highest in one-day internationals. This was South Africa's 10th consecutuve victory in one-day internationals.

Sri Lanka v Kenya (Kandy):
Sri Lanka's 398 is the highest total in one-day internationals (the previous record was 7-363 by England v Pakistan in 1992; the previous Cup record was 4-360 by West Indies v Sri Lanka in 1987). De Silva's 145 was Sri Lanka's first World Cup century, and the highest score by a Sri Lankan in one-day internationals. The match aggregate of 652 set a new record for one-day internationals.

Pakistan v New Zealand (Lahore):
Morrison strained his groin during his second over and took no further part in the competition. Similarly, Wasim Akram strained a side muscle while batting and did not appear again in the tournament. Rashid Latif's five wicketkeeping dismissals equalled the World Cup record.

The Quarter-finals

MARCH 9   India v Pakistan, in Bangalore, India (FIRST QUARTER-FINAL)

*India

NS Sidhu b Mushtaq	93
SR Tendulkar b Ata-ur-Rehman	31
SV Manjrekar c Miandad b Aamir	20
*M Azharuddin c Rashid b Waqar	27
VG Kambli b Mushtaq	24
AD Jadeja c Aamir b Waqar	45
+NR Mongia run out	3
AR Kumble c Miandad b Aaqib	10
J Srinath not out	12
V Prasad not out	0
Extras (3lb, 4nb, 1sw)	22
Total (8 wickets, 50 overs)	**287**

Did not bat: SL Venkatapathy Raju

Fall of wickets: 90, 138, 168, 200, 226, 236, 260, 279

Bowling: Waqar 10-1-67-2; Aaqib 10-0-67-1; Ata-ur-Rehman 10-0-40-1; Mushtaq 10-0-56-2; Aamir 5-0-29-1; Salim 5-0-25-0

Pakistan

Aamir Sohail b Prasad	55
Saeed Anwar c Kumble b Srinath	48
Ijaz Ahmed c Srinath b Prasad	12
Inzamam-ul-Haq c Mongia b Prasad	12
Salim Malik lbw Kumble	38
Javed Miandad run out	38
+Rashid Latif st Mongia b Raju	26
Mushtaq Ahmed c & b Kumble	0
Waqar Younis not out	4
Ata-ur-Rehman lbw Kumble	0
Aaqib Javed not out	6
Extras (1b, 3lb, 5w)	9
Total (9 wickets, 49 overs)	**248**

Fall of wickets: 84, 113, 122, 132, 184, 231, 232, 239, 239

Bowling: Srinath 9-0-61-1; Prasad 10-0-45-3; Kumble 10-0-48-3; Raju 10-0-46-1; Tendulkar 5-0-25-0; Jadeja 5-0-19-0

INDIA WON BY 39 RUNS

MARCH 9   England v Sri Lanka, in Faisalabad, Pakistan (SECOND QUARTER-FINAL)

*England

RA Smith run out	25
*MA Atherton c Kaluwitharana b Vaas	22
GA Hick c Ranatunga b Muralitharan	8
GP Thorpe b Dharmasena	14
PAJ de Freitas lbw Jayasuriya	67
AJ Stewart b Muralitharan	17
+RC Russell b Dharmasena	9
DA Reeve b Jayasuriya	35
D Gough not out	26
PJ Martin not out	0
Extras (8lb, 4w)	12
Total (8 wickets, 50 overs)	**235**

Did not bat: RK Illingworth

Fall of wickets: 31, 58, 66, 94, 145, 171, 173, 235

Bowling: Wickremasinghe 7-0-43-0; Vaas 8-1-29-1; Muralitharan 10-1-37-2; Dharmasena 10-0-30-2; Jayasuriya 9-0-46-2; de Silva 6-0-42-0

Sri Lanka

ST Jayasuriya st Russell b Reeve	82
+RS Kaluwitharana b Illingworth	8
AP Gurusinha run out	45
PA de Silva c Smith b Hick	31
*A Ranatunga lbw Gough	25
HP Tillekeratne not out	19
RS Mahanama not out	22
Extras (1lb, 2w, 1nb)	4
Total (5 wickets, 40.4 overs)	**236**

Did not bat: WPUJC Vaas, HPDK Dharmasena, M Muralitharan, GP Wickremasinghe

Fall of wickets: 12, 113, 165, 194, 198

Bowling: Martin 9-1-41-0; Illingworth 10-1-72-1; Gough 10-1-36-1; de Freitas 3.4-0-38-0; Reeve 4-1-14-1; Hick 4-0-34-1

SRI LANKA WON BY 5 WICKETS

FACTS AND TRIVIA FROM THE QUARTER-FINALS

India v Pakistan (Bangalore): Pakistan were penalised one over in their innings because of their slow over-rate in India's innings. This was the second time India and Pakistan had met in the World Cup; the other was in 1992. India have won both matches.

Sri Lanka v England (Faisalabad): Jayasuriya scored 82 off 44 balls (13 fours, three sixes). His half-century came in 30 balls, equalling the World Cup record shared by CM Old, Imran Khan and MD Crowe. England's defeat meant that, for the first time in Cup history, they did not reach at least the semi-finals.

West Indies v South Africa (Karachi): The victories of Australia and West Indies meant that the four teams remaining in the tournament after the quarter-finals were all from the original Group A. The four losing quarter-finalists had been the semi-finalists in 1992. This match featured the two bowlers

Continued

MARCH 11 South Africa v West Indies, in Karachi, Pakistan (THIRD QUARTER-FINAL)

*West Indies		
S Chanderpaul c Cullinan b McMillan	56
⁺CO Browne c Cullinan b Matthews	26
BC Lara c Pollock b Symcox	111
*RB Richardson c Kirsten b Symcox	10
RA Harper lbw McMillan	9
RIC Holder run out	5
KLT Arthurton c Hudson b Adams	1
JC Adams not out	13
IR Bishop b Adams	17
CEL Ambrose not out	0
Extras (2b, 11lb, 1nb, 2w)	16
Total (8 wickets, 50 overs)	**264**

Did not bat: CA Walsh

Fall of wickets: 42, 180, 210, 214, 227, 230, 230, 254

Bowling: Pollock 9-0-46-0; Matthews 10-0-42-1; Cronje 3-0-17-0; McMillan 10-1-37-2; Symcox 10-0-64-2; Adams 8-0-45-2

South Africa		
AC Hudson c Walsh b Adams	54
G Kirsten hit wkt b Ambrose	3
DJ Cullinan c Bishop b Adams	69
*WJ Cronje c Arthurton b Adams	40
JN Rhodes c Adams b Harper	13
BM McMillan lbw Harper	6
SM Pollock c Adams b Harper	6
⁺SJ Palframan c & b Harper	1
PL Symcox c Harper b Arthurton	24
CR Matthews not out	8
P Adams b Walsh	10
Extras (1b, 4lb, 2w, 4nb)	11
Total (49.3 overs)	**245**

Fall of wickets: 21, 118, 140, 186, 196, 196, 198, 227, 228, 245

Bowling: Ambrose 10-0-29-1; Walsh 8.3-0-51-1; Bishop 5-0-31-0; Harper 10-0-47-4; Adams 10-0-53-3; Arthurton 6-0-29-1

WEST INDIES WON BY 19 RUNS

MARCH 11 Australia v New Zealand, in Madras, India (FOURTH QUARTER-FINAL)

*New Zealand		
CM Spearman c Healy b Reiffel	12
NJ Astle c Healy b Fleming	1
**⁺LK Germon c Fleming b McGrath	89
SP Fleming c SR Waugh b McGrath	8
CZ Harris c Reiffel b Warne	130
RG Twose b Bevan	4
CL Cairns c Reiffel b ME Waugh	4
AC Parore lbw Warne	11
SA Thomson run out	11
DN Patel not out	3
Extras (6lb, 3w, 4nb)	13
Total (9 wickets, 50 overs)	**286**

Did not bat: DJ Nash

Fall of wickets: 15, 16, 44, 212, 227, 240, 259, 283, 286

Bowling: Reiffel 4-0-38-1; Fleming 5-1-20-1; McGrath 9-2-50-2; ME Waugh 8-0-43-1; Warne 10-0-52-2; Bevan 10-0-52-1; SR Waugh 4-0-25-0

Australia		
*MA Taylor c Germon b Patel	10
ME Waugh c Parore b Nash	110
RT Ponting c sub (RJ Kennedy) b Thomson	31
SK Warne lbw Astle	24
SR Waugh not out	59
SG Law not out	42
Extras (lb, 6lb, 3w, 3nb)	13
Total (4 wickets, 47.5 overs)	**289**

Did not bat: MG Bevan, ⁺IA Healy, PR Reiffel, DW Fleming, GD McGrath

Fall of wickets: 19, 84, 127, 213

Bowling: Nash 9-1-44-1; Patel 8-0-45-1; Cairns 6.5-0-51-0; Harris 10-0-41-0; Thomson 8-0-57-1; Astle 3-0-21-1; Twose 3-0-23-0

AUSTRALIA WON BY 6 WICKETS

---

who would finish as the tournament's most economical bowlers. BM McMillan conceded 127 runs during the Cup from 43 overs — a runs-per-over rate of 2.95. Next best was CEL Ambrose, who conceded 170 runs from 56.3 overs, a rate of 3.01. Lara's century was the 10th by a West Indian in World Cup cricket, a new record. The other West Indian century makers are IVA Richards (3), CG Greenidge (2), CH Lloyd, DL Haynes, RB Richardson and PV Simmons.

Australia v New Zealand (Madras): ME Waugh became the first player to score three centuries in one Cup tournament and the third player (after IVA Richards and Rameez Raja) to score three World Cup centuries. Waugh's century was the 10th by an Australian in World Cup cricket, bringing Australia back level with the West Indies. The other Australian century makers are GR Marsh (2), DC Boon (2), A Turner, TM Chappell, RT Ponting.

The Semi-finals

MARCH 13   India v Sri Lanka, in Calcutta, India (FIRST SEMI-FINAL)

Sri Lanka

ST Jayasuriya c Prasad b Srinath	1
⁺RS Kaluwitharana c Manjrekar b Srinath	0
AP Gurusinha c Kumble b Srinath	1
PA de Silva b Kumble	66
RS Mahanama retired hurt	58
*A Ranatunga lbw Tendulkar	35
HP Tillekeratne c Tendulkar b Prasad	32
HPDK Dharmasena b Tendulkar	9
WPUJC Vaas run out	23
GP Wickremasinghe not out	4
M Muralitharan not out	5
Extras (1b, 10lb, 4w, 2nb)	17
Total (8 wickets, 50 overs)	**251**

Fall of wickets: 1, 1, 35, 85, 168, 206, 236, 244
Bowling: Srinath 7-1-34-3; Kumble 10-0-51-1; Prasad 8-0-50-1; Kapoor 10-0-40-0; Jadeja 5-0-31-0; Tendulkar 10-1-34-2

⁺India

SR Tendulkar st Kaluwitharana b Jayasuriya	65
NS Sidhu c Jayasuriya b Vaas	3
SV Manjrekar b Jayasuriya	25
*M Azharuddin c & b Dharmasena	0
VG Kambli not out	10
J Srinath run out	6
AD Jadeja b Jayasuriya	0
⁺NR Mongia c Jayasuriya b de Silva	1
AR Kapoor c de Silva b Muralikharan	0
AR Kumble not out	0
Extras (5lb, 5w)	10
Total (8 wickets, 34.1 overs)	**120**

Did not bat: V Prasad
Fall of wickets: 8, 98, 99, 101, 110, 115, 120, 120
Bowling: Wickremasinghe 5-0-24-0; Vaas 6-1-23-1; Muralitharan 7.1-0-29-1; Dharmasena 7-0-24-1; Jayasuriya 7-1-12-3; de Silva 2-0-3-1

SRI LANKA WON BY DEFAULT
(crowd violence, match referee intervened)

March 14   Australia v West Indies, in Chandigarh, India (SECOND SEMI-FINAL)

⁺Australia

ME Waugh lbw Ambrose	0
*MA Taylor b Bishop	1
RT Ponting lbw Ambrose	0
SR Waugh b Bishop	3
SG Law run out	72
MG Bevan c Richardson b Harper	69
⁺IA Healy run out	31
PR Reiffel run out	7
SK Warne not out	6
Extras (11lb, 5w, 2nb)	18
Total (8 wickets, 50 overs)	**207**

Did not bat: DW Fleming, GD McGrath
Fall of wickets: 0, 7, 8, 15, 153, 171, 186, 207
Bowling: Ambrose 10-1-26-2; Bishop 10-1-35-2; Walsh 10-1-33-0; Gibson 2-0-13-0; Harper 9-0-47-1; Adams 9-0-42-0

West Indies

S Chanderpaul c Fleming b McGrath	80
⁺CO Browne c & b Warne	10
BC Lara b SR Waugh	45
*RB Richardson not out	49
RA Harper lbw McGrath	2
OD Gibson c Healy b Warne	1
JC Adams lbw Warne	2
KLT Arthurton c Healy b Fleming	0
IR Bishop lbw Warne	3
CEL Ambrose run out	2
CA Walsh b Fleming	0
Extras (4lb, 2w, 2nb)	8
Total (49.3 overs)	**202**

Fall of wickets: 25, 93, 165, 173, 178, 183, 187, 194, 202, 202
Bowling: McGrath 10-2-30-2; Fleming 8.3-0-48-2; Warne 9-0-36-4; ME Waugh 4-0-16-0; SR Waugh 7-0-30-1; Reiffel 5-0-13-0; Bevan 4-1-12-0; Law 2-0-13-0

AUSTRALIA WON BY 5 RUNS

FACTS AND TRIVIA FROM THE SEMI-FINALS

Sri Lanka v India (Calcutta): Both Sri Lankan openers were dismissed in the semi-final's opening over. Mahanama retired hurt (leg cramps) at 5-182. Match referee Clive Lloyd awarded the match to Sri Lanka after crowd disturbances prevented the match being played to a conclusion.
Australia v West Indies (Chandigarh): After 41.1 overs, West Indies were 2-165, requiring a further 43 runs. In the next 8.2 overs they lost eight wickets for 37 runs. Healy's two catches took his career Cup dismissals tally to 21 (18 caught, 3 stumped from 14 matches) second only to Pakistan's Wasim Bari (18 caught, 4 stumped from 14 matches).

The Final

MARCH 17   Sri Lanka v Australia, in Lahore, Pakistan

Australia

*MA Taylor c Jayasuriya b de Silva	74
ME Waugh c Jayasuriya b Vaas	12
RT Ponting b de Silva	45
SR Waugh c de Silva b Dharmasena	13
SK Warne st Kaluwitharana b Muralitharan	2
SG Law c de Silva b Jayasuriya	22
MG Bevan not out	36
*+IA Healy b de Silva	2
PR Reiffel not out	13
Extras (10lb, 1nb, 11w)	22
Total (7 wickets, 50 overs)	**241**

Did not bat: DW Fleming, GD McGrath

Fall of wickets: 36, 137, 152, 156, 170, 202, 205

Bowling: Wickremasinghe 7-0-38-0; Vaas 6-1-30-1; Muralitharan 10-0-31-1; Dharmasena 10-0-47-1; Jayasuriya 8-0-43-1; de Silva 9-0-42-3

+Sri Lanka

ST Jayasuriya run out	9
+RS Kaluwitharana c Bevan b Fleming	6
AP Gurusinha b Reiffel	65
PA de Silva not out	107
*A Ranatunga not out	47
Extras (1b, 4lb, 5w, 1nb)	11
Total (3 wickets, 46.2 overs)	**245**

Did not bat: HP Tillekeratne, RS Mahanama, HPDK Dharmasena, WPUJC Vaas, M Muralitharan, GP Wickremasinghe

Fall of wickets: 12, 23, 148

Bowling: McGrath 8.2-1-28-0; Fleming 6-0-43-1; Warne 10-0-58-0; Reiffel 10-0-49-1; ME Waugh 6-0-35-0; SR Waugh 3-0-15-0; Bevan 3-0-12-0

SRI LANKA WON BY 7 WICKETS

FACTS AND TRIVIA FROM THE FINAL

Sri Lanka v Australia (Lahore): Taylor's 74 is the highest score by an Australian captain in the World Cup. De Silva became the third century maker in a World Cup final, after CH Lloyd (102 in 1975) and IVA Richards (138 not out in 1979). Sri Lanka became the first team batting second to win a Cup final.

The final was SR Waugh's 25th World Cup match, equalling the Australian record held by AR Border. The overall appearance record is held by Javed Miandad, with 33, followed by Imran Khan (28), Kapil Dev (26), then Waugh, Border, DL Haynes and A Ranatunga (all with 25).

SR Waugh is one of only three men to score more than 500 runs and take more than 20 wickets in World Cup matches. He has scored 580 runs and taken 24 wickets. The other two to achieve this feat are Imran Khan (666 runs, 34 wickets) and Kapil Dev (669 runs, 28 wickets).

MAN OF THE MATCH AWARDS

Group matches

Match	Winner
New Zealand v England	NJ Astle (NZ)
South Africa v UAE	G Kirsten (SA)
West Indies v Zimbabwe	CEL Ambrose (WI)
New Zealand v Holland	CM Spearman (NZ)
India v Kenya	SR Tendulkar (I)
England v UAE	NMK Smith (E)
Sth Africa v New Zealand	WJ Cronje (SA)
Sri Lanka v Zimbabwe	PA de Silva (SL)
India v West Indies	SR Tendulkar (I)
England v Holland	GA Hick (E)
Australia v Kenya	ME Waugh (A)
Pakistan v UAE	Mushtaq Ahmed (P)
South Africa v England	JN Rhodes (SA)
Pakistan v Holland	Waqar Younis (P)
Zimbabwe v Kenya	PA Strang (Z)
New Zealand v UAE	RG Twose (NZ)
Australia v India	ME Waugh (A)
Kenya v West Indies	M Odumbe (K)
South Africa v Pakistan	WJ Cronje (SA)
Australia v Zimbabwe	SK Warne (A)
UAE v Holland	S Dukanwala and S Raza (both UAE)
Sri Lanka v India	ST Jayasuriya (SL)
Pakistan v England	Aamir Sohail (P)
West Indies v Australia	RB Richardson (WI)
South Africa v Holland	AC Hudson (SA)
Sri Lanka v Kenya	PA de Silva (SL)
India v Zimbabwe	AD Jadeja (I)
Pakistan v New Zealand	Salim Malik (P)

Quarter-finals

India v Pakistan	NS Sidhu (I)
Sri Lanka v England	ST Jayasuriya (SL)
West Indies v Sth Africa	BC Lara (WI)
Australia v New Zealand	ME Waugh (A)

Semi-finals

Sri Lanka v India	PA de Silva (SL)
Australia v West Indies	SK Warne (A)

Final

Sri Lanka v Australia	PA de Silva (SL)

Player of the Tournament
ST Jayasuriya (SL)

STATISTICS
The Records

1. AUSTRALIAN AVERAGES

Batting and fielding

Player	Mat	Inn	NO	Runs	HS	100	50	Ave	Ct/St
ME Waugh	7	7	1	484	130	3	1	80.66	1/-
SG Law	7	6	2	204	72	-	1	51.00	-/-
SR Waugh	7	7	2	226	82	-	3	45.20	3/-
RT Ponting	7	7	-	229	102	1	-	32.71	1/-
MG Bevan	7	5	1	125	69	-	1	31.25	3/-
MA Taylor	7	7	-	193	74	-	2	27.57	1/-
PR Reiffel	5	4	3	27	13*	-	-	27.00	3/-
IA Healy	7	5	-	59	31	-	-	11.80	9/3
SK Warne	7	5	2	32	24	-	-	10.67	1/-
S Lee	2	1	-	9	9	-	-	9.00	1/-
DW Fleming	6	1	-	0	0	-	-	0.00	2/-
GD McGrath	7	1	-	0	0*	-	-	-	1/-
CJ McDermott	1	-	-	-	-	-	-	-	-/-

Bowling

Player	Overs	Mdns	Runs	Wkts	Best	Ave	RPO
DW Fleming	45.2	3	221	12	5-36	18.42	4.88
SK Warne	68.3	3	263	12	4-34	21.92	3.84
SR Waugh	31	2	157	5	2-22	31.40	5.06
PR Reiffel	36	4	163	5	2-18	32.60	4.53
GD McGrath	62.2	10	258	6	2-30	43.00	4.15
ME Waugh	48	1	229	5	3-38	45.80	4.77
MG Bevan	32	1	156	3	2-35	52.00	4.86
S Lee	7	2	31	-	0-8	-	4.43
SG Law	5	-	23	-	0-10	-	4.60

2. TEAM RECORDS

Team	Players	Mat	Won	Lost	Batted First	Won	Lost	Batted Second	Won	Lost
Australia	13	7	5	2	5	3	2	2	2	0
England	15	6	2	4	3	1	2	3	1	2
Kenya	13	5	1	4	3	1	2	2	0	2
Holland	13	5	0	5	2	0	2	3	0	3
India	14	7	4	3	3	2	1	4	2	2
New Zealand	14	6	3	3	5	3	2	1	0	1
Pakistan	14	6	4	2	2	1	1	4	3	1
South Africa	14	6	5	1	3	3	0	3	2	1
Sri Lanka	12	6	6	0	2	2	0	4	4	0
UAE	14	5	1	4	2	0	2	3	1	2
West Indies	14	6	3	3	2	1	1	4	2	2
Zimbabwe	13	5	1	4	3	0	3	2	1	1
Totals	**163**	**35**				**17**			**18**	

Team	FOR Overs	Runs	Wkts	Ave	RPO	AGAINST Overs	Runs	Wkts	Ave	RPO
Australia	333.5	1686	44	38.31	5.05	338.1	1568	55	28.50	4.63
England	279.3	1283	42	30.54	4.59	286.5	1321	40	33.02	4.60
Kenya	249.1	960	40	24.00	3.85	219.3	1135	30	37.83	5.17
Holland	250	947	37	25.59	3.78	225	1285	20	64.25	5.71
India	313.4	1544	42	36.76	4.92	347.4	1608	57	28.21	4.62
New Zealand	294.3	1520	49	31.02	5.16	282.2	1331	39	34.12	4.71

Team	FOR Overs	Runs	Wkts	Ave	RPO	AGAINST Overs	Runs	Wkts	Ave	RPO
Pakistan	245.2	1284	26	49.38	5.23	274.5	1268	47	26.97	4.61
South Africa	281.2	1545	35	44.14	5.49	294.3	1155	49	23.57	3.92
Sri Lanka	272.4	1631	29	56.24	5.98	284.1	1349	39	34.58	4.74
UAE	222.5	784	39	20.10	3.51	200	1065	22	48.40	5.32
West Indies	263.1	1119	48	23.31	4.25	288.4	1172	48	24.41	4.06
Zimbabwe	237.5	877	40	21.92	3.68	202.1	923	25	36.92	4.56
Total	**3243.5**	**15180**	**471**	**32.22**	**4.67**	**3243.5**	**15180**	**471**	**32.22**	**4.67**

		First innings	Second innings
Average Runs per Match	433.7	234.8	198.9
Average Runs per Match	13.45	7.37	6.08

	Mat	Overs	Runs	Wkts	Ave	RPO
Group A	13	1201.5	5475	174	31.46	4.55
Group B	15	1375	6349	192	33.06	4.61
Finals	7	667	3356	105	33.22	5.03
in India	17	1595.2	7218	246	29.34	4.52
in Pakistan	16	1461.3	6853	203	33.75	4.68
in Sri Lanka	2	187	1109	22	50.40	5.93

Highest Team Scores

Total		Match	Venue
398	(5 wkts)	Sri Lanka v Kenya	Kandy
328	(3 wkts)	South Africa v Holland	Rawalpindi
321	(2 wkts)	South Africa v U.A.C.	Rawalpindi
307	(8 wkts)	New Zealand v Holland	Baroda
304	(7 wkts)	Australia v Kenya	Visakhapatnam
289	(4 wkts)	Australia v New Zealand	Madras
287	(8 wkts)	India v Pakistan	Bangalore
286	(9 wkts)	New Zealand v Australia	Madras

Notes:
1. *Highest totals for other teams*

England	279 (4 wkts)	v Holland	Peshawar
Kenya	254 (7 wkts)	v Sri Lanka	Kandy
Holland	230 (6 wkts)	v England	Peshawar
Pakistan	281 (5 wkts)	v New Zealand	Lahore
UAE	220 (3 wkts)	v Holland	Lahore
West Indies	264 (8 wkts)	v South Africa	Karachi
Zimbabwe	228 (6 wkts)	v Sri Lanka	Colombo

2. *highest total batting second: 289, as above*
3. *highest total batting first and losing: 286, as above*
4. *highest total batting second and losing: 254, as above*
5. *highest total all out: 258 Australia v India, Bombay*

Lowest Team Scores (completed innings)

Total		Match	Venue
93	(35.2 overs)	West Indies v Kenya	Pune
109	(9 wkts, 33 overs)	UAE v Pakistan	Gujranwala
134	(49.4 overs)	Kenya v Zimbabwe	Patna
136	(48.3 overs)	UAE v England	Peshawar
145	(7 wkts, 50 overs)	Holland v Pakistan	Lahore
151	(9 wkts, 50 overs)	Zimbabwe v West Indies	Hyderabad
152	(44.3 overs)	England v South Africa	Rawalpindi
152	(8 wkts, 50 overs)	UAE v South Africa	Rawalpindi

Notes:
1. *India's 120 (8 wkts) v Sri Lanka in the semi-final is excluded because the innings was uncompleted*
2. *Lowest totals (completed innings) for other teams:*

Australia	207	(8 wkts, 50 overs)	v West Indies	Chandigarh
India	242	(48 overs)	v Australia	Bombay
New Zealand	177	(9 wkts, 50 overs)	v South Africa	Faisalabad
Pakistan	242	(6 wkts, 50 overs)	v South Africa	Karachi
South Africa	230	(50 overs)	v England	Rawalpindi
Sri Lanka	251	(8 wkts, 50 overs)	v India	Calcutta

3. *Lowest total batting first and winning:*
       166   (49.3 overs)   Kenya v West Indies   Pune
4. *Lowest total in Sri Lanka:*
       228   (6 wkts, 50 overs)   Zimbabwe v Sri Lanka   Colombo

Highest winning margins

Runs margin	169	South Africa beat UAE	Rawalpindi
	160	South Africa beat Holland	Rawalpindi
	144	Sri Lanka beat Kenya	Kandy
Wickets margin	9	Pakistan beat UAE	Gujranwala
	8	Pakistan beat Holland	Lahore
	8	Australia beat Zimbabwe	Nagpur
	8	England beat UAE	Peshawar
Overs to spare	20.3	West Indies beat Zimbabwe	Hyderabad

Closest winning margins

Runs margin	5	Australia beat West Indies	Chandigarh
	11	New Zealand beat England	Ahmedabad
Wickets margin	4	West Indies beat Australia	Jaipur
Overs to spare	1.1	West Indies beat Australia	Jaipur
	1.2	Sri Lanka beat India	Delhi

Match aggregates

Highest	652	(12 wkts, 100 overs)	Sri Lanka v Kenya	Kandy
	575	(13 wkts, 97.5 overs)	Australia v New Zealand	Madras
	543	(7 wkts, 98.4 overs)	Sri Lanka v India	Delhi
Lowest	276	(12 wkts, 81.3 overs)	England v UAE	Peshawar
	271	(15 wkts, 92 overs)	Zimbabwe v Kenya	Patna
	259	(20 wkts, 84.5 overs)	Kenya v West Indies	Pune

Note: Pakistan v UAE at Gujranwala was restricted to 33 overs per innings. 221 runs were scored for the loss of 10 wickets, off 51 overs.

3. BATTING

Centuries (16, by 12 players)

Score	Batsman	Match
188*	G Kirsten	South Africa v UAE
161	AC Hudson	South Africa v Holland
145	PA de Silva	Sri Lanka v Kenya
137	SR Tendulkar	India v Sri Lanka (Delhi)
130	ME Waugh	Australia v Kenya
130	CZ Harris	New Zealand v Australia
127*	SR Tendulkar	India v Kenya
126	ME Waugh	Australia v India
111	Admir Sohail	Pakistan v South Africa
111	BC Lara	West Indies v South Africa
110	ME Waugh	Australia v New Zealand
107*	PA de Silva	Sri Lanka v Australia
106	VG Kambli	India v Zimbabwe
104*	GA Hick	England v Holland
102	RT Ponting	Australia v West Indies (Jaipur)
101	NJ Astle	New Zealand v England

Notes:
1. Highest scores for other teams:

Holland	64	KJ van Noortwijk	v England
Kenya	96	S Tikolo	v Sri Lanka
UAE	84	Salim Raza	v Holland
Zimbabwe	75	ADR Campbell	v Sri Lanka

2. SR Tendulkar's 127* (above) was the highest score for a team batting second, and the highest proportion of an innings (62.56% of India's 203)
3. The highest score by a captain was 93* by RB Richardson, West Indies v Australia, Jaipur

Highest score for each batting position

Pos	Score	Batsman	Match
1	126	ME Waugh	Australia v India
2	188*	G Kirsten	South Africa v UAE
3	111	BC Lara	West Indies v South Africa
4	145	PA de Silva	Sri Lanka v Kenya
5	130	CZ Harris	New Zealand v Australia
6	70*	HP Tillekeratne	Sri Lanka v India (Delhi)
7	36*	MG Bevan	Australia v Sri Lanka
	36	AC Parore	New Zealand v Pakistan

Pos	Score	Batsman	Match
8	35*	DA Reeve	England v Pakistan
9	47*	JA Samarosekero	UAE v New Zealand
10	40*	S Dukanwala	UAE v South Africa
11	12	PS de Villiers	South Africa v England

Most scores of 50 and over

No.	Batsman
5	SR Tendulkar (India)
4	ME Waugh (Australia), PA de Silva (Sri Lanka)
3	AP Gurusinha (Sri Lanka), SR Waugh (Australia), Saeed Anwar (Pak), Aamir Sohail (Pak)

Most runs

Runs	Batsman	Mat	Inn	NO	HS	100	50	Ave
523	SR Tendulkar (India)	7	7	1	137	2	3	87.16
484	ME Waugh (Australia)	7	7	1	130	3	1	80.66
448	PA de Silva (Sri Lanka)	6	6	1	145	2	2	89.60
391	G Kirsten (South Africa)	6	6	1	188*	1	1	78.20
329	Saeed Anwar (Pakistan)	6	6	2	83*	-	3	82.25
307	AP Gurusinha (Sri Lanka)	6	6	-	87	-	3	51.16
276	WJ Cronje (South Africa)	6	6	1	78	-	2	55.20
275	AC Hudson (South Africa)	4	4	-	161	1	1	68.75
272	Aamir Sohail (Pakistan)	6	6	-	111	1	2	45.33
269	BC Lara (West Indies)	6	6	1	111	1	1	53.80
255	DJ Cullinan (South Africa)	6	6	2	69	-	2	63.75
254	GP Thorpe (England)	6	6	2	89	-	2	63.50

Notes:

1. Most runs for other teams:

Team	Runs	Batsman	Mat	Inn	NO	HS	100	50	Ave
Kenya	196	S Tikolo	5	5	-	96	-	2	39.20
New Zealand	193	SP Fleming	6	6	-	66	-	1	32.16
Holland	168	KJ van Noortwijk	5	5	1	64	-	1	42.00
Zimbabwe	159	AC Waller	5	5	-	67	-	1	31.80
UAE	137	Salim Raza	4	4	-	84	-	1	34.25

2. Highest batting average:

Average	Batsman	Mat	Inn	NO	Runs	HS	100	50
120.50	A Ranatunga (Sri Lanka)	6	6	4	241	75*	-	1

Highest partnerships

Runs	Wkt	Batsmen	Match
207	3rd	ME Waugh, SR Waugh	Australia v Kenya
186	1st	G Kirsten, AC Hudson	South Africa v Holland
184	3rd	AP Gurusinha, PA de Silva	Sri Lanka v Kenya
175	3rd	SR Tendulkar, M Azharuddin	India v Sri Lanka (Delhi)
172	3rd	AP Gurusinha, PA de Silva	Sri Lanka v Zimbabwe
168	4th	LK Germon, CZ Harris	New Zealand v Australia
163	1st	AD Jadeja, SR Tendulkar	India v Kenya

Highest Partnership for each wicket

Wkt	Runs	Batsmen	Match
1st	186	G Kirsten, AC Hudson	South Africa v Holland
2nd	138	S Chanderpaul, BC Lara	West Indies v South Africa
3rd	207	ME Waugh, SR Waugh	Australia v Kenya
4th	168	LK Germon, CZ Harris	New Zealand v Australia
5th	138	SG Law, MG Bevan	Australia v West Indies (Chandigarh)
6th	80*	Salim Malik, Wasim Akram	Pakistan v New Zealand
7th	44	H Modi, T Odoyo	Kenya v West Indies
8th	62	DA Reeve, D Gough	England v Sri Lanka
9th	80*	A Laeeq, S Dukanwala	UAE v South Africa
10th	17	CR Matthews, PS de Villiers	South Africa v England

Notes:
1. There were 28 century partnerships in the tournament. Sri Lanka, with 6, had the most, followed by Australia (5) and South Africa, New Zealand and India (3).
2. AP Gurusinha and PA de Silva each participated in four century partnerships, three with each other.

4. BOWLING

Most wickets

Wkts	Bowler	Match	Overs	Mdns	Runs	Best	Ave	RPO
15	AR Kumble (India)	7	69.4	5	280	3-28	18.66	4.02
13	Waqar Younis (Pakistan)	6	54	5	253	4-26	19.46	4.69
12	PA Strang (Zimbabwe)	6	42.1	4	192	5-21	16.00	4.55
12	RA Harper (West Indies)	6	58	6	219	4-47	18.25	3.78
12	DW Fleming (Australia)	6	45.2	3	221	5-36	18.42	4.88
12	SK Warne (Australia)	7	68.3	3	263	4-34	21.92	3.84
10	CEL Ambrose (West Indies)	6	56.3	11	170	3-28	17.00	3.01
10	Mushtaq Ahmed (Pakistan)	6	57	2	238	3-16	23.80	4.18
9	R Ali (Kenya)	6	36.2	3	176	3-17	19.55	4.84
8	AA Donald (South Africa)	4	34	-	126	3-21	15.75	3.71
8	SLV Raju (India)	4	40	4	158	3-30	19.75	3.95
8	DG Cork (England)	5	48	2	216	2-33	27.00	4.50
8	J Srinath (India)	7	65.4	3	293	3-34	36.63	4-46
8	V Prasad (India)	7	65	1	313	3-45	39.13	4.82

Notes:

1. Most wickets for other teams

Country	Wkts	Bowler	Match	Overs	Mdns	Runs	Best	Ave	RPO
Sri Lanka	7	M Muralitharan	6	57.1	3	216	2-37	30.85	3.77
	7	ST Jayasuriya	6	51	1	231	3-12	33.00	4.52
New Zealand	6	DJ Nash	4	35	4	153	3-27	25.50	4.37
UAE	6	S Dukanala	5	33	1	153	5-29	25.50	4.63
	6	S Azhar Saeed	5	31	1	157	3.45	26.16	5.06
Holland	5	SW Lubbers	4	36	-	187	3-48	37.40	5.19

2. PA Strang, with 21.08, finished the tournament with the best strike rate (balls per wicket).

Most wickets in a Match

Total	Bowler	Match	Total	Bowler	Match
5-21	PA Strang	Zimbabwe v Kenya	4-36	SK Warne	Australia v West Indies (Chandigarh)
5-29	S Dukanwala	UAE v Holland			
5-36	DW Fleming	Australia v India	4-40	PA Strang	Zimbabwe v West Indies
4-26	Waqar Younis	Pakistan v Holland	4-47	RA Harper	West Indies v South Africa
4-34	SK Warne	Australia v Zimbabwe			

Notes:

1. Best bowling for other teams:

Team	Total	Bowler	Opponent
South Africa	3-11	BM McMillan	UAE
Sri Lanka	3-12	ST Jayasuriya	India (Calcutta)
Kenya	3-15	M Odumbe	West Indies
New Zealand	3-20	SA Thomson	UAE
India	3-28	AR Kumble	Kenya
England	3-29	NMK Smith	UAE
Holland	3-48	SW Lubbers	New Zealand

2. Two bowlers, AR Kumble (India) and R Ali (Kenya) took three or more wickets in a match three times. Six bowlers did it twice. In all, there were 41 instances, by 31 players.

5. FIELDING

Most dismissals in a match by a wicketkeeper

Total	Keeper	Match
5 (4ct, 1st)	JC Adams	West Indies v Kenya
5 (4ct, 1st)	Rashid Latif	Pakistan v New Zealand

Most dismissals in the tournament by a wicketkeeper

Total	Keeper	Matches
12 (9ct, 3st)	IA Healy (Australia)	7
9 (7ct, 2st)	Rashid Latif (Pakistan)	6
8 (8ct)	SJ Palframan (South Africa)	6
8 (7ct, 1st)	RC Russell (England)	6

Notes:

1. The most catches by a fieldsman in a match was four (including one caught-and-bowled) by CL Cairns for New Zealand against UAE.
2. The most catches by a fieldsman in the tournament was eight (including one caught-and-bowled), in seven matches, by AR Kumble of India.